CALLED UNTO LIBERTY

Distributed in Great Britain by Oxford University Press, London

Publication of this book has been aided by a grant
from the Ford Foundation

Library of Congress Catalog Card Number 64–21783

Printed in the United States of America

FOR ELEANOR

ACKNOWLEDGMENTS

THE MAJOR part of the research for this book was done in the libraries of Boston University, the Massachusetts Historical Society, and Harvard University. I am indebted to their staffs for many hours of patient and friendly assistance. In addition, I wish to thank the following institutions for their cooperation: American Antiquarian Society; Museum of Fine Arts in Boston; Boston Public Library; British Museum; John Carter Brown Library; William L. Clements Library; Columbia University Library; Congregational Library, Boston; Duke's County Historical Society; Henry E. Huntington Library; Institute of Early American History and Culture; Library of Congress; McCartney Library, Geneva College; New York Historical Society; New York Public Library; Princeton University Library; Public Record Office, London; Rhode Island Historical Society; Royal Society of Arts, London; Unitarian College, Manchester; University of Aberdeen; University of Bristol; Dr. Williams's Library, London; Wisconsin State Historical Society; Yale University Library.

The generosity of Mark Bortman made possible the acquisition of a collection of Mayhew's personal papers by the Chenery Library of Boston University. A grant from the Penrose Fund of the American Philosophical Society enabled me to conduct a search for Mayhew documents in this country and in England. A leave for study from Geneva College was instrumental in the completion of the manuscript.

I have profited from suggestions made on various sections

of the manuscript by Clinton Rossiter, Edmund S. Morgan, Conrad Wright, Kenneth A. Bernard, and J. G. Vos. I am obligated to Clifford K. Shipton, not only for the limitless treasures of the *Harvard Graduates,* but for indefatigable patience in answering my queries.

Most of all, I owe a debt of gratitude to Robert E. Moody, a scholar, teacher, and friend, who guided my early work on Mayhew and has inspired it at every stage.

C. W. A.

Beaver Falls, Pennsylvania
5 September 1964

CONTENTS

ILLUSTRATIONS

frontispiece
Portrait of Jonathan Mayhew, painted between 1747 and 1752 by John Greenwood. (Courtesy of the Congregational Library, Boston)

page 36
The first page of a long letter of advice written by Experience Mayhew to his son, November 1741. (Courtesy Chenery Library, Boston University)

page 107
Letter of Jonathan Mayhew to Dr. John Clarke, seeking permission to court his daughter Elizabeth. (Courtesy of Chenery Library, Boston University)

facing page 112
Portrait, painted by John Hazlett, of Ebenezer Gay, Congregational Minister at Hingham, Massachusetts, who encouraged Mayhew's theological studies. (Courtesy of Ebenezer Gay)
Portrait of Charles Chauncy, Arminian minister of the First Church (Congregational) of Boston from 1727 to 1787, painted by an unknown artist. (Courtesy of the Massachusetts Historical Society)
Portrait, by John Singleton Copley, of Samuel Cooper, politically minded minister of the Boston Brattle Street Church (Congregational) from 1746 to 1783. (Courtesy of Harvard University)
Portrait of Robert Treat Paine, by Edward Savage and John Coles, Jr. A future member of the Continental Congress and signer of the Declaration of Independence, Paine attended the West Church in the 1750's and became a great admirer of Mayhew. (Courtesy of the Massachusetts Historical Society)

facing page 113
Title page of Mayhew's first volume of sermons. (Courtesy of the Massachusetts Historical Society)
Title page of Mayhew's major contribution to the struggle against an Anglican episcopate. (Courtesy of the Massachusetts Historical Society)

facing page 144

Thomas Hollis, painted in 1752 at Rome by Richard Wilson, while Hollis was on his tour of Europe. (Courtesy of Harvard University Library)

Title page of the copy of John Locke, *Two Treatises of Government* presented by Thomas Hollis to Harvard College in 1764. Hollis edited and published this sixth edition, which remained the best in English until 1960. (Courtesy of Harvard University Library)

facing page 145

Etching commissioned in 1767 by Thomas Hollis in commemoration of Mayhew's death. It was made from a crayon portrait drawn the day before he died (by John Singleton Copley?). Despite the difficulties under which it was executed, Mrs. Mayhew regarded this as the best portrait of her husband. The device under the picture, contrived by Hollis, shows Mayhew's pens crossed over an archbishop's miter, which hangs from a wreath enclosing a quotation from *Remarks on an Anonymous Tract*. (Courtesy of the Massachusetts Historical Society)

The West Church in 1775, as seen from the top of Beacon Hill. From a watercolor by a British officer, who copied from the sketch of a fellow officer. (Courtesy of the Massachusetts Historical Society)

CALLED UNTO LIBERTY

PROLOGUE

In late summer, 1765, the American colonies were waiting apprehensively for the Stamp Act to go into effect the following November 1. On Sunday afternoon, August 25, Dr. Jonathan Mayhew climbed into his pulpit at Boston's West Congregational Church and preached from the text, "I would they were even cut off which trouble you. For, brethren, ye have been called unto liberty; . . ."

The preacher who read these prophetic words (inflammatory words to victims of the Stamp Act riots) was Boston's most conspicuous personality. From his ordination in 1747 until his death in 1766, no other townsman received such sustained attention in the newspapers, was covered simultaneously with so much invective and adoration, participated in so many widely publicized controversies, or kept gossipy tongues so busy. This fame was not confined to Boston or even to New England, for his was one of a very few American names well known in England at the time of the Stamp Act crisis.

In their grief over his death at only forty-five years of age, Mayhew's partisans concluded that greatness had departed from their midst. This feeling is best expressed in one stanza of the spate of bad verse that drenched his grave for the next quarter century:

> MAYHEW the Great is dead! His eyes are clos'd
> From mortal things! His soul has soar'd aloft,
> On wings celestial, to the realms of bliss!
> And leaves a world to mourn the general loss![1]

More prosaic voices of the Revolutionary generation echoed this theme. Robert Treat Paine, a signer of the Declaration of Independence, called the Boston preacher "the father of civil and religious liberty in Massachusetts and America." John Adams freely acknowledged the influence of Mayhew on his youthful development. After the Revolution his reputation waned slowly except among the leaders of the Unitarian movement, who regarded him as the foremost pioneer of liberal Christianity. Yet, in the second half of the nineteenth century, a few voices could be heard maintaining in Massachusetts that Jonathan Mayhew was a greater and more eloquent American than Daniel Webster.[2]

Mayhew's reputation had grown out of nineteen years of battle for what he conceived to be the cause of American liberty. He was the boldest and most articulate of those colonial preachers who taught that resistance to tyrannical rulers was a Christian duty as well as a human right. He directed his great polemical skill against the efforts of the Church of England to export its bishops to America. And he brazenly proclaimed his abandonment of Puritan theology in favor of a "pure and undefiled" version of Christianity. With all the fervor of the most intense Puritan, Mayhew preached his gospel of the Enlightenment to a Boston that still sought to govern the spirit of Benjamin Franklin with the conscience of John Winthrop.

The fame of the man together with the explosive nature of the issues on which he took his stand in unmistakably clear prose assured his writings a wide reading by his generation and by future scholars. But, however deeply mined by historians in search of quotable nuggets, the twenty-three printed sermons and polemical works he left behind do not fully explain the fame and infamy he received in his day, nor do they disclose the whole man.

John Adams once suggested that a dozen volumes would be

required to delineate the character of Mayhew.[3] Regrettably, much of the material to fill these volumes died with his intimates, who behind closed doors probed the depths of his personality, but whose letters and diaries contain only general and laudatory references.[4] In newspapers, in hundreds of scattered manuscripts, and in a small collection of personal papers, however, enough has survived to make possible for the first time a full exploration of the career and personality as well as the mind of this important intellectual leader of pre-Revolutionary New England.

CHAPTER I

Martha's Vineyard

God speaks to us daily in all his providences; even in the
most common of them, in order to excite us to that reverence of, and obedience to him, which is our greatest good.

Jonathan Mayhew, 1755[1]

JONATHAN MAYHEW was a fifth-generation American. In
outline his family's history is the familiar story of hopeful
migration to the New World, slow and often painful adaptation
to the wilderness, and eventual establishment on a new foundation. In detail, however, the Mayhew history was duplicated
nowhere in the American colonies. Many Englishmen dreamed
of securing a tract of land from the new continent's unlimited
acreage on which to erect themselves as lords of the manor in
a rebirth of medieval feudalism. Other Englishmen, fewer in
number, saw the American Indians as additional human souls
to be wrested from a wily Satan. Only the Mayhews of Martha's
Vineyard fused these two interests into an enduring family
enterprise. At Jonathan's birth in 1720, he was the heir of this
mixture of suzerainty and piety.

Thomas Mayhew, a merchant originally from Tisbury Parish
in Wiltshire, left England in 1631 during the Great Migration
that brought 20,000 persons to Massachusetts in thirteen years.
While engaged in business ventures in the vicinity of Boston,
he acquired the title in 1641 to Martha's Vineyard, an island of
one hundred square miles located four miles south of Cape
Cod. The following year he sent his only son, Thomas Mayhew,
Jr., to assume control of the island, where, after some business
setbacks, the father soon joined the son.[2]

Through a maze of conflicting land grants, changing political allegiances, and settler unrest, Thomas Mayhew—self-styled "Governour Mayhew"—ruled his island with an iron hand for forty years. The most serious threat to his control came in 1665 when Martha's Vineyard was included in the lands placed under the Duke of York. After much delay a settlement, worked out in 1671, confirmed the Mayhew patent and named Thomas Mayhew "Governour and Chiefe Magistrate" for life. At the same time a patent was issued erecting the Manor of Tisbury in the southwestern part of the island. The Governour and his grandson were made "joint Lords of the Manor of Tisbury," and the inhabitants became manorial tenants subject to the feudal political jurisdiction of the Mayhews. This full-fledged feudal manor appears to have been the only such institution actually established in New England.

The attempt of the Mayhews to create an hereditary aristocracy on the Vineyard met with increasing opposition as more and more colonists arrived. When the Dutch temporarily recaptured New York in 1673, open rebellion broke out and lasted until the English rewon New York and restored the authority of the Mayhews on the island. The old patriarch died in 1682 at eighty-nine. Nine years later the political rule of the family ended when Martha's Vineyard was annexed by Massachusetts after the Glorious Revolution, but the problem of manorial tenancy remained. Although some of the Mayhews clung to the "pleasant fiction" of their manorial rights almost until the American Revolution and received token quit rents as late as 1732, feudalism on Martha's Vineyard died the same slow, lingering but certain death it did elsewhere in the colonies.[3]

Kenneth Scott Latourette has concluded that the Missionary Mayhews of Martha's Vineyard represent what is likely the longest and most persistent family missionary endeavor in the annals of all Christendom.[4] Thomas Mayhew was not concerned for Indian souls when he settled on his island; he sought only to improve his social and economic position. The son rather than the father receives credit for launching the Indian mission. Thomas Mayhew, Jr., had emigrated from England with the elder Mayhew. Somewhere he had received a liberal education, apparently from private tutors. After moving to the Vineyard to begin the white settlement there, he became pastor of the small English church as well as acting governor in his father's absence. He soon discovered that he could not refuse the challenge he found among the three thousand Pokanauket Indians on Martha's Vineyard. The Pokanaukets, a branch of the mainland Narragansetts, far outnumbered the whites, so an effective settlement required friendly relations with the Indians. But Thomas Mayhew, Jr., appears to have been motivated largely by spiritual concern, while his father and other members of the family enjoyed the practical results of the Indian mission. The younger man gradually abandoned most of his secular tasks and spent the remainder of his life among the natives. Progress was slow at first, but by the end of 1652 there were 283 converts, a school for Indian children, and two Indian meetings each Sabbath. The Praying Indians of Martha's Vineyard who said grace before meals became a topic of conversation on both sides of the Atlantic.[5] Thomas Mayhew, Jr., carried on his missionary work with little heed to his personal fortunes. As the elder Mayhew put it, his son had followed this work "when 'twas bare with him for food and rayment, and when indeede there was nothing in sight any waies but Gods promises." The situation was improved somewhat by the formation in 1649 of a London missionary society, usually called the New England Company, which in a few years began to provide substantial aid for the Mayhews and other missionaries.[6]

In the fall of 1657, Thomas Mayhew, Jr., sailed for England

on a trip combining an appeal for missionary funds with personal business. After leaving Boston Harbor, the ship was never seen again. The death of his only son at thirty-six was a heavy blow to the father and greatly increased the burdens he must carry in old age. He made repeated efforts to find a replacement to continue his son's ministry to the Indians, but no minister who knew the language or was willing to learn could be induced to settle permanently on the island. So Thomas Mayhew, who had started out as a merchant, then turned landed proprietor, became at the age of sixty a missionary in his son's place. For the next twenty-five years he traveled on foot as far as twenty miles to preach once a week at an Indian assembly or to visit the native camps.[7]

From the beginning the elder Mayhew had worked to preserve the original political institutions of the Indians. Religion and government are distinct matters, he told the chiefs. When one of your subjects becomes a Christian, he is still under your jurisdiction. Indian land was guarded against further encroachment by white settlers. So successful were these policies that during the bloody battles of King Philip's War, in 1675–1676, the Vineyard Indians never stirred, although they outnumbered the English on the island twenty to one. By practicing as well as preaching the gospel and by understanding the value of native institutions, the Mayhews gave Martha's Vineyard a felicitous pattern of Indian-White relations seldom duplicated in the conquest of the North American continent.[8]

When the venerable Governour Mayhew became ill one Sunday evening in 1682, he calmly informed his friends and relatives that "his Sickness would now be to Death, and he was well contented therewith, being full of Days, and satisfied with Life." His great-grandson, Experience Mayhew, Jonathan's father, was only eight at the time, but he remembered clearly being led to the bedside to receive from the dying man a blessing "in the Name of the Lord." Family leadership now passed to the three grandsons, two of whom deserted the mission, leaving John, youngest grandson and grandfather of Jonathan, to care for Indian souls. John possessed all the zeal and aptitude for missions exhibited by his father, Thomas Mayhew, Jr., but like his father he died in the prime of life, only seven years after Governour Mayhew. At John's death in 1689, the Indian mission had reached its summit. Four or five Indian congregations met for worship each week under ministers of their own race. Never again would the outlook be so bright.[9]

John left behind a family of eight children, the eldest of whom was Experience, age sixteen. Experience's feminine name had been given him by his grandmother, who had expected a girl and had died shortly before his birth revealed her mistake. He had grown up among the Indians and had learned their language as a second native tongue. Within five years following his father's death, he was preaching to the Indians, the fourth successive generation of his family to carry on the work. At about the same time he was invited to become pastor of an English church on the island, but he chose the Indian mission, and there he remained for sixty-five years. Without formal education and in an isolated field of labor, Jonathan's father must be ranked as one of the ablest men of his day. By 1698, Boston's Cotton Mather was singing his praises. Another of the town's ministerial great, Charles Chauncy, later suggested that with an education Experience Mayhew would have found a place among the "first worthies of New England."[10]

Even without a university education, Experience was inclined toward scholarship. His first scholarly efforts were the production of Christian literature in the Indian language. He translated three of Cotton Mather's sermons, and in 1709 he published the *Massachuset Psalter,* a translation of the Psalms and the Gospel of John. Containing parallel columns of Indian and English, the *Psalter* enabled the natives to read the Scriptures in their own language and at the same time encouraged the more ambitious to learn English. The missionary gained a friend and advocate when in 1699 Judge Samuel Sewall of Boston became the treasurer and most active member of the Commissioners, the American agents for the New England Company. Sewall was the first treasurer to take a sincere interest in the mission work of the Company. The two men worked together on programs to strengthen the mission and protect the Indians. Experience Mayhew gradually became the acknowledged expert on New England Indian missions. His account of the Vineyard Indians published in 1720 was a best seller of the day.[11] In 1723 Harvard College bestowed its master of arts degree on him, a signal honor for a self-educated man.[12]

At home, Experience Mayhew had to face hard times in the Indian mission. The native population had dropped nearly 50 percent since the English settlement. White traders, with an eye to profit, continued to ply the Indians with liquor—"poison to their Souls as well as destructive to their bodies." Experience voiced the despair he felt so poignantly in a letter to Cotton Mather in 1723: Were it not for the encouragement of seeing "here and there a truly pious person among the Indians" and knowing that hundreds of them had gone to heaven, he would have "given out" long before. The "memorable experiment of God's power and grace amongst the Indians," as Thomas Mayhew, Jr., had described his missionary work in 1648, had become an effort that "goes on heavily." That it went on at all was a tribute to the unselfish and devoted service of four generations of Missionary Mayhews—Thomas, Thomas, Jr., John, and Experience.[13]

In late November 1724, Experience Mayhew journeyed northward to Boston. He had been making this pilgrimage nearly every winter for the last fifteen years to collect the funds

given him by the New England Company and to order supplies
from Boston's swarm of shopkeepers. Sometimes he had business to bring before the winter session of the Massachusetts
General Court. This year he was petitioning the Court to declare him a regularly established minister so that he might
qualify for the clerical exemption from taxation. There were
usually invitations to fill pulpits of Boston churches whose
congregations hungered for the sound of a new voice from the
sacred desk. Most of all he looked forward to seeing such
Boston friends as his nephew, Thomas Prince of the Old South
Church, Judge Samuel Sewall, or the great Cotton Mather. A
few hearty dinners around heavily laden, richly set tables and
a fortnight of stimulating contact with the social and intellectual elite of the town did much to compensate for long months
spent in the isolation and bleakness of Martha's Vineyard.[14]

This year Experience had accepted an invitation to deliver
the Boston Thursday Lecture on December 3. The Thursday
Lecture was a distinctive feature of the town's religious life,
an additional weekly meeting at the First Church where
theological topics could be presented with a subtlety beyond
the grasp of the typical Sunday congregation. Ordinarily, each
of the Congregational clergy lectured in turn, but Thomas
Foxcroft of the First Church had invited the missionary to
speak in his place. In recent years the Thursday Lecture had
lost much of its lay following and had developed into little
more than a ministers' club, but on this occasion the usual
audience was swelled by the presence of the General Court,
whose members had stopped their legislative deliberations long
enough to honor Puritan tradition by their presence at the
lecture.

Experience Mayhew was not noted for eloquence.[15] After
arguing for nearly an hour that all men are equally under the
bondage of sin—a very typical Thursday Lecture topic—he
reached the main point of his discourse, although he disguised

it as an aside, an incidental matter that possibly should not be permitted to intrude. "HERE I cannot but think it proper to make a more particular Application of what I am saying under this Head, unto the case of a miserable People dwelling among us, and bordering upon us: I mean the Aboriginal Natives of this Land." One of the glories of early New England has been the successful effort to convert the Indians—"GOD Himself has been Glorified on account of it." But alas, today the spirit of the past is gone, and some people are saying that Indian missions are hopeless ventures! "BUT why should we be so discouraged about them! They are no worse by nature than others, or than we ourselves. They are as capable Subjects of good impressions, as the People of any other Nation; and when it pleaseth God to bless means for their good, there are the same effects produced thereby, as the same means do produce on others." Many among us, he went on, regard the Indians as a vicious people. Although this may be generally true, yet there are "a considerable number of Godly People among them." It is time for a revival of this work! Indeed, this is "an Affair worthy of the serious consideration" of the General Court. In this aside in the Thursday Lecture, Experience Mayhew laid bare his heart to the clergy and legislators. That his appeal produced some response is evidenced by the subsequent publication of the sermon, for only the best of the Thursday Lectures were so honored.[16]

Experience remained in Boston for several more days. The following Sunday morning he attended that most unusual communion service at the Old South Church where Judge Sewall blushed to see Madame Winthrop served first by Deacon Checkly—a deliberate slight in Sewall's eyes. At the afternoon service at Old South, Experience preached on "Follow peace with all men," a more appropriate text for the occasion than he realized. On Monday the General Court "Resolved in the Affirmative" the question of tax exemption on which he had petitioned. One might wonder how much the presence of the Court at the Thursday Lecture had influenced its decision. His business concluded, he was free to return home.[17]

The farm to which Experience Mayhew returned was in Chilmark, a wild section in the southwestern part of the island which had been incorporated as a town in 1714. John Mayhew had been the first white settler in Chilmark, where he had moved in the 1670's to a flat neck of land between two of the many large ponds that fill the southern coast of the Vineyard. John had selected this spot, known as Quenames, because it offered some of the best available farm land on which to support his family while he ministered to the nearby Indians. Here, a mile and one-half from the south coast, he had erected a modest but comfortable frame house. Under its roof Experience had first seen the light of day. He had inherited the property on the death of John, and here, likewise, a fifth generation of Mayhews had been born.[18]

Experience was glad to get back to Quenames, for his children were special objects of affection and care. He devoted a considerable portion of the last fifty years of his life to their education, guidance, and material and spiritual welfare. In the children the father hoped to compensate for personal shortcomings, failures, and lack of opportunity. After a series of severe disappointments, he finally succeeded. Jonathan, the youngest son, became the man Experience Mayhew had dreamed of being. Unlike many such fathers, he lived to enjoy this vicarious fulfillment.

Experience had married well. His first wife had been Thankful Hinckley, daughter of the last governor of Plymouth Colony. The older children, Reliance, Samuel, and Mary, were Thankful's offspring. Reliance, "a pious prudent woman of blameless conversation," had been a great aid and comfort to her father, sometimes even accompanying him on his trips to Boston. The two daughters would soon marry local Vineyard men and settle near Quenames. Samuel, a mental defective, is seldom mentioned in the Mayhew records or correspondence. Thankful had gone to her grave in 1706 at only thirty-three, and for five years Experience had farmed, preached to the Indians, and cared for his three small children without the aid and comfort of a wife.[19]

The second marriage in 1711 to Remember Bourne had united two of New England's oldest missionary families. The Bournes had been ministering to the Indians at Ma'shpee on Cape Cod since 1658. Remember's father, Shearjashub Bourne, seems to have been more interested in Indian trade than in Indian souls, but he was a highly respected and influential man in the public affairs of southern Massachusetts. He had married Bathsheba Skiffe, daughter of James Skiffe of Sandwich, who, although he had never lived on the Vineyard, was one of its largest landowners. Thus, when Remember Bourne had come to Quenames at the somewhat spinsterish age of thirty, she had brought with her a pedigree of which a country minister with ambitions for his children need not be ashamed.

Remember had borne children for Experience as regularly as the calendar, one every two years for ten years—Nathan, Abigail, Eunice, Zachariah, and Jonathan. Little Jonathan, only four when his father returned from delivering the Boston Thursday Lecture, could not remember his mother. The combination of her sixth pregnancy and an epidemic of "Feaver" then raging on the island had overtaxed her physical resources. A child had been born alive on March 1, 1722, but did not live, and the following afternoon Remember had joined her baby in death.[20]

Experience, fifty at the death of his second wife, never remarried. The family was large enough, the farm could support a servant or two to help with the work, and the father was so occupied with preaching, writing, farming, and the education

of his sons that he had no inclination to go courting again. The
care of the younger children was left to the older sisters, although there is no record of which one played the mother role
to Jonathan. Perhaps it was Reliance, the oldest sister, who was
at home until she married in 1729. (She died in childbirth the
following year.) In any case, the father was the dominant influence on the first twenty years of Jonathan's life.

Experience kept busy in the period following Remember's
death. It was then that he wrote *Indian Converts: Or Some
Account of the Lives and Dying Speeches of a Considerable
Number of the Christianized Indians of Martha's Vineyard . . . ,*
to which the Rev. Thomas Prince added an *Account* of the
Missionary Mayhews. *Indian Converts* was published in London in 1727 with an "Attestation" signed by eleven of the
Boston clergy, Cotton Mather's name heading the list. It was
an attempt to interest an international audience in Indian missions by what amounted to human-interest stories about the
religious experiences of the Indians and, thereby, to promote
the revival of this work asked for in the Boston Thursday
Lecture of 1724.

The main concern of the father in these years was the education and preparation for the ministry of his son Nathan, the
first of Remember's children, almost ten at her death. From
childhood Nathan had been set aside for the Indian ministry.
Experience saw clearly the need for better qualified missionaries. The efforts to train native preachers had largely failed,
and the few whites who had aided in the work had often done
as much harm as good. A recent example was Josiah Torrey,
pastor at Tisbury, who had drawn a salary from the New
England Company for preaching to the Indians. Torrey had
died in 1723 of an ailment aggravated by drinking "too freely
and too frequently of spirits." [21]

Experience was determined that Nathan should not repeat
the familiar Mayhew pattern of drifting into the Indian work

CHAPTER II

Harvard College

As to which principles [of civil government], excepting what
I learnt from nature, from the ancient greeks & romans, &
from the holy Scriptures, I own I learnt them from such
writers as Sidney, Locke, and Hoadley.

Jonathan Mayhew, 1762[1]

ZACHARIAH and Jonathan were now the men of the family.
Life on Martha's Vineyard offered exciting possibilities for
these teen-age boys: hunting in the woods surrounding Quenames, fishing in the salt-water ponds almost at their doorstep,
swimming in the rough surf on the South Beach, or playing
football with the young Praying Indians, a sport that produced
occasional casualties. On rarer occasions there were trips to the
harbors on the north and east sides of the island to see the ships
from all parts of the world that during the eighteenth century
put in at the Vineyard and to talk with their crews, who
brought news directly from England or the West Indies. The
boys often accompanied the aging father as he traveled to one
of the several Indian services held on Thursday and Sunday.
More routinely, there was work on the farm, and the few acres
of Vineyard land tilled by Experience Mayhew and his sons
were as stony, as backbreaking, as those on the mainland of
New England.[2]

It would be easy to attribute Jonathan Mayhew's adult personality to the twenty years of his youth spent in the isolation
of a Vineyard farm and Indian mission. A biographer may
wish that such a simple thesis were tenable, but if he attempts
to demonstrate that Jonathan's boldness, eloquence, brilliance,
and ambition were so produced, he must also explain the older

brother as a product of the identical environment. Zachariah was everything Jonathan was not—slow, inarticulate, retiring, a plodder in all he attempted. Not until 1767 did he decide to enter the Indian ministry to preserve the family tradition through five generations.

The cultural pattern imposed upon young Jonathan by the accident of birth was that of the typical New England village, a pattern duplicated with monotonous regularity wherever the lineal or spiritual descendants of the first American Puritans penetrated the vast continent. Chilmark, last of the three original Vineyard towns to be founded, had few inhabitants before the eighteenth century. During Jonathan's youth it could have boasted of not more than three hundred residents including the Indians. Town life centered around the meetinghouse. Here, as always, young people had to be rebuked occasionally for "their irreverent and profane deportment in the time of God's publick worship." The meetinghouse was also the scene of special religious services, for example, public fasts held to pray for rain or to seek the meaning in divine providence of a recent earthquake. And here assembled Chilmark's version of New England's peculiar institution, the town meeting. Jonathan's friends and neighbors were humble folk, but their lives give abundant evidence of the Puritan's equal passion for spiritual and material concerns.[3]

New Englanders were widely known in the colonial period for their litigious spirit, and the people of the Vineyard, including Jonathan's relatives, were no exception. The much-used court system proved a particular blessing to the Indians, who through it were spared the worst rigors of a white man's justice. Not even the Chilmark schoolmaster escaped the web of litigation. Francis Bryan was taken to court in 1732 because he did "Neglect and Refuse to teach Sundry Children" of the town, and particularly the servant girl of Zephaniah Mayhew. Apparently Bryan thought the town was sending him more pupils

than his contract specified. Five years later the selectmen were
forced to answer to the county courts for failing to maintain
a schoolmaster. Whether Experience Mayhew's sons learned
the rudiments of reading and writing in this poorly maintained
school is uncertain; the records fail to provide a single important clue to Jonathan's precollege education.[4]

Nathan may have tutored the boys during his vacations from
Harvard and in the short period he was at home before his
death. Certainly, a major source of Jonathan's early education
was his father and his father's library. Experience Mayhew had
assembled a small collection of theological works and a few
other books, a modest library which was enlarged from time
to time by gifts of contemporary sermons and newspapers from
his Boston friends. One does not have to indulge in sentimen-
tality to imagine the boy before the fireplace on a winter
evening poring over such items from his father's bookshelves as
Increase Mather's sermon, *Do thy self no harm,* or going
through the papers and books Nathan had brought home from
Cambridge, perhaps the *Lyra Prophetica David,* a volume of
Psalms in Hebrew and Latin. The teen-age lad was sometimes
engaged in what might be loosely described as literary pursuits.
He transcribed letters for his father, whose "feeble and shaking
Hand" was unequal to his correspondence. The beginning of
an "Indian Grammar," undated but in Jonathan's handwriting,
suggests that he was sufficiently acquainted with the language
to assist his father in the Indian mission. Yet Experience Mayhew gave no outward sign that he was thinking of sending
either son to college.[5]

In 1738, Jonathan at seventeen was already well past the
age at which most students entered Harvard. On February 14
of that year he gathered together a few scraps of lead and cast
them into a crude inkstand. He inscribed on its sides, "J.M.
Feb. 14, A.D. 1738," as if to commemorate some important
moment in his life—possibly the time he began seriously to
prepare for admission to college. According to a contemporary

account, Experience Mayhew had concluded he was too impoverished to send another son to Cambridge. At last, however, his younger son's "genius Superior" to farming and his expression of "a great desire for learning" had convinced the father that he must see Jonathan through college, whatever the sacrifice. Where or under whose tutelage the boy prepared for the Harvard entrance examinations is unknown, but it is usually assumed he did so without leaving the Vineyard.[6]

In a pathetic mood, the father petitioned the General Court in December 1739, to grant him some of the "unappropriated Lands of this province, which may hereafter be a Benefit to his Children." In support of his petition he cited forty-five years of work among the Indians at great financial sacrifice. The General Court answered the petition with an annual grant of £10 for five years and the privilege of selecting six hundred acres of land. The grant of £50 was directly useful in paying Jonathan's college expenses, but the tract of land had no immediate cash value. It did, perhaps, help to compensate for the personal holdings in Chilmark which the father sold in 1740 and 1741 to raise cash. Experience was land poor, and his usual way of obtaining funds was to sell some of his ancestral holdings.[7]

Experience Mayhew was not sending a son to Harvard to follow in the family's footsteps by entering the Indian ministry. In 1740, Jonathan had not yet settled on the ministry as a career. The father's increasing discouragement over "the miserable Indians," his neglecting to seek funds for his son's education from the New England Company, and his intense interest in the theological controversies of the day, all point to a determination that his last son should seek a field of service less obscure and more promising than his own.

Jonathan Mayhew moved into the mainstream of New England society in the first week of July 1740, when he presented himself for examination to the President and Tutors of Har-

vard College. He had narrowly escaped from the oblivion of a
life on a Vineyard farm.[8]

Educational prerequisites for admission to Harvard in 1740
were largely classical; every candidate was required to demonstrate proficiency in Latin and offer at least a smattering of
Greek. Such requirements were more than a vestige of a past
civilization, for Latin and to a lesser degree Greek and Hebrew
were functional in the eighteenth-century society of scholars.
When Governor Shirley visited the college during Jonathan's
second year, he was greeted by a student oration in Latin, to
which the Governor replied in "an elegant Latin Speech."
Those present at the Harvard commencement in 1747 did not
think it incredible to hear a graduate student present the argument that in the future world articulate communication would
be in Hebrew.[9]

If he survived the oral examination, the candidate was assigned to write a simple theme in Latin. After this hurdle came
more mundane considerations. He must furnish evidence of
good character, sign a pledge to abide by the rules, and make
the inevitable financial arrangements. Finally the freshman
was sent home until the fall term opened, usually about the
middle of August. Jonathan had completed this process and
was back on the Vineyard by August 17, if not before, for on
that day he was received into the communion of the Chilmark
Church.[10]

An epidemic of "throat distemper" delayed the reopening
of Harvard until the end of August. When the doors finally
opened, Jonathan found himself considerably older than most
of the thirty-three freshmen admitted in 1740. The average age
of the class was about sixteen, yet there was one "20-1/2" and
several seventeen or eighteen, so his nineteen years were not
as conspicuous as they would have been in some freshman
classes. Harvard freshmen were expected to run errands for
the upperclassmen and tutors and "to carry themselves to there

seniors in all Respects so as to be in no wise saucy to them."
It is difficult to picture Jonathan, who chafed so easily at any
restraint, fetching the morning "cue" of beer for some of the
fifteen-year-old lads who were his "seniors," but the records
suggest nothing other than acquiescence to this pattern of
academic aristocracy.[11]

Harvard Yard in 1740 was hardly more than a country field
on which three modest college buildings outlined a small common, but here in this academic community of some 150 students and staff, Jonathan Mayhew joined the generation of
New England leaders who were soon to initiate the drive for
independence from Great Britain and to force the Old Testament God of the Founding Fathers to share His direction of the
new American destiny with the God of nature and reason of the
European Enlightenment. During the seven years he was to
spend in Cambridge, Jonathan lived, studied, prayed, and
played with such future leaders of the Revolution as James
Otis, Jr., Samuel Cooper, James Bowdoin, James Warren, and
Thomas Cushing. Although he maintained permanent friendships with Otis and Cooper, he was closer during college days
to future religious liberals, particularly Lemuel Briant, John
Brown, and James Wellman. Educationally more important,
he saw represented in classmates he knew personally the important segments of New England life and both sides of the issues
for which men contended. Few generations in American history were to be confronted with so many questions on which
division would be inescapable. Far from forming an enclave of
peace in troubled times, Harvard in the 1740's inadvertently
provided in embryo the very world in which this fateful generation would live.[12]

The most nerve-racking event in the life of every freshman
class was the spring day on which the class was placed.
Placing was a serious matter, for it determined the question
of precedence at all public and private college functions for

the entire stay at Cambridge. It was done, as one freshman remarked, "to the great uneasiness of a great many." The basis of placing was unrelated to scholarship and did reflect the supposed social status of the student's father, with preference being given to public service. When the Class of 1744 was permanently placed on May 1, 1741, Jonathan landed in eighth position, testimony to the esteem in which his father was held. Joshua Gee, son of the pastor of Boston's influential Second Church (the Mather Church), preceded him on the list. At the head of the class was Samuel Welles, whose father was a member of the Massachusetts Council and wealthy enough to pick up the check for the dinner which the top man was bound by tradition to give for the class.[13]

The Harvard rules, which Jonathan had copied as part of his admission procedure, required the young scholars "to behave themselves blamelessly, leading Sober, righteous & godly Lives." College students in the 1740's were no worse, no better, than those of most periods: they shot firecrackers in the yard at night, made "indecent Noises" at all times, stole chickens from neighboring farmers, and sometimes took part in what was described in the Faculty Records as an "Extravagant drinking Frolick." Undergraduates were permitted beer and some other hard beverages, but only in the amount and at the time and place stipulated by the college authorities. Illegal drinking was common, but few students seem to have been contaminated by the philosophy of the college servant who, a student concluded, had made rum his "summum bonum." A favorite stunt was to send a freshman to town for rum or some such liquor to quicken the brain during study hours. Shortly after the beginning of the school year in 1741, Tutor Joseph Mayhew, Jonathan's cousin, caught a group enjoying rum fetched by three freshmen, obedient to their seniors' commands. Although his cousin was in the number, Tutor Mayhew reported the incident to the faculty, with the result that Jonathan was fined three shillings, the first of a long series of fines for various items of misconduct during his undergraduate days.[14]

Jonathan's most serious embroilment with the college authorities came at the beginning of his senior year. One evening the senior class met to select officers to perform certain duties at commencement. Someone brought along a supply of liquor, which may have contributed to an inability to conclude their business. At ten o'clock, one hour after the meeting was required to disband, they were still "deliberating." Tutor Mayhew attempted to send the seniors to their chambers, but with slight success, and finally three of the tutors issued a direct order for the class to return to their individual quarters. This order got the young men out of the room in which they were meeting, but on the way to their chambers they gathered in the yard and appointed a delegate to ask the tutors for an extension of time "to Tarry together to do their business in." Two days later the faculty fined the seniors seven shillings each for drinking and issued an "Admonition" for their contempt of the tutors. When Jonathan learned of the punishment, he "in a very imprudent manner made an impertinent recrimination upon some of the imediate Governors of the House they all being present." As he was to do so often in the future, the scion of the feudal lords of Martha's Vineyard said boldly what his fellows only dared think. This was his first and most unsuccessful defense of "liberty" against "tyranny." [15]

The penalty for this "recrimination" was degrading—a punishment second in severity only to expulsion. After evening prayers on September 26, the entire college witnessed the ceremony of Jonathan's name being moved from eighth to fifteenth place on the buttery table, a board where the names of the students were posted according to rank. Although his reaction to degrading is not recorded, the culprit's reformation was less than complete, for the following March he was again

fined for illegal drinking. Acting under Tutor Flynt's policy
that wild colts often make good horses, the authorities eventually forgave Jonathan the affront for which he had been
degraded. In June the faculty voted to accept his "humble
Petition for his restoration" accompanied by "an humble confession of his Crime," and he was graduated in his original
place. As a postscript to this incident, the Class of 1744 never
succeeded in electing the officers they had met to select, and
in desperation the faculty finally made appointments, among
whom was the author of the "impertinent recrimination." [16]

Thanks to his father's reputation as a missionary, Jonathan
was permitted to defray part of his expenses with grants and
jobs given him by the College Corporation. After his freshman
year he was able by his own efforts to pay perhaps one quarter
of the yearly college bill of slightly more than £20. Except for
a summer vacation of six weeks, the college kept its doors open
the year round. Students were allowed to go home or to visit
friends for certain periods, the duration and frequency of
which were determined by the distance of the student's home
from Cambridge. Jonathan was seldom able to take advantage
of such vacations because of the length and expense of a trip
to the Vineyard. Nevertheless, he saw his father once or twice
each year, for Experience, although entering his seventies, was
still making trips to Boston.[17]

When he arrived in Cambridge, Jonathan had made no
definite decision to go into the ministry. As far as the curriculum was concerned, an immediate choice of a life's work
was unnecessary, for the undergraduate was pushed through
the same course of study regardless of career plans; even
Hebrew was required of all. A freshman class was turned over
to a tutor, who for four years guided the young scholars pro-
gressively through the classics, rhetoric, logic, natural philosophy, geography, ethics, divinity, metaphysics, mathematics,
and astronomy. The tutor assigned readings and disputations,
and sometimes encouraged his students to read independently

in the library. The Class of 1744 was given to Tutor Thomas
Marsh, who had been graduated with Jonathan's brother
Nathan in 1731. There were rumors that Marsh's theology was
heretical, but evidence is lacking to show any lasting influence
on his pupil from Martha's Vineyard by this sincere, patient
man, who bore the brunt of so much undergraduate impudence.
Lectures by two professors, Edward Wigglesworth in theology
and John Winthrop in science, supplemented the tutorial system.[18]

Under its moderately liberal president, Edward Holyoke,
the college was rapidly eliminating the remnants of medieval
scholasticism from its curriculum. The old standard works
were being replaced with newer books incorporating the ideas
and spirit of Newton and Locke. Jonathan prepared an alphabetical list of some of the books he read, with page and line
references for each. Not one title on this list had been used at
Harvard in the seventeenth century. Doubtless he read many
of the older books, but the authors of whom he took special
note were recent imports. Prominent among these were writers
who explored the relation between morality or moral philosophy and revealed religion. New England Puritans had usually
placed religion and ethics in separate categories, consequently
preparing the way for the acceptance of rationalistic works on
moral philosophy at the same time rationalistic ideas in theology were rejected. Intellectually curious undergraduates could
read such books as William Wollaston's *The Religion of Nature
Delineated,* an attempt to discover the extent to which nature
and reason could produce "true religion" without the aid of
revelation. As the century moved on, more and more Harvard-
educated clergymen admitted nature and reason to a partnership with Biblical religion. So firm was the foundation of revelation, however, that for Mayhew and nearly all others the
relation remained a coordinate one, and few in New England
were to advocate a dependence on natural religion alone for
another half-century.[19]

Most of the commonplace books (notebooks) Jonathan used at Harvard are missing, but a nineteenth-century biographer reports that one contained a passage copied from a work by Samuel Clarke, England's most influential liberal divine of the past generation. In a fragment of one commonplace book that has been preserved, Mayhew transcribed an innocuous quotation from John Tillotson, the rationalistic Archbishop of Canterbury. When evangelist George Whitefield visited New England in 1740, he accused the Harvard faculty of encouraging students to read "Bad books" by Tillotson and Clarke instead of more orthodox "Evangelical writers." Professor Wigglesworth replied that Tillotson's works had not been borrowed by an undergraduate for nearly nine years, nor Clarke's for more than two years. Benjamin Colman, pastor of Boston's Brattle Street Church, tried to quiet the controversy by telling Whitefield that "Our College supplies us with many worthy Ministers, notwithstanding the New Books of Morality with Infidelity, wch. has possibly hurt some." Since Jonathan took his extract from Tillotson after Whitefield made his charges, it is possible that the controversy advertised the "Bad books" to Harvard undergraduates.[20]

Whatever the critics may have said, the Harvard system in the 1740's encouraged ambitious students to read widely and freely and to develop a lifelong dependence on imported books. The significance of this "intellectual revolution" in a society that only sixteen years before had still made life miserable for booksellers can hardly be exaggerated.[21] Mayhew always gladly acknowledged his debt to the European writers he began reading in college. He would soon be speaking publicly of Clarke as an "admirable writer" and quoting Voltaire to show the folly of persecuting heretics.

In later life Jonathan expressed great interest in the scientific work of John Winthrop, Hollis Professor of Mathematics and Natural and Experimental Philosophy, but their relation while the younger man was a resident in Cambridge has eluded biographers. Winthrop was the preëminent colonial scientist of his day, and his lectures at Harvard introduced receptive students to the universe of Newton. A courageous scholar who refused to let Biblical interpretations discourage experimentation and scientific thinking, he was at the time of his installation spared an examination of his theological views for fear of the consequences. A friendship between the Professor and Jonathan is suggested by brief references in Winthrop's diary, but the younger man was no scientist; he could make only a layman's effort to understand the practical implications of his great teacher's work. It is possible that their common bond was religion and not science, for they were moving simultaneously away from the doctrines of Puritanism.[22]

Into Mayhew's commonplace book went long extracts from Thomas Burnet's *Sacred Theory of the Earth* and Pascal's *Pensées;* and he noted such books as John Woodword's *Natural History of the Earth,* Samuel Parker's *A demonstration of the divine authority of the law of nature,* and John Ray's *The Wisdom of God manifested in the Works of the Creation.* But his interest here was in the popular "physico-theology" of the day rather than the science of Professor Winthrop. With a practical, utilitarian mind that had no capacity for theory, he copied passages that appealed to him because of their metaphorical qualities and common-sense rationality. He was giving signs of a scholarship that would be diligent and eclectic but seldom profound or original. Mayhew's role as a disseminator of ideas in America required no higher level of scholarship. It was sufficient that in his years at Harvard he learned that "the more a man habituates himself to intellectual employments, the greater will be his aptness and facility in discovering truth, and detecting error."[23]

CHAPTER III

Great Awakening

Blessed are our Eyes and our Ears, for they see & hear such Things as many Prophets and wise men have desired to see & hear, but could not—How thankful should we be to our Glorious Redeemer that he is thus riding forth in the Chariot of his Word, conquering and to conquer: But happy, yea thrice happy, shall we be, if made Partakers of these Blessings ourselves.

Jonathan Mayhew, 1741 [1]

JONATHAN MAYHEW's years at Harvard were the most turbulent Massachusetts had witnessed since the turn of the century. Between the witchcraft hysteria of the 1690's and the torturous decision for independence in the 1770's, no experience proved so traumatic for so many as the religious revivals known as the Great Awakening.

New Englanders had read with wonder Jonathan Edwards' description of the 1735 revival a hundred miles west in the Connecticut Valley. As a result, they listened eagerly to the reports that began to circulate in 1738 of the English evangelist George Whitefield's "flaming Piety and Zeal for the Power of Godliness," and in 1740 they hailed the news that this "most importunate Wooer of Souls" had arrived in their midst. Three weeks after Jonathan began his freshman studies at Harvard, Whitefield proclaimed from Boston's Brattle Street pulpit "that all our Learning and Morality will never save us; and without an experimental Knowledge of *God* in *Christ* we must perish in Hell for ever." Out of curiosity, out of boredom, out of piety, out of fear for their souls, people of all ranks crowded into Boston to hear him repeat this warning on the Common

and in church after church. His histrionic magic seemed a gift
from heaven. "It is a pleasant and wondrous Thing," wrote
Benjamin Colman, pastor of the Brattle Street Church, "to see
Souls flying to Jesus Christ." One week later the evangelist
crossed to Cambridge and preached to seven thousand persons (by his own count) in Harvard Yard. Whitefield was
gone in ten days, but he was followed almost immediately by
Gilbert Tennent, a New Jersey evangelist, whose sermons
were even more "searching and ranging." By 1741 "the very
Face of the Town seemed to be strangely altered." Churches
were crowded, people rushed into membership and to the
communion table, private homes as well as churches were
thrown open to weekday services, and the taverns were emp-
tied. The community rejoiced: "Let the guardian Angels carry
the News to Heaven of the numerous Converts; the Millen-
nium is begun, Christ dwells with Men on Earth." [2]

Harvard students found the excitement of the revival a
welcome release from academic monotony. Some heard
Whitefield with "wonder and affection," but Tennent produced the "great shock." After both evangelists had preached
at the college, Tennent wrote to Whitefield that "the shaking
among the dry Bones was general; and several of the Students
have received Consolation." Observers reported that "the
Scholars in general have been wonderfully wrought upon,
and their Enquiry now is, What shall we do to be saved?" and
"divers Gentleman's Sons, that were sent there only for a more
polite Education, are now so full of Zeal for the Cause of
Christ, and of Love to Souls, as to devote themselves entirely
to the Studies of Divinity." Benjamin Brandon, Jonathan's
fellow student and intimate friend, witnessed all-night services in which people were "blessing and praising God, or
bewailing their lost and undone Condition by Nature." No
one was surprised when in June 1741, the Harvard Overseers
spent a special meeting "in humble thanksgiving to God for

the Effusion of his holy Spirit & in the earnest Supplication
that the good work so graciously begun may be abundantly
carryed on." [3]

Tutor Henry Flynt recorded in his diary that "many Schol-
lars appeared to be in great concern as to their souls & Eternal State." Some, he noticed, had been first affected by Whitefield's preaching, others by Tennent's, and still others had
been moved by the sermons of Nathaniel Appleton, pastor of
the Cambridge Church, "who was more close & affecting in
preaching after Mr. Whitefields being here." Flynt observed
a group of thirty students, including Jonathan Mayhew, Samuel Cooper, and James Otis, who "prayed together, sung
Psalms, and read good books." One had a vision of hell opening wide; another was concerned lest his father's "formal &
insipid" prayers were evidence of his unconverted state. The
majority "look serious & concerned," said Flynt, who had
heard that some students were fasting in addition to praying
and singing. Most of them mean well, he concluded, but they
suffer from the "Extravagances & Errors of a weak & warm
Imagination." [4]

There is no record of Mayhew's religious experience before
this reference in Tutor Flynt's diary, but one year later he
wrote his brother a letter which, except for one short postscript, was devoted entirely to the wonders of the Awakening.
Evidently, under the influence of the revival, Jonathan had
decided to enter the ministry, for he explained to Zachariah,
"God has been pleased for holy Ends, to visit me with Sickness; but thro' his tender Compassion he has raised me again;
but what shall I render to the Lord for all his Benefits?—he
would write a Law of Gratitude on my Heart and encline me
to devote my Spared Life, yea all the Powers and Faculties of
my Soul, to his Service. He has done great Things for me
whereof I am Glad." [5]

Sometime in the three months following this letter to his

brother of December 26, 1741, Jonathan and another student journeyed seventy miles from Boston to York, Maine (then Massachusetts) because of "an earnest Desire . . . to see and get a right Understanding of Affairs there with Respect to Religion." His account of this trip, as related to Zachariah, is important evidence of his initial attitude toward the Great Awakening and also one of the best descriptions of the religious phenomena associated with that movement:[6]

The Spirit seems to set the Word home in a very extraordinary Manner; so that some Persons who have scarcely thought of God, Heaven or Hell, seriously in all their Lives, have been not only pricked to the Heart, and forced to cry out in Meeting-Time *What shall we do,* &c; but some have been struck to the Ground in an Instant, as Paul was, and have remain'd for some Time wholly speechless. Others have had their Sins so set in Order before them, that they were render'd incapable of expressing any Thing distinctly; and would seem to be in as much Distress as you could imagine a Person to be, who was cast into a Furnace; which Distress they express'd by their hideous Cryings and Yellings, and all the Distortions of Body which the acutest Torments could throw them into; but these who have been in such Agonies have not continued long without Consolation; some Three Weeks, (tho' not all the while in such Extremity) some a Fortnight, some a Week, some a few Days, and some but a few Hours: And when they receiv'd Joy, it came in no less an extraordinary Manner; some being so overcome with the Love of Christ, that their Bodily Strength quite failed them; they would fall to the Ground, and lay panting as though their Souls were dissolving, and ready to take their Flight, and leave the lifeless Clay. Others would cry out *Comfort me with Apples, slay me with Flaggons for I am sick of Love—This is my beloved and this is my Friend, O ye Daughters of Jerusalem!* They are generally young Persons who are thus wrought upon; and some of them are even Babes and Sucklings, and from the Mouths of these does God ordain Praise. Their Words who have seen cannot express, nor their Thoughts conceive, who have not seen, with what Agonies of Soul, and Aptness of Expression, they . . . pray and exhort. When I have seen & heard them blessing and praising the adored Jesus, I have frequently thought of the Children crying out Hosanna to the Son of David, Hosanna in the Highest!

After this description, Jonathan attempted to explain what he had seen on the trip: "Some have been much stumbled at the Degrees of Sorrow and Joy which many have experienced." But he saw nothing strange in sinners trembling "for Fear of God" nor in their great rejoicing "when they see themselves rescued from Destruction from that amazing Place of Torment where the Worm dies not and the *fire* is not quenched, where the Smoke of their Torment ascendeth up forever and ever; when they have a glimmering Prospect of those Mansions above, and some Prelibations and Foretastes of the Joys of the new Jerusalem." He concluded in a passage so eloquently evangelical that it would have fitted nicely into a Whitefield sermon:

Let us, my Dear Brother, look upon every Thing below with an Holy Scorn & Contempt, with an Air [of] Unconcernedness: Let us look forward beyond Death and the Grave, and let the thoughts of Death, instead of being terrible to us, comfort and support us under all the Toils and Fatigues of Life. Let us look upon the Time of Death as the kind and courteous Moment that shall give us a Discharge from our Shackels and Prison; that shall at once launch us into the Ocean of Eternity, that Sea without a Shore, and land us safe at the thrice happy Haven of the Blessed. . . . Surely there are Joys in Religion which neither the Sensual & carnal World, nor the self righteous Pharisee know any Thing of, Joys which those Strangers intermeddle not with. . . . May our Souls be more & more inflamed with the Love of Christ, and grow warmer and warmer in our Devotions to him, till we arrive at the Regions of Immortal Glory, where we shall never know any Coldness of Affection, and where Hosannas shall never languish on our Tongues; where Glory shall irradiate every Face, and perfect Love & Friendship reign in every Heart, and [a] smile in every Eye, and our Tongues shall ever utter the melting Language of redeeming Love.

Five years later, after hearing Whitefield's farewell sermon

on Copp's Hill in Boston, Jonathan Mayhew again reported
on the progress of the revival, this time with marked antago-
nism. He wrote to his father, "As to Mr. Whitefield, when he
was in Town there were many Persons that attended his
preaching; but chiefly of the meanest sort, excepting those
that heard him from a Principle of Curiosity—I heard the last
Sermon he preached, which was a very low, confused, puerile,
conceited, ill-natur'd, enthusiastick, &c. Performance as ever
I heard in my Life." [7] This is one of the most quoted opinions
of the Great Awakening in New England, with the result that
Mayhew has been branded as an archopponent of the revival.
Written in 1747, it has often been cited as an opinion of the
movement in general with no reference to date. In fact, the
revival was then a memory; Whitefield was no longer at the
center of a large community manifestation. During the peak
of the New England Awakening, 1740–1742, young Mayhew
was playing the part of the enthusiast he was later to denounce.

The father was instrumental in the transition that occurred
during these five years, as he was so often in the crucial stages
of Jonathan's development. Experience Mayhew had hoped
for the best from the Great Awakening, even desiring the
Indians to participate in "such Blessings." As time went by,
he became increasingly doubtful of any permanent results,
and these doubts were confirmed when he read Whitefield's
autobiography, in which he found reason to believe the evangelist still unregenerate long after he had testified to being
in a state of grace. He concluded that Whitefield was "under
the Power of *Satanical* Delusions" and unable to distinguish
these "Delusions" from the true voice of God. When under
such "Delusions" the preacher became a *"Miserable Enthusiast"* dependent upon "Immediate *Revelations,* rather than
on the *Scriptures* to direct him in his Duty." There was great
danger that Whitefield's example would lead New Englanders

My Son,

That divine Sentence uttered by the wise Man in Proverbs g. 10. The Knowledge of the holy is Understanding, is worthy of your most serious Consideration.

The Design of your Education in the School of the Prophets, where for the present you are placed, is, that your Mind may be furnished with useful Knowledge; and that particularly which will be necessary for the Service of the Sanctuary, if it should please the great Master of Assemblies to call you thereunto: And to this the Knowledge of divine Things will be especially necessary, & this such a Knowledge as is in the Nature and Exercise of it divine & spiritual.

That I may my self do something to encourage and

Experience Mayhew writes his son in November 1741

to think they were converted while still living wicked lives.[8]

In November 1741, three months after Jonathan had returned to Cambridge for his second year at Harvard, he was handed a letter from his father. Written in one of the small booklets in which New England ministers scribbled their sermons, this letter was in reality a sermon of fatherly advice to the son, who carefully preserved the manuscript throughout his lifetime. Although couched in Biblical language, the point of this letter-sermon was unmistakable. Faith and reason, as criteria of religious truth, must be supplemented by experiential evidence. "The Knowledge of the Holy is Understanding," and such knowledge "delivers the Souls of Men from those Clouds of Ignorance & Darkness" which hide religious truth and spiritual duties from man in his natural state. This sobering admonition from the father reached Cambridge at the very time the son was most absorbed in the revival.[9]

The influence of the Harvard community was also tranquilizing. President Holyoke and Professor Wigglesworth hesitantly approved the revival in the beginning, but Tutor Flynt always regarded Whitefield as "a composition of a great deal of good & some bad." Among the bad was that the evangelist "seems to be a man not much acquainted with bookes & indeed has had but Little time for it wch makes mee wonder at his positive & dogmatical way of Expressing himself in some things." It was soon apparent to Flynt and others that the supporters of the revival hoped to stifle freedom of inquiry at the college. Whether or not they agreed with his aims, the faculty found Whitefield—young, poorly educated, heedless of ecclesiastical order, intolerant, scornful of reason, dependent on histrionics—the antithesis of the ministerial type they sought to produce. Worst of all, he set the stage for ever wilder evangelists, such as James Davenport, who, when brought to trial in 1742 for slandering the Boston clergy, was declared *non compos mentis*. The same Benjamin Colman

who had opened his arms to Whitefield in 1740 came to
Harvard two years later to urge prospective ministers "to give
Light and Heat together, in . . . well composed and delivered
Sermons" in emulation of the "Learning and Labours of the
present Pastors" rather than "these noisie Exhorters" who
begin preaching without even knowing their topic. Harvard's
sympathy seemed to be with neither the supporters (New
Lights) nor the opponents (Old Lights) of the Awakening,
but with the "regular lights" who understood both the power
and danger of revivalism. In December 1744 every faculty
member signed *The Testimony of the President, Professors,
Tutors and Hebrew Instructor of Harvard College in Cambridge, against the Reverend Mr. George Whitefield, and his
Conduct.* This document labeled Whitefield "an Enthusiast,
a censorious, uncharitable Person, and a Deluder of the People." Samuel Bird, Jonathan's classmate, was expelled the
same year for calling his pastor an unconverted "Dumb Dog"
who "had not one Qualification of a Gospel Minister." Harvard Yard did not shield its undergraduates from these "blasts
of enthusiasm" of the early 1740's, but it did furnish a sanctuary where students were encouraged to apply tests other than
emotional response to determine the validity of the religious
contagion they saw all around them.[10]

As Jonathan read the increasing number of testimonies de-
nouncing the excesses of revivalism and diagnosed his own
emotional response to the preaching of the evangelists, he
developed a mistrust of religious enthusiasm that was to follow him throughout his life. Much later he admitted that
some of the itinerant preachers of the Awakening might have
meant well and in particular cases have done "some real good,
contrary to the more direct tendency, and the far more common effects, of such irrational, and anti-scriptural preaching."
It was unfortunate, he concluded, that after the great conviction of the revival had evaporated, the masses returned to

their sinful ways "like the Dog to his vomit." [11] The aftermath of the Great Awakening left him persuaded that he must check his powerful emotions and in religion be a calm, clear-headed rationalist.

But Jonathan Mayhew's emotional power was too excessive to be confined to an inner reservoir. It must find other outlets; and it did, initially in application to intensive and serious study for the ministry, and throughout his career in religious and political controversy. He became a man who was never happy unless he was in a fight. In his own words, "My natural temper is perhaps too warm." [12] He was to become the Luther and not the Erasmus of eighteenth-century New England, but such harsh qualities are the stuff out of which reformers are made.

On Wednesday, July 4, 1744, less than eleven years after the death of Nathan, Experience Mayhew saw another son graduated from Harvard. Unlike Nathan, this son was not intended for the Indian ministry. After receiving his bachelor's degree, a young man thinking of the ministry as a calling usually spent some time in additional study to prepare himself to preach. If he was not taken into the parsonage of a friendly parson, who served as mentor, the candidate would often remain in residence at the college until he was settled in a church of his own. In October 1744 the Harvard Overseers voted Jonathan a grant from the Saltonstall foundation "on condition of his residing at the College & pursuing such Study as may best fit him for the Service of the Ministry." This grant was repeated for the two following years, with the result that Jonathan remained in residence until the spring of 1747.

Except for the restrictions of a small income, this was a happy period in his life. He was free to study as he pleased; and he was addressed as "Sir," a title Harvard gave to its candidates for the master's degree. Most of the undergraduate

restrictions did not apply to him—even so, he was fined twice
during these three years for breaking college rules. There
were trips to hear Boston's best preachers, carriage rides with
Tutor Flynt, and occasional opportunities to preach. Best of
all, there was ample time for discussion and fellowship with
his friends also in residence during these months. Benjamin
Brandon, a jolly lad "more bulky . . . than two ordinary men,"
had already developed something of a local reputation as a
literary wit. Samuel Cooper, whose youthful eloquence had
moved the Brattle Street Church to invite him to take the
place of his deceased father as colleague of the aging Benjamin Colman, was on leave of absence to complete his
theological study before being ordained. The humor and poise
of Gad Hitchcock and John Brown were perfectly at home
in this impressive group of young scholars whose zest, charm,
and family connections opened to them many of the important
doors in the area. Yet, the more they moved in Boston circles,
the louder grew the whispers that Harvard had bred a pack
of young heretics. Brandon soon escaped to his father's count-
ing house, but Mayhew, Cooper, and Hitchcock prepared to
face the ire of the ultraorthodox at their ordinations.[13]

Tradition has attempted to place Jonathan sometime between 1744 and 1747 in the home of Ebenezer Gay, pastor at
Hingham, twenty miles south of Boston. In his sermon at
Mayhew's ordination, Gay spoke of "frequent Conversation"
with the younger man.[14] The Hingham parson was fond of
taking candidates for the cloth under his wing and opening his
pulpit to their first sermons. By the early 1750's he had succeeded in filling some of the neighboring churches with men
who shared his moderately liberal theology, which stressed the
essentials of Christianity on which all Christians agreed rather
than "the offensive peculiarities" of any one party. There is no
further evidence of Gay's influence on Mayhew, nor is it certain
that he spent more time in the Hingham parsonage than an
occasional overnight lodging on trips to and from Martha's

Vineyard. If Mayhew was indebted to Gay for theological nurture, he owed him nothing for political philosophy, an area where their ideas clashed sharply.[15]

In March 1746 Jonathan informed his father that he was forced to cancel a projected visit to the Vineyard during the coming spring, as he expected to begin preaching in three or four months. "I shall Need," he explained, "to improve all my Time with the greatest Diligence to prepare for such a difficult Work." Three weeks later he again wrote his father, this time with the good news that the Commissioners for Indian Affairs had voted to increase the missionary's annual salary. The opportunity was too tempting to resist, and Jonathan closed with a familiar plea: "If you could any Way let me have some Money, I should be very glad, being at the present out of Money & pretty much in Debt." [16] A young man in such financial straits was in need of a job, which in this case meant finding a church that would accept him as its pastor.

As Jonathan penned these lines to his father, the church at Worcester, thirty-five miles west of Boston, was seeking a new minister, a task made more difficult by a history of unhappy relations with former pastors. The first shepherd of the flock, noted chiefly for the practical jokes he played on his parishioners, at last had been dismissed. Isaac Burr, the second pastor, had been ousted in 1746 after a long struggle against the revivalistic party in the town. The church was divided between a majority of New Lights and a small minority of liberals who went so far as to tamper with the doctrine of original sin. After agreeing on one candidate, only to have him decline the call, the church heard a score of prospects without making a choice, notwithstanding a day of prayer and fasting to seek divine guidance. Jonathan was one of the aspirants heard by the church, although there is no record of when he first preached in Worcester.[17]

By October 1746 the congregation had narrowed the field

to Thaddeus Maccarty and Jonathan Mayhew. Maccarty, a tall, slender man with a "black penetrating eye" and "loud sonorous voice," had been graduated from Harvard in 1739 and had spent the three years prior to November 1745 as pastor of the Kingston, Massachusetts, Church, where finally his approbation of the Great Awakening had resulted in his dismissal. To the New-Light faction in Worcester he seemed the natural selection to replace the anti-Whitefield Burr. Mayhew was very likely the candidate of the liberal group. The congregation arranged a competition between the two candidates. Each was invited to preach four Sundays in succession, Mayhew during November and Maccarty during December. January 19 was the date of the final choice. The previous Sabbath both men preached, one in the morning and the other at the afternoon service. Whatever Mayhew said or did failed to impress his hearers. When the day of election came, forty-four indicated their preference for Maccarty and only two voted for his rival. When the news of his rejection reached Cambridge, Jonathan's spirits were low. The £100 annual salary at Worcester had seemed a small fortune after nearly seven years of financial struggle to finish college and prepare for the Lord's work.[18]

Historians of Worcester are fond of speculating on the possibilities of Mayhew's settling there, but they ignore the difficulty of picturing the impetuous liberal laboring in harmony among the people of central Massachusetts, who apparently preferred their preachers loud and not overly scholarly. Whatever Worcester may have lost by its votes for Maccarty, Jonathan Mayhew left there his last shred of respect for George Whitefield.

Jonathan did not have long to mourn his failure at Worcester. The Cohasset Church was erecting a new building and seeking a minister. Mayhew along with several other young men preached during the interim. This time he was better

received, and the church invited him to settle. An answer was
not easy. Cohasset was a small town, hardly more than a
village separated from Hingham a few years before. It was
true that Cohasset was only a short walk from Ebenezer Gay's
home in Hingham, and the circle of ministers of whom Gay
was the center was made up of the most enlightened clergymen of the province. Yet, had Experience Mayhew's son left
Martha's Vineyard only to bury himself in a small country
parish? Would the bleak, parsimonious life of a country parson
offer a challenge to the talents his classmates and teachers at
Harvard had admired? These were difficult questions for a
young scholar in need of a regular income. He had not found
the answers by the first week in March when he received word
that the West Church of Boston had also invited him to become its minister.[19]

CHAPTER IV

West Church

It has been the remark of many persons, and, I suppose, not wholly without foundation, that among my honoured and beloved hearers of this society, there is a pretty large proportion of "young men"; a larger proportion, perhaps, than in most of the other assemblies in the town.

Jonathan Mayhew, 1763[1]

IF ONE stood on the summit of Boston's Beacon Hill in 1747 and looked directly north across the Charles River, his view of Charlestown on the opposite bank would be intersected by a steeple rising some sixty feet above the roof of the frame structure of the West Church that rested on a strip of elevated ground at the foot of the hill. The land surrounding the church was West Boston, sometimes called New Boston. Most of this area was still empty of houses or other buildings in 1747, although several streets had been already laid out, and here and there could be seen a handsome, spacious dwelling encircled by well-cared-for grounds. Just to the right of the church was a small cluster of eight or nine houses at the point where Green Lane branched from Cambridge Street—later called Bowdoin Square. Beyond the steeple could be seen a square-tipped point of land jutting into the river. One corner of this tip, called Barton's Point, was the site of Captain Henry Berry's shipyard, and another shipyard was visible nearby. Not far from the church to the east, along the shore of the Mill Pond which filled the area where North Station now stands, were several "still houses" busy turning West Indian sugar into rum, some of which New England ships would carry to Africa as payment for slaves.

West Boston had contained little more than a few rope-
walks and a windmill in the first two decades of the eighteenth century, but beginning about 1719 it had rapidly become along with the (old) South End a haven for those who
had the financial means to escape the congested North End.
"Large and substantial residences" and such luxuries as a
bathhouse and a public garden made their appearance.[2] Out
of this situation grew the demand for a neighborhood church,
since Bostonians found the interval between the morning
and afternoon services all too short as it was—the closer the
church, the longer one could linger over Sunday dinner. William Hooper landed in Boston in 1734 at the very time a
demand for a church in West Boston began to be heard.
Hooper, educated at the University of Edinburgh, had come
from his native Scotland to serve as a tutor for the son of a
Boston aristocrat. Before long the Scotsman's attractive personality and exceptional talent for preaching won him a considerable personal following.[3] The coincidence of Hooper's
arrival and the need for a meeting house in West Boston
brought results. A group led by two prominent merchants,
Hugh Hall and Harrison Gray, arranged for the erection of
a house of worship with the intention of inviting Hooper to
accept the pastorate. Before the building was completed,
the seventeen founders met for organization at Hugh Hall's
mansion on January 3, 1737, and elected Hooper to the pastoral office. To make its invitation more palatable, the newly
gathered church voted Hooper a salary larger than that paid
to any other Congregational minister in town, notwithstanding
his lack of a family to support.[4]

On April 17 the West Church met for the first time in its
new meeting house, which, although slightly smaller than
the town's largest churches, seemed "beautiful and commodious" to contemporaries. Dr. Alexander Hamilton described it
succinctly: "This meeting house is a handsome, new, wooden

building with a huge spire or steeple att the north end of it. The pulpit is large and neat with a large sounding board supported att each side with pilasters of the Dorick order, fluted, and behind it there is a high arched door over which hangs a green curtain. The pulpit cushion is of green velvet, and all the windows in the meeting are mounted with green curtains." [5] All that remained to complete the formation of the church was to ordain a pastor, and May 18 was set for this ceremony. William Shirley, an Anglican, soon to become Governor of Massachusetts, attended the ordination service and came away impressed with Hooper's talents. It was slightly irregular for a minister to preach at his own ordination, and the refusal of other ministers to preach suggests that they were already irked at Hooper and his congregation. One likely source of this hostility was that some of those who had left the older churches to unite with the West Church did not live in its vicinity but had been drawn by the personal appeal of Hooper.[6]

Before the year was over, Hooper gave further offense to the Boston clergy by some remarks in his prayer and sermon at a Thursday lecture. Again in 1740 the ministers called Hooper to account, this time for an "insinuation" in another lecture that "the Doctrines of Grace and Holiness as presented in this Country serve to lead the people into apprehension of God as a peevish, vindictive or revengefull Being." He vigorously denied that he had any intention of making such an insinuation, and the matter was hushed, thanks largely to the conciliatory spirit of Benjamin Colman. For the next five years Hooper remained outwardly on good terms with his ministerial brethren. He was extremely popular with his parishioners, who thoroughly approved of his "strenuous opposition to Mr. Whitefield and his enthusiasm." [7]

On November 19, 1746, Boston was stunned by the report that Hooper had accepted the pastorate of Trinity Church,

an Anglican congregation less than half a mile across Beacon
Hill from the West Church. Tongues began to wag. Supporters of the revival accepted the news as evidence that Hooper
had opposed Whitefield out of an unconverted heart. The
Congregational clergy saw their suspicions confirmed. Even
the Anglican clergy of Boston were unhappy at this development, for Hooper was too popular and they doubted the
sincerity of his "instantaneous" conversion. They reported
their suspicions to the Bishop of London only to have the
laymen of King's Chapel, Boston's oldest Anglican church,
come out in support of Hooper against the clergy. The person
mainly responsible for the change was Governor William
Shirley, who had surmised the minister's drift toward the
Church of England several years before. As Hooper had been
about to accept an Anglican mission at Salem, Trinity Church
became vacant and Shirley proposed his friend for the position. So the popular preacher sailed for London on December
1 to secure Episcopal ordination, and the West Church was
left without a pastor.[8]

Hooper's defection hit the West Church hard. Ebenezer
Gay expressed the feelings of the congregation when he said,
"had it been possible, ye would have almost *plucked out your
own* Eyes, rather than have parted with him." [9] How or when
the parish first became interested in Mayhew is not on record,
but the ultraorthodox later suspected that Charles Chauncy,
copastor of the First Church, had pushed a liberal friend into
West Boston to draw attention from his own leanings toward
heresy. Jonathan preached his first sermon at the West Church
on January 25, 1747, the Sunday following his rejection at
Worcester, and he preached there as well as at Cohasset
several times in the next six weeks. On Friday, March 6, the
West Church elected Mayhew its pastor with only two dissenting votes out of forty-six. The same meeting set the pastor's salary at £15 (old tenor) per week, a full woodbox, and

house rent, and appointed a dozen gentlemen of the parish to wait upon Mayhew with the news of his election. Experience Mayhew's son had little difficulty in deciding between the two churches. Both were new and still small in membership, but there the similarity ended. The West Church was affluent and located in Boston; the Cohasset Church was modestly supported and isolated. It is easy to understand the thoughts of the young man who sought escape from poverty and the wilderness. When the church received an acceptance, it set Wednesday, May 20, for the ordination.[10]

An ordination was no light matter in eighteenth-century New England. In theory, each congregation ordained its own minister, but in practice an advisory council from neighboring churches was called in to conduct the service, so it was necessary to secure the approval of at least some of the Congregational clergy before the candidate could be ordained in the accepted manner. As "Philanthropos" sarcastically noted in the *Boston Evening Post*, "any Man may practice Physick who thinks himself fit for it, without a *Diploma;* but no Man can, consistently with good Order in Society, pray and preach publickly without *Approbation* and *Licence* for so doing."[11]

Boston in 1747 contained ten Congregational churches, of which the West Church was ninth in order of founding. The dean of the town's clergy was Benjamin Colman of the Brattle Street Church. He had been considered somewhat liberal when he assumed the pastorate of his innovating congregation in 1699, but since then had spent his time resisting further ecclesiastical change and working for peace and harmony among the clergy at all costs. Thomas Foxcroft and Charles Chauncy were copastors of the influential First Church. Foxcroft, the senior pastor, had been a disciple of Cotton Mather and had supported the Great Awakening. Chauncy, who already was revolting privately against Puritan theology,

had been Whitefield's chief antagonist in Boston. Yet the two
men, so unlike in outlook, seemed to work together in perfect
peace. The Old South Church, where Joseph Sewall and
Thomas Prince had colabored for over thirty years, was the
citadel of orthodoxy. These divines, with Joshua Gee of the
Second Church, Samuel Checkly of the New South, and John
Webb of the New North, formed the "old guard" of the Boston clergy, to whom the West Church would be expected to
turn for advice and counsel in the ordination of its new
pastor.[12]

Had the elder Boston divines been invited to form the
ordination council and the other pastors to assist, as was the
custom, it is possible the event would have gone off without
mishap. There was nothing these reverend gentlemen desired
less than a renewal of the ecclesiastical strife that had shaken
the town in the early 1740's. Instead, only two Boston
churches, Brattle Street and First Church, were invited to
attend, and the others were ignored. Ebenezer Gay of Hingham, Nathaniel Appleton of Cambridge, and Experience Mayhew would complete the council. As soon as he received the
invitation, Benjamin Colman dashed off a note to Thomas
Foxcroft expressing his great "Uneasiness" at the failure to
invite the other Boston churches. "Our Peace & Edification
at home," he told Foxcroft, "is I fear threatned whether we
send, or not." Although the church usually decided by vote
whether to send delegates to an ordination, it was led by the
recommendation of the minister. Colman did not, as he put
it, have "Light to lead the Brethren of the Church to which
I am related, into their sending Messengers . . . to act in the
Ordination of Mr. Mayhew." He gave his congregation and
the West Church two reasons for his lack of "Light": the
infirmities of mind and body which greatly curtailed his
activities, and the failure to invite the other churches and
pastors "in our Neighbourhood."

At the First Church the question of whether to send delegates to the ordination was voted on several times, but the
congregation was so divided and the debate so heated that
no action resulted, despite Chauncy's friendship for Mayhew.
Its short history had already made the West Church suspect
in the eyes of the clergy, and now the invitation to only two
of the Boston Congregational churches on the unprecedented
excuse that Mayhew had not preached in the others, was
further evidence of the congregation's lack of respect for
ecclesiastical order. Furthermore, it was common gossip that
the candidate to be ordained was not only heterodox but—
and more serious in clerical eyes—could not be silenced. The
combination threatened the ecclesiastical peace which Colman
and his party labored so steadfastly to maintain.[13]

An ordination was a top social event. As most pastoral
settlements were for life, an average congregation would in-
stall a new minister only once each generation. In the seventeenth century ordinations had emphasized the fasting and
prayer that preceded the actual ceremony, but increasingly
in the eighteenth century the banquet which concluded the
day's activities became the central event. Only one year before
the Brattle Street Church had raised £300—more than many
ministers received in salary for an entire year—to defray the
expense of Samuel Cooper's ordination as associate pastor
with Colman. The wealthier congregations rivaled each other
in providing choice cuts of meat, rare delicacies of all kinds,
and the best liquors for the visiting clergy, who, critical observers reported, sometimes returned home in a state of
spiritual joy. Naturally, the prosperous West Church would
not neglect its duty.[14]

May 20 was a beautiful day. A sumptuous feast was in
preparation. When the hour appointed in the afternoon for
the ordination service arrived, only two of the five ministers
invited were present. It was known that Colman and Foxcroft

would be missing, but the other three, as a majority of the council, would be able to conduct the ceremony. Unfortunately, Experience Mayhew had been delayed in travel and did not arrive until early evening. After much consultation, Gay and Appleton, the two members of the council present, decided that it would be improper to proceed without a majority, and they advised the congregation to postpone the ordination until a more representative council could be assembled. The feast was perishable and could not be postponed, so in the late afternoon the congregation and guests dined with the still unordained pastor.[15]

After the boycott of May 20, the West Church leaders were more determined than ever to settle Mayhew as their pastor. Wednesday, June 17, was announced as the date for the second attempt. This time the Boston churches were ignored and invitations sent to fifteen congregations, which, as the *Boston Evening Post* flung in the face of the town's divines, were all from the country.[16] Eleven of the churches accepted, so the West Church was assured of an adequate representation for June 17. On the day of the second ordination, Colman replied to a "kind brotherly Enquiry" as to why he had not accepted the invitation for May 20. His answer was evasive but conciliatory: "I heartily wish the Revd. Council to Day conven'd the Divine Presence & Conduct in all that comes before them." He prayed for peace among the churches of the town, but he still refused to endorse Mayhew. His final word to the West Church was Romans xvi, 17, a verse that summarized his attitude toward the new pastor: "Now I beseech you, brethren, mark them which cause divisions and offences contrary to the doctrine which ye have learned; and avoid them." [17]

The ordination service was a long, solemn, and formal affair. Originally, it had been a final test of the candidate's qualifications for the ministry, but this element of trial had all but disappeared by 1747. The candidate was no longer expected to preach the main sermon; instead, an elder divine delivered a message of admonition to congregation and new minister. Ebenezer Gay was a natural choice to preach at this ordination. After the introductory prayer, he arose and addressed the West Church and its guests in a remarkably candid sermon that answered the challenge of Colman and the Boston ministers yet also cautioned Mayhew to curb his impetuosity. But Gay's final word to his young friend left no doubts as to the road that lay ahead: "Be valiant for the Truth against all Opposition from the Lusts of Men, and Powers of Darkness. . . . So that from the Blood of the uncircumcised Slain, from the Fat of the Mighty, the Bow of *Jonathan* turn not back empty!" [18]

As an aftermath of the religious controversies of the Great Awakening, ordination councils of the last few years had often enquired into the theology and religious experience of the candidate. Only the year before Samuel Cooper had been forced to give a confession of faith to the entire church a few weeks prior to his ordination. Since Mayhew's council had been selected from the most broad-minded ministers in the area, it encountered no difficulty in agreeing in a private session on the soundness of his theology and the regularity of the entire proceedings. So the service continued without reference to Mayhew's beliefs or the requirement that he make a public profession of faith. Jonathan's elderly father, who had remained in Boston since May 20 to be certain to be on hand for the second ordination, now read the charge, which was designed to impress upon the candidate the solemn responsibility he was assuming. Then followed the official welcome to the candidate from his brother ministers—the right hand of fellowship—extended by the Reverend Benjamin Prescott of Salem. The ceremony was over and at last Mayhew was settled as pastor of the West Church. Another "handsome Entertainment" was ready, and the *Boston Gazette* announced to the missing clergy that "the whole Affair was finished with great Decency and perfect Unanimity." [19]

One Sunday in the spring of 1738, a servant boy from the North End was discovered picking pockets during the afternoon service at the West Church. Although the thief was promptly committed to jail, he had selected a likely place to ply his trade. From its foundation, the West Church was known as a society of prosperous and enterprising persons, many of whom represented the younger generations of old Boston families. The congregation was composed largely of merchants, great and small, their families and servants, and those engaged in occupations closely allied to trade, such as shipbuilders, sea captains, lawyers, printers, and artisans.[20] There were a few men with large amounts of property and high incomes, for example, Samuel Waldo, whose property at his death was inventoried at over £70,000; Harrison Gray, who enjoyed a comfortable income as treasurer of the province in addition to that derived from his own business and holdings; or John Spooner, who, Mayhew once boasted, was "one of the Wealthiest Merchants in this Town." [21] More typical were the smaller merchants and shopkeepers—men such as Daniel Jones, a hatter who also sold clothes and other English goods at the sign of the "Hatt and Helmit" on Newbury Street and whose advertisements in the press promised easy credit to soldiers and recruiting officers; Thomas Walley, who ran a grocery store in Dock Square where he offered for sale sugar, indigo, coffee, fish, spices, "Sweet Oyl," and other foodstuffs; or Henderson Inches, whose shop displayed such assorted commodities as cloth, twine, porter, pipes, and saddles.[22]

It was typical for these merchants to have spent their early years in cramped second-story quarters over their shops in the business districts of the North End and then to have moved into newly constructed houses in the open spaces of south and west Boston, where they devoted their profits to living in a

style to which they were unaccustomed. Household furnish-
ings, private gardens, and feminine draperies became symbols
of their new life. When Dr. Alexander Hamilton visited the
West Church in 1744 he was impressed by the "genteel congregation" in which most of the ladies were in "high dress."
While in Boston, the physician called on his countrywoman,
Mrs. Blackador, a wealthy widow, who with her two beautiful
but cross-eyed daughters, attended services at the West
Church in "glaring" dresses. Copley's portrait of the buxom
Mrs. Henderson Inches of the same congregation illustrates
what the doctor may have meant. Mayhew witnessed an excellent illustration of the composition of his parish when in
one of his first weddings he united in marriage Samuel Waldo's
daughter Lucy and Isaac Winslow, thereby uniting in business
two of the province's most ambitious families. The newlyweds
were the first members to be received into the West Church
after Mayhew's ordination.[23]

Other Boston churches had members who followed mercantile pursuits, of course, but the West Church, because it was so
new and situated in an area where few of the poorer classes
lived, was more exclusively made up of merchants than the
older churches. More than any other in Boston it was the
church of ambitious and often self-made men who lived by
their wits, who were cosmopolitan in their business and social
worlds, and who were impatient of restraining traditions. Such
men had come to respect success more than social status, and,
consciously or not, they now regarded religion as the chief
bulwark of private property and Christian liberty as the freedom to pursue profits. Mayhew's task was to adapt the Puritan
heritage to his segment of commercial Boston. The direction
he took was not inherent in the nature of the society to which
he ministered, for the so-called merchant class exhibited no
unanimity on religious and political issues beyond agreement
on the sanctity of the profit motive and the obvious acceptance
of the ethic of success. His theology and political philosophy

were not dictated by his milieu, yet they were compatible with and adapted to the mercantile environment in which he found himself. Personally, he soon discovered that a childhood spent in the wilderness had not rendered him incapable of being at home among the enterprising folk of his parish.[24]

The ordination safely past, the now Reverend Jonathan Mayhew faced the weekly routine of an eighteenth-century parson, the most important part of which was the two Sabbath services, one in the morning at ten o'clock, the other at three in the afternoon. It soon became evident that his growing reputation for heresy would force him to carry an increased load of preaching. The local ministers were noted for exchanging pulpits—a practice by which a preacher could avoid the wearisome task of preparing two new sermons for each Lord's Day—for the same sermon could be repeated in church after church. Congregations did not object; exchanging ministers involved no extra expense and broke the monotony of hearing the same voice twice each week throughout one's lifetime. It was not uncommon for a typical preacher to exchange for one-third of the year's services. Few of Mayhew's colleagues cared or dared to invite such a controversial figure into their pulpit while they in turn preached at the West Church. Chauncy was inhibited by the presence of Foxcroft; and Samuel Cooper, the only other supporter among the local clergy from the beginning, had to wait until after Colman's death in the fall of 1747 before he ventured to become the sole pastor to exchange with his college friend. The difficulties of travel to the country churches that would have welcomed Mayhew meant that for the most part he had to settle down to the preparation of two fresh messages each week.[25]

Sometime between 1682 and 1725 the New England clergy had lost the commanding position in society they had held during the seventeenth century. The "Fall of the Theocracy," as this loss of influence has been rather inaccurately described, did not mean that a minister could no longer occupy a place

of importance in New England affairs. It meant that the clergy
as a body must compete with a rising tide of secularism that
refused to accept them as ex officio leaders. The newspaper in
general had replaced the pulpit as the most influential public
platform in the larger towns, but a dynamic speaker who dealt
with vital topics of the day from the sacred desk was a
powerfully persuasive force. A few ministers continued to exert
widespread influence late into the century.[26] By 1748 Boston
contained eleven Congregational churches, three Anglican, two
Baptist, one Presbyterian, and one French Huguenot. These
churches, particularly the Congregational and Anglican, openly
competed with each other for the unchurched or those with
only loose church affiliations. Bostonians still flocked to hear
popular preachers, often to the dismay of the advocates of the
old ecclesiastical order. As late as 1754 effigies of New England
ministers done in mezzotint were advertised for sale in Boston;
and in the 1760's, printed sermons sold in such quantities that
printers encouraged their publication as a source of profit.[27]

Jonathan Mayhew was more fortunate than most ministers
in having an unusually homogeneous congregation. As a result
he was able to take a consistent point of view on controversial
issues without risking serious dissension among the people of
his parish. Aside from the topics of his sermons, a considerable
share of his effectiveness as a preacher and writer resulted from
a natural directness in speaking and an unadorned literary
style. The aim of preaching, he once declared, is "to express,
not to disguise, a man's real sentiments." [28] He spoke in a bold,
blunt, direct manner that left no doubt as to his meaning. Perry
Miller's description of Mayhew's style as "colloquial ease" fits
perfectly, as the many passages quoted in the following chap-
ters will bear out.[29] Harrison Gray, who heard Mayhew preach
regularly for nineteen years, described his conduct in the pulpit
as sober rather than light: "He had . . . a grave manly solemn
delivery which very much commanded the Attention of his

Audience." [30] His enemies were often critical of his oral abilities. Chief Justice Peter Oliver said that "In Conversation he
was an awkward Disputant, as well as in his extempore Pulpit
Effusions. . . . Both were so unharmonious and discordant, that
they always grated upon the Ears of his Auditors." [31] Such
extremes illustrate the difficulty contemporaries experienced in
evaluating Mayhew. Few could be neutral or objective; he
made either friends or enemies. Scores of New England ministers in the 1740's gave up the practice of reading their sermons after they witnessed the persuasiveness of Whitefield's
extemporaneous preaching. Mayhew continued to write out
each sermon in a manuscript booklet as his predecessors in the
ministry had done for more than a century, and his pulpit
discourses were not noteworthy for brevity. On important
occasions, at least, he also wrote prayers in advance. In his
hands the old Puritan formalism, which had made even the
most devout New Englander nod occasionally in the meeting
house, became a massive battering ram with which to beat
down the stone walls of orthodoxy.

In addition to the time-consuming sermon preparation, the
new minister began an endless round of baptisms, weddings,
funerals, lectures, and other events that demanded his presence
and usually an entry in the church records. Since the churches
were the chief welfare agencies of the day, his oversight included the care of the poor, although the West Church was
much freer from this burden than the congregations in the
older sections. He spent many hours calling on his parishioners,
who had taken their bachelor pastor to their heart as they had
done Hooper ten years before. The former parson's defection
had cost the West Church no more than two members. In
October, Jonathan wrote his father, "The People of my Parish
seem to be well united—none having left since my Ordination."
Hooper had returned from England and assumed his duties at
Trinity Church. "He has been to visit the Principal Families

of his former Parish," Mayhew noticed, "where he was well
entertained, not a word being mentioned on either side concerning his going over to the Church of England." [32]

The personal popularity and forensic talents of Mayhew and
Hooper could not overcome the unwillingness of the vast
majority of their congregation to become church members.
After a century of controversy over the terms of admission to
membership, the old Puritan distinction between the saints of
the church and the unredeemed of the congregation had largely
disappeared by the time of the Great Awakening. Most Congregational ministers were now willing to admit anyone of sound
character and nominal faith, thus qualifying almost any adult
in the congregation for membership. Still they hung back.
During Mayhew's ministry, the West Church seems to have
served altogether approximately 200 families representing perhaps 450 adults, of whom not more than one-sixth were members.[33] Such a proportion was typical of New England Congregational churches, but the West Church did differ in one
important way: the ratio of male to female members was
always about even, whereas typically it was two or three
women to one man. Only church members could take communion, but in most other respects little distinction was made
in the West Church between church and congregation. On
important questions such as calling a new minister, both had
to concur. Hooper and Mayhew baptized children freely without strict concern for the status of parents, thereby eliminating
one of the most pressing inducements to membership. The
challenge remained, nevertheless. Twice each Sabbath, Mayhew had to face an audience that came voluntarily to hear him
preach and contributed generously to his support, yet that for
the most part did not feel moved or qualified to join his
church.[34]

A few days after his ordination, Jonathan went to Cambridge
to complete requirements for the master of arts degree. The

second degree, as Harvard referred to its M.A., was usually granted three years after the first or bachelor's degree to those graduates who had done some further study in a particular field, who had led a blameless life for the three years, and who were prepared to defend a thesis of their own selection. For his thesis, Jonathan defended the affirmative side of the question, "Does reason correctly accord with faith?" Abraham Williams, his classmate, responded that the argument was fallacious, but for a shocking reason: a religion that taught the doctrine of original sin could hardly be rational. According to one witness, Mayhew's reply came as even more of a shock: "Sir, it is true." [35]

The young parson, so recently come from rags to riches— from poor theological student to pastor of Boston's highest salaried church—may have been unduly conscious of his new-found success as he mingled with the crowds on Commencement day, July 1. Benjamin Walker, Jr., who recorded most of Boston's scandal in his voluminous diary, wrote of "An Affront Put on . . . Edward Holyoke President of the Colledges at Cambridge by Mr. Jonathan Mayhew minister at New or West Boston meeting." As this unconfirmed account relates the story, Mayhew wrapped a £4 bill, the fee for the M.A., together with a gratuity of two copper halfpence in a paper and handed them to Holyoke. When "the President seem'd angry at the Copper," Jonathan insisted that "if he did not take all he'd pay him none." [36] There was some truth in Walker's tale, for three weeks later Jonathan informed his father, "As to the President, That affair remains just as it was when you was in Town." [37] Was this "Affront" a reminder that he still remembered the "impertinent recrimination" and subsequent degrading of 1743? Or was it merely a misfired attempt to show gratitude for the President's repeated generosity over the past seven years? In any event, the activities of the West Church's pastor had become first-rate material for gossip, and he would keep Boston tongues wagging at a record pace for the remainder of his life.

CHAPTER V

Out of Nazareth

To inquire into evidence, is to no purpose, unless we follow it wherever it leads, and chearfully receive the truth wherever it is to be found; whatever notions it may contradict; whatever censures it may expose us to.

Jonathan Mayhew, 1749[1]

WHEN JONATHAN Mayhew celebrated his twenty-seventh birthday on October 8, 1747, the important forces that would shape his life were already present and working. A choleric temperament, tightly reined since the Great Awakening, had made him bold, impatient, outspoken. His father had carefully guided his pre-college development but in the process had raised major questions concerning the New England Way, questions to which Experience Mayhew could give only shallow answers. Harvard had encouraged him to mine fully the vein of rationalism inherent in Puritanism and to explore widely and freely the ideas of the European scholars who struggled to keep Christianity alive in the Age of Reason. Against the wishes of the town's divines, the West Church had placed him in its prominent pulpit from which he could now turn loose his tongue and pen against the pillars of orthodoxy. For the most part, the Boston clergy resolved to ignore the upstart, but this proved to be a difficult task in a town whose four weekly newspapers encouraged religious controversy in the hope of increasing circulation. Finally, he was discovering the weakness of his congregation's defenses against the allurement of Anglicanism as the gentleman's path to heaven. The mixture of these elements proved explosive. Before his thirtieth birthday, he had knocked down the creeds of Puritanism and on

their ruins had erected a monument to the rational Christian
who never neglected his sacred duty to resist poth political
and ecclesiastical tyrants.

By the time of his ordination Mayhew had become an
Arminian, although he disliked to use the word in reference to
himself. To the original Puritan the term had denoted both
religious and political subversion; Arminians not only denied
the Calvinistic doctrines of salvation, but also, under Charles
I, they had won control of the Church of England. The Puritans
who resisted Charles and his archbishop, William Laud, had,
it was true, embraced many of the Reformation doctrines
stated in their classical form by John Calvin. Puritanism, at
heart, however, remained a native English movement that
pragmatically adapted continental theology to serve the requirements of strategy in the long struggle with the House of
Stuart.

To guard the masses against the Arminianism they saw entrenched in high places, Puritan theorists placed more and
more emphasis upon the doctrine of the covenant of grace. By
this contractual arrangement between omnipotent God and
impotent man, the Puritan could cling to the belief that God
saved only His elect and yet leave room for man's will and
good works in the process. Technically, only God could bestow
the faith needed to claim the covenant and thus hold Him to
His bargain. But in practice the covenant of grace became the
answer to the Arminian promise of salvation to anyone who
would seek it. Although not all Puritans followed the leaders
who made covenant theory the central tenet of faith, those who
came to New England were imbued with the doctrine. In their
tightly knit communities in the wilderness, Congregational
preachers stressed "preparation" for salvation at the same time
they preached against the soul-damning notions of the Arminians.[2]

An amalgam of elements taken from revelation, theology,

common law, logic, reason, and the science of the day, covenant theology contained the seeds of its own destruction. However well-fused these disparate elements had seemed early in the seventeenth century, they began to separate in the eighteenth. In the face of Newton's physics and Locke's psychology, and amid the secularization of the state and the growth of materialism, the eighteenth-century Massachusetts clergy had made a brave and prolonged effort to hold the covenant scheme together, but in most cases they could do little more than deny that a problem existed. By the 1730's there was sufficient evidence of a growing undercurrent of Arminianism to alarm the pillars of ecclesiastical order, many of whom then turned to the Great Awakening as the God-sent answer to their fears.[3] When Whitefield first arrived in Boston, Benjamin Colman greeted him as a new witness for the doctrines of Calvinism. Such a spirit made it easy to associate the revival with the orthodox theology and to label its opponents Arminians. Jacob Green, Jonathan's classmate, plainly understood this association: "And when I got my religion in the *New Light* time, I became a more zealous Calvinist. I had a great aversion to the opposers of New Light religion; and those opposers in New England, . . . were generally supposed to be Arminian, or tinged with Arminian principles." This view ignored the many moderate Calvinists who drew back in horror from the excesses of revivalism and who in desperation finally realized that the radical New Lights would call any minister, however evangelical, who concerned himself with reason, learning, or morality, "a dry, husky, *Arminian* Preacher, and conclude for certain that he was not converted." [4]

After the peak of the Great Awakening had passed, it gradually became apparent that the New England Way was irreparably fractured. Although most of the clergy remained for the time moderate Calvinists, two new factions came into the open. On one extreme, a group took its cue from Jonathan Edwards, who removed the emphasis from the covenant of grace and moved back toward unmitigated Calvinism. On the other extreme, the New England Arminians, spearheaded initially by Mayhew and later by Chauncy, became the historical link between New England Puritanism and nineteenth-century Unitarianism. A third possibility, the evangelical Arminianism of John Wesley in England, made no progress in New England at this time, for the Calvinistic followers of Whitefield had preëmpted the ranks of the evangelistic and the local Arminians saw no affinity between themselves and a religious movement that refused to accept reason as the key to revelation.[5]

Jonathan Mayhew's theological development had begun in the Indian mission on Martha's Vineyard, where Experience Mayhew had found it impossible to teach the complexities of Calvinism to the primitive Indians. A God who chooses to save only a portion of mankind (His elect) could not be the basis of a widespread appeal to the Indians to become Christians and to give up their heathen ways. Jonathan's father told the natives, "All that truly Believe in Christ, Christ will save, let them be Indians or English, High or Low, Bond or free." The reason why people are not saved is because they do not come to Christ, who is willing to save all, even drunkards or those who have "often committed Whoredom, or Stole or lyed." God "is infinitely Good & Mercifull, or else man would never have bin saved." To this generous invitation to salvation he would sometimes add a Calvinistic footnote: the hearts of men are so bad that they cannot "worship and serve God, as they ought unless he did renew them and assist them by his spirit." The simplification of doctrine in the interest of missions was not regarded as heresy. No less a person than Cotton Mather had urged missionaries to present to the heathen "first of all these most important articles of which true Christianity primarily consists."[6]

The elder Mayhew found it difficult to keep his English and Indian theology separate. In 1718 he preached a sermon in Boston which emphasized the reasonableness of God's covenant with man.[7] During the next twenty years—the period of Jonathan's boyhood—Experience read books that "embrace or incline to the *Arminian Hypothesis*" as well as the writings of the Calvinists, and he devoted his study time to speculation on the question of God's grace in salvation. By the time Jonathan entered Harvard in 1740, his father had reached the edge of Arminianism, although loyalty to the old doctrines obscured his true bearings. He took violent exception to a book published in 1741 by Jonathan Dickinson, pastor at Elizabeth Town, New Jersey and soon to be the first president of the College of New Jersey, in which Dickinson argued for a very narrow definition of human liberty. A controversy between the two ensued through the medium of Thomas Foxcroft of the Boston First Church. The climax of this exchange was the publication of Experience Mayhew's *Grace Defended* in 1744.[8]

Grace Defended, its author stated, was not an attack on Calvinism, but an attempt "to remove some Things out of the Way," which were not necessary to the "principal Articles in that Scheme," and which "render it the more difficult to be received and defended." The difficulty with the Calvinistic doctrine of predestination, the missionary wrote, is that it makes impossible any effective appeal to sinners:

If Salvation be not promised conditionally unto Sinners, then they have no Ground of Assurance, that on the Performance of the Duties which God requireth of them, in order to their Salvation, they shall certainly be saved. . . .

Now, if sinners are invited to go to Christ for this Principle of Life, or Grace, how can it be possibly imagined that their first having it is necessary in order to their doing it? For must they first have the Life they should go to Christ for, before it is possible for them to go to him for it? I cannot yet understand this![9]

Man is unable to come to Christ unaided, but this inability is of a lower type than the extreme Calvinists assert. It comes not from divine election, but from corruption, ignorance, temptations, and other man-made inabilities which can be overcome by the instruments of man—"Instructions, Exhortations, and convincing Arguments." This truth, he concluded, removes all excuse from those who refuse to seek God, and yet enables one to be "fully persuaded of the Truth of the Doctrine of God's Decrees of *Election* and *Reprobation,* as the same is revealed in Scripture; and for the Substance, as it is explained in our *Confessions of Faith* and *Catechisms,* and by our orthodox Divines." [10]

Such was Jonathan Mayhew's theological heritage. The father had raised the right questions, but had provided no answers. He recommended in 1741 that his student son study all the regular treatises on Puritan theology, but he further urged, "neglect not the Writings of the great Dr. *Twisse.*" This was the William Twisse who, in debate with John Cotton, had flatly denied that the covenant scheme had any foundation. As so often, freedom of inquiry brought results, but not the intended results. Jonathan submitted one of his father's writings on justification, likely *Grace Defended,* to Professor Edward Wigglesworth, an honest and able scholar, who spent some time reading the work in 1741. If it was *Grace Defended,* the verdict was not favorable, for the Professor sharply criticized that long treatise as "a Medley of Arminianism and Pelagianism." Thus Jonathan was forced to face the inconsistency of believing in free grace and election at the same time. He could not go backward, so he followed the logical path forward to Arminianism. He had taken this final step by the time of his ordination, if not before. Experience Mayhew's unhappiness over his son's theological defection could not be concealed. In the charge he gave at the ordination he pleaded with Jonathan to "know the GOD of thy Fathers." The son was apologetic but not in the least inclined to retreat.[11]

In spite of the religious feuds of the Great Awakening, public disputes were now few, for the Congregational clergy agreed to debate their differences behind closed doors, lest their congregations become involved.[12] The recent revival had made plain the disruptive effects of theological disputes among laymen. Jonathan Mayhew broke this conspiracy of public silence. By blurting out what the clergy were thinking he embarrassed some and angered others, but he did force them to take sides. His refusal to be quiet and to maintain the uneasy peace can in part be attributed to his temperament, but it was also the result of his unprecedented ostracism by the Boston Association of Congregational Ministers. Chauncy worked for his admission, but the majority could not bring themselves to accept him as a colleague. There was little incentive to cooperate with a group that did not consider him an equal, and "thro' God's Goodness," he determined to live "very happily and contented without them." [13] He explained the situation to his congregation, who shared his persecution complex: "the most favourable Treatment that a small Party can expect, is to have the terrible artillery of Creed & Confession levell'd against them, & a whole Volley [of] reverend Anathemas discharged at their Head. For this is the Method in which reigning & vicious Priests, who delight in cursing rather than blessing, constantly vent their Fury: and then they very modestly call it Zeal for God & Religion." The West Church seemed to take comfort when their pastor told them, "Indeed, it is more glorious to stand by true primitive Christianity contrary to prevailing Custom, than to do it when it is fashionable & so suits our Interest." "Fear not little flock, for it is your Father's good pleasure to give you the Kingdom." [14]

The clergy's hopes for theological peace were further thwarted by the town's four weekly newspapers, which had discovered that religious controversy was an easy way of snaring readers. On June 22, 1747, the *Boston Evening Post* carried the story of Mayhew's ordination. The following week it published a long anonymous letter explaining the five points of Calvinism and charging the clergy with a plot to keep out of the ministry "all who have not *New Light* enough to declare their *unfeigned Assent & Consent* to them," however excellent their other qualifications. From then on, every radical idea voiced in the West Church pulpit found its way in one form or another into the local press, and in turn, replies, refutations, and personal attacks were given equal space. Unless distracted by military and political crises, the editors encouraged religious clash. Unfortunately for the historian, these contributions were always anonymous. If each piece could be identified, the resulting list of authors would feature Mayhew and Chauncy and their clerical opponents, but it would also include the town's wags, not a few prankish Harvard undergraduates, and editors with space to fill and a deadline to meet.

One feature of Mayhew's ostracism was his exclusion from participation in the Boston Thursday Lecture. Not to be outdone, he gave lecture series of his own from time to time. The first was presented in the summer of 1748, when on alternate Thursdays during June, July, and August at five in the afternoon he lectured to audiences noticeably larger than those attending the regular Thursday Lecture. Here was an opportunity for the curious of the other congregations to hear the notorious new minister without being conspicuous by absence from their own Sabbath meetings. This may have been the time when Paul Revere, still in his teens, listened to a sermon by Mayhew. Paul's enthusiasm for what he heard, according to tradition, resulted in a beating at the hands of a strict father, fearful that the lad would stray into heresy. The seven lectures given during this summer series were printed by subscription in

Boston the following year and reprinted in London in 1750.
Mayhew's first volume of printed sermons turned out to be one
of his most famous. It remained such a guide and inspiration to
religious liberals for the next century that in the 1830's the
American Unitarian Association reprinted a portion of the
work.[15]

In the *Seven Sermons* and in his regular preaching program
during the first three years of his ministry, Mayhew was most
concerned in establishing a partnership between reason and
religion, a position that is best described as supernatural rationalism.[16] If one understands that this cause was his great passion, the failure of his theology to develop systematically, far
from being a problem, can be anticipated. Brought up in the
optimism of the century ushered in by the discoveries of Newton and Locke, Mayhew had little difficulty deciding that truth
was not relative. There is an absolute truth, he believed, that
"exists independently of our notions concerning it." This truth
is "one, simple, uniform; and always consistent with itself."
Opposed to truth is falsehood, and between the two are "precise
boundaries" which are "determined by the real nature and
properties of things, whether they are perceptible to us, or
not." It follows that the difference between right and wrong
cannot be a matter of indifference, for there is a true side and
a false side to every proposition. With such a faith in the
objectivity of truth, he could follow the pragmatic tendencies
of his environment and his father's emphasis upon the criterion
of experience only to the limits of everyday practice. He never
doubted that Christianity in its purest form was this "one,
simple, uniform," consistent truth.[17]

How then, Mayhew asked, does one find this "noble Treasure" of religious truth? Is he to find it in the creeds of Christendom—the practice of "setting up human tests of *orthodoxy,*
instead of the infallible word of God"? The answer was directed

to those who for a century had held to the Westminster Confession as a standard of faith:

[Creeds] are imperious and tyrannical: and contrary to the spirit and doctrines of the gospel. They are an infringement upon those rights of conscience, which ought to be sacred; they have an apparent tendency to prevent all improvements in religious knowledge, and to entail ignorance, error, and superstition upon future generations. What improvements can we suppose would have been made in the several arts and sciences comparable to the present, had the study of them been incumbered with such restraints, and almost insuperable difficulties? . . .

Error may indeed become *venerable* and *gray-headed* with length of time: but a falshood of a thousand years standing, remains as much a falshood as ever, although it may have been consecrated by the church, and transmitted to posterity in a creed. . . . There is nothing more foolish and superstitious than a veneration for *ancient* creeds and doctrines, *as such;* and nothing more unworthy a reasonable creature, than to value *principles* by their *age,* as some do their *wines.*[18]

Is religious truth to be found on the side of the majority? Again the answer was an emphatic no! Can one discover this truth by looking to persons of authority and position in the world? No, a religion nursed by a king or a queen or directed by a pope or a "Right Reverend Father in God" is no more, indeed less, likely to be true than another. As to the clergy, they in general have been "the greatest Enemies to true Religion."[19]

The answer to this quest for religious truth, Mayhew concluded, is found in the individual. Human reason varies widely in persons according to native intelligence and education, but "all men are capable of discerning truth and right in some degree." Man's limited "rational faculties" require guidance from divine revelation, but even here reason is necessary to determine whether the credentials of alleged revelation are valid. By reason man must interpret the meaning of a genuine bit of revelation, as he does any other writing. Man's divine reason, imperfect as it is, is the chief instrument for the perception of religious truth.[20]

Not only does man have the faculties for discerning between truth and falsehood, it is his sacred duty to do so. Mayhew explained fully what he meant by "The Right and Duty of private Judgment." Except for a few first principles which do not concern religion, "private judgment" requires a suspension of judgment on all issues until one is able to determine where the truth lies.

Thus, for example, we ought not to believe that there is, or that there is not a God; that the Christian religion is from God, or an imposture; that any particular doctrine fathered upon it, is really contained in it, or not; or that any particular sect of christians, is in the right, or in the wrong; 'till we have impartially examined the matter, and see evidence on one side or the other. For to determine any point without reason or proof, cannot be to judge *freely,* unless it be in a bad sense of the word.[21]

The second step in "private judgment" is to activate one's reason, "for truth is coy, and must be courted." Next, a man must honestly embrace truth wherever he finds it and wherever it leads. Finally, the seeker after truth must give his assent to any proposition "in proportion to the degree of evidence that appears to support it" and, accordingly, contend for some truths more than others. There can be no substitute for "private judgment," for the big questions of life "are too interesting and important to be submitted to the determination of a second person." "Our obligation, therefore, to inquire after truth, and to judge what is right, may be found within us, in our own frame and constitution." It is true, he added, that every man is not obliged to study all branches of science for himself, but one does have an obligation to inform himself of his duty to God and others. No man can escape his duty to think for himself in religious matters.[22]

Jesus Christ taught "the right and duty of private judgment," Mayhew declared to his lecture audience. Christ "did not demand of men an implicit and blind belief in himself, without offering matter of conviction to their understandings." The Apostle Paul, although an inspired writer, was not so dogmatic as many today who have no claim to inspiration. He was rather "a reasonable, catholick man, and a friend to the rights of private judgment." In short, the essence of the Christian religion is reason. It follows that, since every man has a right to private judgment, no one may exercise that right for another nor force his own judgments on his fellow men.

To attempt to *dragoon* men into sound orthodox *Christians,* is as unnatural and fruitless as to attempt to *dragoon* them into good *poets, physicians* or *mathematicians.* A blow with a club may fracture a man's skull; but I suppose he will not think and reason the more clearly for that; though he may possibly believe the more *orthodoxly,* according to the opinions of some. . . .[23]

This right is given them by God and nature, and the gospel of Christ: And no man has a right to deprive another of it, under a notion that he will make an ill use of it, and fall into erroneous opinions. We may as well pick our neighbour's pocket, for fear he should spend his money in debauchery, as take from him his right of judging for himself, and chusing his religion, for fear he should judge amiss and abuse his liberty.[24]

Mayhew could not resist making a final application of "our *indispensible duty"* to exercise private judgment in religion:

Let us all *stand fast in the liberty wherewith Christ has made us free;* and not suffer ourselves to be *intangled with any yoke of bondage.* If we have submitted to the yoke hitherto, and ingloriously subjected ourselves to any human impositions in religious matters; it is better to throw off the yoke even now, than to let it gall us all our life-time: It is not yet too late to assert our liberty, and free ourselves from an ignominious slavery to the dictates of men.[25]

With this plea for action Mayhew, scarcely out of Harvard, served notice that the theological war had been declared. How much of the traditional Puritan theology would stand the young liberal's rational test? The answer would require a generation of Arminian scholars, but at least one dogma had to go immediately. Using arguments gleaned from English writers, he made short work of the doctrine of original sin. Sin, he taught his congregation, is the transgression of law. When Adam and Eve, our first parents, transgressed the law God promulgated to them, they sinned. Since they were the only violators of this law, they alone were guilty, for "There can be no sin, but where there is some sinful Act itself, or a transgression of the Law." It would be both unjust and impossible for God to impute the sin of the first parents to their posterity. It is impossible because "The Sin of any Act cleaves necessarily to the act itself, and cannot be extended beyond it." An extension of sin to others "is a contradiction; and so exceeds the Power of omnipotence itself." Such an extension "would be plainly unjust, tyrannical, and arbitrary," and we know God is "a compassionate Parent; a gentle Master, a righteous Judge." It becomes obvious, then, that the doctrine of original sin "is not agreeable to truth, Reason or Scripture." As God "is the *father of all,* so his government is *paternal,* free from all unnecessary rigor;—uniform and steady, in opposition to all capriciousness and arbitrary proceedings." With the other contemporary Arminians, Mayhew regarded human nature as neither inherently good nor evil. Man differs from the animals chiefly in his faculties for reason, and in this sense it can be said that man is created in the image of God. Each man must stand or fall on the basis of whether he uses his reason to find for himself true religion or whether he allows it to be corrupted by vice, ignorance, or superstition. "Let us therefore mourn and amend our own Faults; and not trouble our Consciences about the Sins of Adam. We have Sins enough of our own to bewail, without taking those of others upon ourselves." [26]

After clearing away the dead wood of original sin, the youthful divine turned to what soon became the central theme of his preaching, the relation between Christianity and morality, a practical issue of far greater and more immediate significance to him than the deeper philosophical problem of free will with which so many of his contemporaries wrestled. Mayhew's interest in this problem had developed out of the peculiar course of New England history. Since about 1660 the clergy had been decrying the decline of religion. Their jeremiads were in part nostalgia for the seemingly godly life of first-generation Massachusetts, but they also reflected concern over the growing number who were now either unwilling or unqualified to join the visible saints in church membership. To meet this challenge the Congregational clergy had increasingly stressed Christian nurture through church affiliation, if not full membership, a move toward an institutional and formalistic emphasis. The Great Awakening, in part a reaction against such formalism, had once again attempted to draw a clear line between the saints and sinners by demanding an inner, personal relationship with God as the test of conversion. In Mayhew's eyes, both positions fell far short of "true primitive Christianity," and the practices of both groups were "subversive . . . of natural Religion, and plainly tend to root all virtue & goodness out of the world."[27]

On the one hand, "Some are pleasing themselves with a round of empty formalities, imagining that religion consists chiefly in frequent fastings, attending upon the sacraments, and worshiping God with a great deal of outward pomp and ceremony. They forget that *God is a spirit;* and to be *worshipped* chiefly *in spirit:* and love all kinds of ordinances much better than they love their neighbours."[28]

As for the New Lights, on the other hand, they "place religion chiefly in having frequent raptures, and strange transports of mechanical devotion; in which the less they exercise their reason, the better and more glorious it is. . . . Thus they go on, raising themselves from one degree of religious phrenzy to another, till they run quite *divinely mad;* . . . They then look down with contempt upon all *moral duties,* as being below such *spiritual men.*" [29]

Each party had avoided the central point in Mayhew's definition of the Christian religion: "Christianity is principally an institution of life and manners; designed to teach us how to be good men, and to show us the necessity of becoming so." Man's obligation to live a moral life is not dependent upon Christianity alone, for antecedent to the Christian religion is an universal religion—natural religion or the law of nature— common to all mankind. "And, indeed, it is plain beyond dispute, that the substance of true religion must necessarily be the same, . . . in all countries, to all rational creatures, in all parts of the universe, in all periods of time." "The Law of Nature is obligatory upon all Mankind without exception; because it is promulg'd to all," and inscribed upon the heart of every man. Christianity is more than "a re-publication of the law of nature," yet its most important objective is the enforcement of natural religion by the added authority of the commands of Jesus Christ and the inspiration of His life on earth. "In short, the whole tenor of our Lord's preaching was *moral.*" When one knows only the theological subtleties of Christianity, or when one uses Christianity as an excuse for not performing his moral obligations, his religion has become a sham and not only useless but a force subversive of all true religion. Mayhew told a New England in which it had become difficult to identify God's elect, "It is practical religion, the love of God, and a life of righteousness and charity, proceeding from faith in Christ and the gospel, that denominates us good men and good christians." It is vital that you *"let no man deceive you with vain words. He that doth righteousness,* and he only, *is righteous.*" [30]

Mayhew was not preaching a religion of works alone. "Real

piety," he reminded his parishioners, "necessarily supposes, that the heart is touched, affected, warmed, inflamed." He could not entirely forget the emotions he had felt during the Awakening, though with the passage of time he had concluded that there was no method of judging "Real piety" other than by its effects upon human behavior—the test of religious experience is experience. Experience Mayhew's son had learned well his father's counsel that "a knowledge . . . of the holy will have a mighty Influence on the Lives of those who are the Subjects of it." [31]

The lecture series in the summer of 1748 and the publication of these lectures as the *Seven Sermons* the following year served notice on New England that here at last was one of Professor Wigglesworth's students who was going to say publicly what he believed. Other divines might dispute behind closed doors, but this one was determined to be heard. He had developed a sense of mission, a conviction that Christianity could be stripped of its corruptions only by a few brave souls such as he: "in time of general Desertion from true Religion; when Superstition, Vice & falshood are triumphant, and the Doctrines of Christ despised & trampled upon, & called heresy & schism; when folly is thus set in great dignity, & truth is left almost friendless & solitary; this is a time for a Man to show what he is." [32] With the exception of Chauncy and Cooper and later Andrew Eliot, the Boston clergy treated him with a cold, stony silence; it would be years before a man of the cloth would dare to challenge publicly the darling of the West Church merchants. In the meantime an anonymous attempt to discipline the young agitator appeared from time to time in the local press. The most potent of such efforts was a long letter to Mayhew from *Philanthropos*, published a few months after the lecture series. The letter warned him against the dangers of pride and charged him with ingratitude to his

"Mother," New England's religious and political institutions. He was following the "Hottentottonian" custom which required young men to beat their mothers as a way of proving their manhood. The writer even reminded Mayhew of his youthful indiscretions.[33]

If Mayhew's ego needed buttressing after this dressing-down at the hands of *Philanthropos,* who obviously knew his subject well, the reception of the *Seven Sermons* in England quickly restored self-assurance. The tide of rationalism that had swept over England late in the seventeenth century had further variegated English Christianity both within and without the established church. The Deists had rejected all revelation in favor of natural religion, and at the other extreme strict Calvinists had held stubbornly to their doctrines. In between were several groups willing to make compromises, including the moderate Calvinists and, nearer to the Deists, a school of liberal and scholarly Arminians who sought to amass overwhelming rational evidence to support the validity of the few revealed truths they regarded as central to true Christianity. The *Seven Sermons* delighted this last group, and they encouraged its republication in London. There was nothing new in this volume; every idea in its 157 pages had already seen the light of day in England. But coming from New England, considered by English theologians to be the stronghold of seventeenth-century Puritanism, Mayhew's rational Christianity offered evidence that a new wind was blowing on the other side of the Atlantic. The more liberal dissenting clergy and even Benjamin Hoadley, a low-church Anglican bishop, greeted the Boston divine as a comrade-in-arms in their war against "Enthusiasm & Infidelity." Mayhew admitted that he could understand their surprise upon reading the *Seven Sermons:* "It is no little mortification to me to find what a mean Opinion Gentlemen abroad entertain of my Country's Taste. But it is a much greater, to know that this

opinion is just and well grounded. It cannot be denied that
the general Taste of N.E. and the manner of writing here,
have been such, that any Production from hence, which was
but just tolerable, might naturally excite some degree of wonder and appear almost as strange as *any good Things' coming
out of Nazareth."* [34]

The author did not fully realize how favorably his book
had been received in England until April 1750, when he heard
the unexpected news that the University of Aberdeen had
conferred on him the degree of Doctor of Divinity. Late in
May a huge sheepskin diploma arrived in Boston to confirm
what had at first seemed unbelievable. A circle of Dissenters,
he learned, had secured the honorary degree for him as a
reward for the *Seven Sermons* and as a stimulus to fight on
in the future. Prominent among those instrumental in obtaining this honor for him were George Benson, Nathaniel
Lardner, and James Foster, scholars and preachers and all
friends of John Taylor of Norwich, from whose book, *The
Scripture-Doctrine of Original Sin,* Mayhew had drawn much
of his ammunition against that doctrine. Governor William
Shirley of Massachusetts, who was in London at the time,
had joined in the recommendation at the request of the sponsors. Honorary degrees from Scottish universities could usually be obtained for any suitable person upon the payment of
a small fee and perhaps a few bribes to influential members
of the faculty—a total of £20 in one actual case on record.
The Dissenters used honorary degrees from Scotland to
counterbalance those bestowed on Anglicans by Oxford and
Cambridge. Only three years before Mayhew's degree, Ebenezer Miller, Anglican missionary at Braintree, Massachusetts,
had been given an Oxford D.D.[35]

Doctor Jonathan Mayhew belonged to a select company.
Only three other Congregational ministers in the vicinity of
Boston could display the same title—Charles Chauncy, Joseph

Sewall, and Professor Wigglesworth. It was a "Bright Occasion" for his friends and followers, but the Boston clergy was not overjoyed at the preferment of one they had attempted to keep out of the West Church pulpit three years before. Mayhew had been denied ministerial fellowship in Boston only to find it in London. During the remainder of his life he carried on a continual correspondence with friends across the ocean, and letters of introduction written in the West Church study would cross the Atlantic in the baggage of numerous Bostonians who sailed for the mother country. More important, he was now in touch with the heart, soul, and mind of the English liberal Arminians to whom his own intellectual and spiritual development was so deeply indebted, and a cross-fertilization of ideas could begin.[36]

The Boston divines had failed to silence Mayhew, but his friend Lemuel Briant, pastor at Braintree, Massachusetts was less fortunate. Nearly the same age, the two had met at Harvard. Both were Arminians, and both were determined to voice their convictions. They enjoyed exchanging pulpits occasionally. In June 1749, Briant preached a sermon in the West Church on *The Absurdity and Blasphemy of depretiating Moral Virtue*. Thomas Foxcroft and several other ministers took violent exception to this anti-Calvinistic sermon which Briant repeated in a number of churches in the area. They warned that the "Growth of *Arminianism* and loose Principles in Religion" in New England threatens "the utter Ruin of these Churches, in Point of Faith, Worship, and vital Godliness." Mayhew and Briant, declared Foxcroft, had formed a new sect whose distinguishing tenet was "That Christ always preached the Law, and never the Gospel." [37]

In the ensuing controversy Briant's congregation split into two hostile factions. To make matters worse, his wife left him and spread "evil Reports" concerning his conduct. Charges and countercharges of immorality were hurled by the clerical opponents in the struggle. Richard Cranch, Mayhew's friend and parishioner, had just moved to Braintree from Boston, and he hastened to Briant's defense. Cranch asked his former pastor for an immediate transfer of membership so that he might throw additional weight on the side of "the friends of Christian liberty." Against Briant's wishes, an ecclesiastical council met in January 1753 and charged him with failure to attend fasts, "renouncing the Assembly's Catechism, and declaring his Resolution never to instruct the Children in it," and recommending "the prayerful Perusal" of John Taylor's work on original sin, "which we esteem very erroneous." The council implied that Briant's refusal to clear himself of his wife's charges amounted to an admission of guilt. In the spring a committee from the Braintree Church exonerated their pastor and defended the right of a clergyman to exercise independent judgment. Supported by Gay and other liberals on the South Shore, Briant seemed to be winning the battle to remain in the Braintree pulpit. At this point his health broke; he resigned in October 1753, and died the following year. There is little evidence concerning the cause of death, but in the eyes of "the friends of Christian liberty" Lemuel Briant died a martyr for rational Christianity.[38]

Briant's death was sad news to Mayhew, who had been confident that "Time will probably bring Truth to Light" and with it a full vindication of his friend. It would have been easy for the situations of these two ministers with so much in common to have been reversed. Mayhew would have fared no better than Briant in a small country church with a congregation of conflicting theological views. At the same time he could not have been without a sense of satisfaction as he surveyed the results of eight years' labor at the West Church. Shortly after he moved to Braintree, Richard Cranch wrote to Mayhew, "There is no circumstance of our removall from

Boston that gives me so much pain as that of leaving your Ministry, from which (without flattery) I must confess I have learnt more genuine Christianity than from any other I ever attended." Such a tribute from a man raised and educated in England made Jonathan Mayhew more certain than ever that the cause for which he fought was right.[39]

CHAPTER VI

Catechism of Revolution

Now when Iniquity comes to be thus established by a Law;
it cannot be any iniquity to transgress that law by which it
is established. On the contrary, it is a sin not to transgress it.

Jonathan Mayhew, 1749[1]

O N OCTOBER 17, 1750, a servant dusting books in Mayhew's study might have seen the minister at his desk, pen in
hand and an anxious look upon his face. Before him lay a
sheet of paper on which he was composing a letter to Governor Shirley, who was then in Europe, thanking that distinguished gentleman for his aid in procuring the doctorate.
Ordinarily it would have been a simple task—a brief note of
appreciation garnished with the dignities of speech due one
of His Majesty's officials of Shirley's rank—but an event which
had occurred made the writing of such a letter more difficult.
Early in February, months before he knew of his obligation
to Shirley, the West Church pastor had preached what was
to become his most famous sermon, a forthright denunciation
of the doctrine that subjects owe unlimited submission and
nonresistance to the king. He had concluded with some
scathing remarks on the Anglican practice of celebrating
January 30, the anniversary of the death of Charles I at Puritan hands, as a holy day on which a saintly martyr had met
an undeserved death. This sermon, entitled *A Discourse Concerning Unlimited Submission and Non-Resistance to the
Higher Powers,* had been printed and copies were now on
their way to England, where it would possibly be seen by
the Governor, a devout Anglican, before he received the letter
of appreciation.

Eventually, Mayhew found the words he hoped would soften the impact upon the Governor, but he had no intention of retracting the sermon or apologizing for it.[2] Despite all the scholarly speculation on the inherent impossibility of building republican political philosophy on the foundation of the Calvinistic doctrine of man's total depravity, no such nexus in practice has been demonstrated. On another stage, Mayhew's Arminianism might have had few political overtones; but voiced as it was from the pulpit of the West Church, whose first pastor, also an Arminian, had defected to the Church of England and whose congregation was sensitive to social prestige, it dictated a strong stand against Anglicanism and, in turn, the sanctification of the radical Whig political principles of the seventeenth century.

For more than a century the Puritan mind had associated Arminianism with Episcopacy. New England was well aware that nearly all the bishops of the Church had deserted Calvinism by the end of the seventeenth century. In Boston, Anglicanism was rapidly becoming the religion of wealth, fashion, and position. West Church merchants were not immune to the appeal of the impressive organ music and ritual of King's Chapel and Trinity Church. By the 1750's Boston high society centered in Anglican drawing rooms, where more and more the younger generations of some of the old Puritan families were beginning to feel at ease. At the beginning of the decade, Jonathan Edwards estimated with alarm that in all of New England the Church of England had tripled its numbers in the past seven years. *Unlimited Submission* declared to the Puritan world that this Arminian pastor would not follow in Hooper's wake to London for Episcopal ordination; that Anglican authoritarianism was as irrational, as damnable as Calvinistic dogmatism. Mayhew was beginning a lifelong fight to keep his people loyal to the cause of "true religion" in the face of worldly temptations as represented by the increasing grandeur and respectability of the prayer book and miter.[3]

That *Unlimited Submission* was also his major confession of political faith was of secondary importance to the author, who never regarded himself as a political philosopher. His frequent remarks from the pulpit on political questions were always made in application of some Christian duty or principle. He accepted and propagated the political ideas of the Puritan and Glorious Revolutions as annotations to the more basic duty of man to live in a morally and rationally justifiable relation with his Maker and fellow men. Some may think I am preaching politics instead of Christ, he wrote in the Preface to *Unlimited Submission.* Yet, is it not the obligation of a Christian minister to explain and interpret all scripture? "Why, then, should not those parts of scripture which relate to civil government, be examined and explained from the desk, as well as others?" As he grew older Mayhew became bolder in applying his political principles to contemporary events, but he never fully overcame his reticence to discuss political questions per se from the pulpit. His sorties into the world of politics began and ended at the fortress of scripture. Ideas gleaned from the study of the Hebrew theocratic commonwealth and the writings of the holy apostles were used as often in his fight against tyranny as those acquired from the works of Milton, Locke, and Sidney.

Unlimited Submission was the last of a series of three sermons on Romans xiii, 1–7, a passage which begins, "Let every soul be subject unto the higher powers." The first two sermons were briefly summarized in the printed version, to which the author added copious footnotes that often contained the real meat of his argument. In the two sermons preceding January 30 he presented the theoretical foundation for the application to be made in the final sermon preached the Sunday after January 30, 1750. The sole end of government, he told the West Church, is the good, the happiness of society. Man is bound by God to obey civil rulers under any form of government that answers this purpose whether it be monarchy, republic, or aristocracy. "Disobedience to civil rulers in the due exercise of their authority, is not merely a *political sin*, but an heinous *offence against God* and *religion*." On the other hand, "God does not interpose, in a miraculous way, to point out the persons who shall bear rule, and to whom subjection is due." Nor is royal primogeniture supported by Biblical authority. Kings are made by men, not God.[4]

There is, he continued, one point remaining to be considered: "the *extent* of that subjection *to the higher powers*, which is here enjoined as a duty upon all christians." There are those who, in the tradition of the Puritan and Glorious Revolutions, assert the right to rid their nation of a ruler who does not govern for the common good. In opposition, there are men who believe scripture, and the text under consideration in particular, requires "an absolute submission" to a prince under all circumstances, "lest we should incur the sin of rebellion, and the punishment of damnation."[5] For the next twenty-six pages Mayhew blasted every argument he had ever heard or read in support of this doctrine of unlimited submission and nonresistance. His position on this question was not new to his congregation. The preceding March they had been taught that it was a sin not to transgress an iniquitous law. Now they were to hear this theme developed into the most important defense of the right of revolution made by an American before 1776.

The rulers to whom Saint Paul commanded obedience as a Christian duty are good rulers, those who are "benefactors to society." "When once magistrates act contrary to their office, and the end of their institution; . . . they immediately cease to be the *ordinance* and *ministers* of God." After which, "they have not the least pretense to be honored, obeyed and

CATECHISM OF REVOLUTION 85

rewarded." Then followed one of the most quotable sentences Mayhew ever composed: "Rulers have no authority from God to do mischief." Or, in other words, "It is blasphemy to call tyrants and oppressors, *God's ministers*. They are more properly *the messengers of satan to buffet us*." Our Christian duty is not only to obey good rulers but to rebel against those who are "Common tyrants, and public oppressors." [6]

If it be our duty . . . to obey our king, merely for this reason, that he rules for the public welfare, (which is the only argument the apostle makes use of) it follows, by a parity of reason, that when he turns tyrant, and makes his subjects his prey to devour and to destroy, instead of his charge to defend and cherish, we are bound to throw off our allegiance to him, and to resist; . . . Not to discontinue our allegiance, in this case, would be to join with the sovereign in promoting the slavery and misery of that society, the welfare of which, we ourselves, as well as our sovereign, are indispensably obliged to secure and promote, as far as in us lies.[7]

To Mayhew, public office was a public trust. Those who hold office do so because of the *"implicit confidence"* placed in them by the governed, "neither God nor nature, having given any man a right of dominion over any society, independently of that society's approbation, and consent to be governed by him." As no rulers are above human limitations, minor deviations of conduct or administration do not constitute grounds for "legitimate disobedience to the *higher powers*." (Jefferson was to say twenty-six years later, "Governments long established should not be changed for light and transient causes.") "But it is equally evident . . . that those in authority may abuse their *trust* and power *to such a degree,* that neither the law of reason, nor of religion, requires, that any obedience or submission should be paid to them; but, on the contrary, that they should be totally *discarded;* and the authority which they were before vested with, transferred to others, who may exercise it more to those good purposes for which it is given." [8]

At what exact point did revolution become justified by God and nature? Mayhew could give no more definitive answer to this question than any other political thinker of the natural-rights school, but he possessed here, as in religious matters, an abiding faith in the ability of human judgment: "The people know for what end they set up, and maintain, their governors; and they are the proper judges when they execute their *trust* as they ought to do it." He concluded his attack on unlimited submission in a passage that looked back to 1642 and 1688, but also, more than he would live to know, looked forward to 1776:

For a nation thus abused to rise unanimously, and to resist their prince, even to the dethroning him, is not criminal; but a reasonable way of vindicating their liberties and just rights; it is making use of the means, and the only means, which God has put into their power, for mutual and self-defence. And it would be highly criminal in them, not to make use of this means. It would be stupid tameness, and unaccountable folly, for whole nations to suffer *one* unreasonable, ambitious and cruel man, to wanton and riot in their misery. And in such a case it would, of the two, be more rational to suppose, that they that did NOT *resist,* than they who did, would *receive to themselves damnation.*[9]

For Mayhew, resistance to political tyranny had become morality, the hope of eternal life.

Had the sermon ended at this point, it might have attracted little more attention than similar efforts by other Congregational preachers. But, "Much irritated by the senseless Clamors of some Tory-Spirited Churchmen" who still used January 30 as an excuse for worshiping King Charles I and for cursing the Dissenters who "murdered" him, Mayhew went on to make a contemporary application of his political principles. As a result, he touched off a controversy that brought *Unlimited Submission* to the attention of both Old and New England.[10]

Why was Charles I resisted by the Puritans? Mayhew answered his own question with a series of charges against that monarch that has reminded some readers of Jefferson's indictment of George III in the Declaration of Independence. For example:

He levied many taxes upon the people without consent of parliament; and then imprisoned great numbers of the principal merchants and gentry for not paying them. He erected, or at least revived, several new and arbitrary courts, in which the most unheard-of barbarities were committed with his knowledge and approbation. . . . He refused to call any parliament at all for the space of twelve years together, during all which time, he governed in an absolute lawless and despotic manner. . . . He sent a large sum of money, which he had raised by his arbitrary taxes, into *Germany*, to raise foreign troops, in order to force more arbitrary taxes upon his subjects.[11]

Resistance to the archtyrant Charles I was not made by "a small seditious *party*," Mayhew declared, "but by the LORDS and COMMONS of *England*." Thus it was not rebellion, "but a most righteous and glorious stand, made in defence of the natural and legal rights of the people, against the unnatural and illegal encroachments of arbitrary power. . . . Resistance was absolutely necessary in order to preserve the nation from slavery, misery and ruin." Even "God himself does not govern in an absolutely arbitrary and despotic manner," as did Charles I. The Restoration Parliament ordered January 30 to be observed as a national day of humiliation, and the Episcopal clergy "continue to speak of this unhappy prince as a *great Saint* and a *Martyr*," often comparing the life and suffering of King Charles to those of Jesus Christ. The "*church* must be but *poorly stocked* with saints and martyrs, which is forced to adopt such enormous sinners into her *kalendar*, in order to swell the number." [12] In practice, the Anglican clergy are more interested in preaching royal authority than the gospel of Christ:

In *plain english*, there seems to have been an impious bargain struck up betwixt the *scepter* and the *surplice*, for enslaving both the *bodies* and *souls* of men. The king appeared to be willing that the clergy should do what they would, . . . *Provided always*, that the clergy would be *tools* to the crown; that they would make the people believe, that kings had God's authority for breaking God's law; that they had a commission from heaven to seize the estates and lives of their subjects at pleasure; and that it was a damnable sin to resist them, even when they did such things as deserved more than damnation.[13]

This is the real explanation of King Charles' saintship and martyrdom, he concluded. Yet the observance of January 30 may not be a total loss to the cause of liberty: "It is to be hoped, that it will prove a standing *memento*, that *Britons* will not be *slaves;* and a warning to all corrupt *councellors* and *ministers,* not to go too far in advising to arbitrary, despotic measures." [14]

As if this verbal blast set to print were not sufficient to disturb the religious peace of the land, Mayhew added a note in the Preface that was certain to make every Anglican minister in New England fighting mad:

People have no security against being unmercifully *priest-ridden,* but by keeping all imperious BISHOPS, and other CLERGYMEN who love to "lord it over God's heritage," from getting their *foot* into the *stirrup* at all. Let them be once fairly *mounted,* and their "beasts, the laiety," may *prance* and *flounce* about to no purpose: And they will, at length, be so *jaded* and *hack'd* by these reverend *jockies,* that they will not even have *spirits* enough to complain, that their *backs* are *galled;* or, like *Balaam's* ass, to "rebuke the madness of the prophet."

. . . Tyranny brings *ignorance* and *brutality* along with it. It degrades men from their just rank, into the class of brutes. It damps their spirits. It suppresses arts. It extinguishes every spark of noble ardor and generosity in the breasts of those who are enslaved by it. It makes naturally-strong and great minds, feeble and little; and triumphs over the ruins of virtue and humanity. This is true of tyranny in every shape. There can be nothing great and good, where its influence reaches. For which reason it becomes every friend to truth and human kind; every lover of God and the christian religion, to bear a part in opposing this hateful monster.

Earlier in the sermon Mayhew had suggested a simile that made it clear that he regarded some Anglican clergy as "*Reverend* and *Right Reverend Drones,* who *worked not*" but spent their lives in "effeminacy, luxury and idleness." [15]

The publication of *Unlimited Submission and Passive Obedience* unloosed a newspaper controversy that set new records for vituperation in New England and sent both Puritan and Anglican scurrying to dusty library shelves for worm-eaten copies of Neal, Burnet, and Clarendon with which to answer or support Mayhew's charges. As always, Boston newspapers welcomed a fight and printed freely the anonymous letters of both parties.

To the Anglicans the author became that "splenetick" actor "retailing thy Harrangues to get an empty Name"; that "raw youth" who, if he paid for his education, "was cheated of his Money, even to the last *artfully concealed Six pence*"; one of the cheats and imposters that appear in every age; "a misguided Implement, raving about the Danger of Liberty, in a Time of perfect Tranquility and absolute Security"; a "Bully . . . ambitious and vain of proclaiming himself a Friend to Freedom, because she is in no danger"; "one of St. Jude's filthy Dreamers, who despise Dominion and speak evil of Dignities"; and a "wrangling Preacher" who had "belch'd out a Flood of Obloquy."

The sermon itself was labeled "A Scandalous and Invective Pamphlet" containing "the grossest falshoods," "an Over-Load of Abuse and Scurrility" which the lowest man would think below the dignity of an answer, and a blot on the name of New England which "cannot but grieve every good Man." Mayhew was accused by one writer of being a Catholic in disguise, but Boston was far more ready to believe the charge that he was "only acting a Part, to keep his Friends in Tune lest his suspected listing" toward the Church of England become known, as in Hooper's case, before a good opening was found. With more accuracy an Anglican writer predicted that "this *Don Quixote* in *Religion* and *Politics*" would quickly step back from Charles I to an attack on the "*Saintship*" of Jesus Christ and the "*Mystery of the Gospel.*" Mayhew refused to answer the attacks of "these Advocates for Tyranny and Oppression." He publicly announced that "if any person of common sense and common honesty, shall condescend" to reply to the sermon in a signed publication, "he may depend upon having all proper regard shewn to him." As no answer of this description appeared, no defense was necessary.[16]

Charles Brockwell, assistant minister of King's Chapel, assumed that *Unlimited Submission* had been aimed at him, because he had preached on January 30, 1749, a defense of "that Religious & Virtuous Prince," Charles I. He admitted to his ecclesiastical superior in London that he had written several of the anonymous newspaper attacks on Mayhew, and he suggested that the Bishop of London seek damages in Westminster against the "unlicked Cub of Forty One," who was certain to be acquitted by "a Jury of Fanatics" if suit should be brought in Boston. Brockwell also reported that for a time he had been threatened with a libel suit by Mayhew's friends, who finally dropped the matter after presenting a copy of the province laws to the library of King's Chapel.[17]

Mayhew's partisans in the newspaper war agreed that "altho' there was a considerable quantity of Mercury in the Emetick, the stubborn Malady of the patient required it." Many of the letters written in support of the sermon were mild in tone and cited passages from English historians to prove that Charles and Archbishop Laud were all the preacher had charged. One contribution explained that the commotion raised by "Mr. *Mayhew's* ingenious Sermon" was an example of the old proverb, "Touch a gall'd Horse and he will Wince." Another expressed wonderment over "how great a Matter a little Fire kindleth." Boston Congregationalists were not as united in support of this attack on the Church of England as New England's century-old tradition of hatred for Charles I and Laud would lead one to expect. Some thought that his severity and satire ill became a Christian minister. The surviving "old guard" of the Boston clergy never forgave "such *unmannerly behaviour*," which they attributed to "a *thirst* of *superiourity*." Eleven years later they still thought his "*flogging*" of the Anglican clergy to have been "without rhyme or reason," for he had received "no ill or uncatholic treatment" from them. Outside Boston, relations between the Congregationalists and Anglicans were much more strained, and from this time on Mayhew was regarded in many country areas as a new champion of New England's religious independence against the High Church party in England from whose clutches the founders had fled.[18]

The most serious charge hurled at Mayhew during this controversy was plagiarism. The *Boston Evening-Post* devoted its front pages of April 16 and 23, 1750, to a long letter which pointed out that the first part of the *Discourse* had been taken from a sermon on the same topic by Bishop Benjamin Hoadley, and that the second part had drawn freely from two other English publications. The letter writer offered parallel columns from Mayhew and Hoadley to prove his point. All the local preacher had done, he charged, was to add "Wormwood to Gall"—the harshness, the bitterness, the sarcasm were original, but the ideas were all borrowed. There was no question but that much of the political philosophy in *Unlimited Submission* was Hoadley's, for Mayhew was a great admirer of the Whig Bishop and in later life listed him as one of the chief sources of his ideas on civil liberty. The "plagiarism" in this case consisted in paraphrasing thoughts expressed in several of the Bishop's sermons, including one from the same text as *Unlimited Submission*.[19]

In pointing out that Mayhew had borrowed his political ideas, his Anglican detractors apparently hoped to impugn his integrity and to cast on him by association some of the odium Hoadley had suffered in England for being the most pugnacious of the Whig churchmen who had provided a religious sanction for the expulsion of a divine-right king in 1688 and now stood guard against a Jacobite revival in either Church or State. Hoadley had been rewarded with a miter in 1716 for his forceful preaching against the Jacobite rebellion of the previous year. A master of polemic, the Bishop neglected his Episcopal duties to defend his principles. These included private judgment in religion, toleration for Dissenters, a Lockeian theory of civil government, and a rationalistic theology fully as liberal as that of his friend, Samuel Clarke. Anathema to Tories, Hoadley had now become a source of embarrassment to all but the most latitudinarian Anglicans.[20]

Mayhew was not in the least disturbed by the charge. In the fall of 1750, he addressed a respectful letter to Hoadley, now nearing seventy-five, thanking him for his favorable notice of the *Seven Sermons*. With the letter went a copy of *Unlimited Submission*. "You have an undoubted Right to a copy of it," he wrote, if it is true, as some people in Boston have maintained, that "the great Part of it was stolen from Your Lordship's Original." [21] After one more exchange of newspaper volleys, the question of plagiarism was dropped and never revived. To have convicted the author in this case would have been to convict the majority of his contemporaries who wrote for publication. Hoadley's sermons along with the works of Locke and Sidney were becoming textbooks from which American Whigs drew freely.[22]

In October, Mayhew sent copies of *Unlimited Submission* to his new friends in England. Its reception was generally favorable, although George Benson delivered a mild, fatherly rebuke for using such severity on the Anglicans.[23] The more militant opponents of the High Church were quick to make use of Mayhew's pungent style. Richard Baron included the controversial sermon in *The Pillars of Priestcraft and Orthodoxy Shaken,* a two-volume attack on ecclesiastical tyranny, which appeared only two years after the publication of *Unlimited Submission.*[24] Baron had been an intimate of the late Thomas Gordon, one of the authors of *The Independent Whig,* an anti-clerical periodical from which the West Church pastor was accused of having taken "an *over-Dose*" of material for the attack on Charles I. A professional editor, Baron was the most competent person who judged the charge of plagiarism, and his republication of the sermon indicates a verdict of acquittal.

Unlimited Submission was reprinted several times before the American Revolution, and as Englishmen were reading the first glowing reports of the French Revolution in 1789, the *Gentleman's Magazine* offered them extracts from this sermon to point out the nature of tyranny.[25] Today its strongest passages seldom miss an anthology of colonial political thought or history. In his old age, John Adams paid the greatest tributes to *Unlimited Submission.* To it he referred Fourth of July orators who "really wish to investigate the principles and feelings which produced the Revolution." He wrote to Thomas Jefferson that the sermon "was a tolerable Chatechism for The Education of a Boy of 14 Years of Age, who was destined in the future Course of his Life to dabble in so many Revolutions in America, in Holland and in France. . . . This discourse was printed, a Year before I entered Harvard Colledge and I read it, till the Substance of it was incorporated into my Nature and indelibly engraved on my Memory. It made a greater Sensation in New England than Mr. Henrys Philipick against the Parsons did in Virginia." The recollections of an elderly statesman are seldom trustworthy, but in this case the passage of sixty-eight years had not blurred the former president's memory of the impact of Mayhew's most celebrated sermon.[26]

For the next four years Mayhew did not again enter the political arena. His only published sermon in this period was occasioned by the death in 1751 of Frederick, eldest son of King George II and heir to the throne of Great Britain. Boston presses turned out four of the many sermons preached in honor of the deceased Frederick and as a token of loyalty and devotion to the House of Hanover. In contrast to the eulogistical and contrite tone of the other discourses, the West Church heard, "It is better to trust in the Lord than to put confidence in Princes," because "subjects can never have an absolute security, that even the best of kings will not alter their measures; and oppress and devour, instead of defending, them." "Good sense is not entailed with the crown, on the elder branch of the male line." Mayhew went on to say that he was reluctant to eulogize Frederick because he had no firsthand knowledge of the prince and was afraid he might be accused of flattering one in high office. Lest his silence be misinterpreted, however, he would say that all reports he had heard concerning Frederick were favorable and indicated that "the Prince had a due abhorrence of popery and arbitrary government, as being both of them contrary to reason and christianity; inconsistent with the natural rights of mankind, and the truest happiness of human society." [27]

Whatever their private opinions of Mayhew, the leaders of the province had to acknowledge his mounting fame both at home and in England. He was on his way to becoming Massachusetts' most controversial but also best-known figure. A secret desire of the legislators to have a look at him and the tactful suggestions of his admirers produced an invitation from the General Court to preach the election sermon in 1754.

From 1634, when John Cotton began the custom, until it was discontinued in 1884, this unique New England institution served as a public reminder of the ideals of the Puritan founders. Each spring the towns of Massachusetts elected representatives to the lower house of the General Court, and on the last Wednesday in May the newly elected House of Representatives assembled at Boston. After being sworn in, the representatives elected their speaker and heard a sermon by a minister selected in alternate years by each house. Swelling the audience for the annual sermon were the Massachusetts clergy, who held their yearly convention in Boston concurrently with the opening of the General Court.[28]

Most of the election sermons were ordered printed by the Court, and copies were given to each member for distribution in his home district. Country pulpits often echoed the ideas and sentiments of the election sermons brought home at the end of the session. As might be expected, many of the discourses dealt with broad religio-political principles and made applications of those principles to the current problems of the province. One of the few remaining remnants of John Winthrop's "due form of government," the election sermon in the eighteenth century had become an instrument for the dissemination of political ideas second in importance only to the newspaper.[29]

Facing this distinguished audience of lay and clerical representatives from the entire province, Mayhew reiterated his political faith. The ultimate source of civil government is God, but He has not given His blessing to any one form of government: "To say the least, monarchical government has no better foundation in the oracles of God, than any other." Government is "founded in, and supported by, common consent," and the "security and happiness of all members composing the political body" is the objective of political institutions for both God and man. "It is instituted for the preservation of mens persons, properties & various rights, against fraud and lawless violence; and that, by means of it, we may both procure, and quietly enjoy, those numerous blessings and advantages, which are unattainable out of society, and being unconnected by the bonds of it."

It is true, he continued, that monarchs and their deputies are the ministers of God, but "unto whomsoever much is given, of him shall much be required"—rulers must appear before the tribunal of God to give an account of how they have used their God-given talents, just as the meanest slave. Subjects owe reverence and submission to their king as long as he rules by law and not by will: loyalty and slavery are not synonymous. In the course of the sermon he reminded Governor Shirley, "You will never forget, Sir, whose minister you are; what God, the King, and this people, reasonably expect from You, considering the paternal relation in which you stand towards us." [30]

Notwithstanding the reputation of the preacher and the ideas expressed, the House of Representatives voted its thanks for the election sermon and requested a copy for the press. That the Boston edition of 1754 was followed by a London edition the following year pointed once again to growing prestige abroad.[31]

Jonathan Mayhew had added nothing new to the current stock of political philosophy with these early sermons. The two political tenets he had most emphasized—public office as a public trust and the right of the subject to rebel against a ruler who fails to keep the trust—had been formulated long before he entered the West Church pulpit, as he admitted, by such Englishmen as Sidney, Locke, and Hoadley. In America, the Congregational clergy had generally paid lip service to similar concepts while preaching on the ancient Hebrew monarchy or the sins of the House of Stuart. Mayhew had said little of a political nature that could not be found in the sermons of some of his ministerial colleagues.[32]

In politics, as in religion, his significance lay not only in what he said, but in how he said it. His boldness, cutting language, and controversial reputation gave his words a much wider audience than the force of his ideas alone would have commanded. With him, also, there is a new note of caution: no longer is it to be assumed that any monarch can be trusted with the people's liberties. Even the best of kings must be watched constantly. If Mayhew was not antimonarchical, he was at least indifferent to the case for monarchy—"If the *end* [of government] be attained, it is enough." Far more than other Congregational clergymen, he stressed the clear and positive religious obligation of the people to check evil or arbitrary rulers. As he stated the matter so bluntly, "All commands running counter to the declared will of the supreme legislator of heaven and earth, are null and void: And therefore disobedience to them is a duty, not a crime." [33]

Why did Mayhew choose to disseminate and popularize these political tenets in the early 1750's in an empire fighting for its existence under popular King George II? This question puzzled some readers of *Unlimited Submission* who understood neither the religious and social currents that flowed through West Boston nor his passion for religious truth as he saw it through the eyes of the Enlightenment. In only a dozen years, under a new king and a weak, uncertain ministry, with new grievances laid on, such ideas would begin to function as the rationale for American resistance to British imperial policy.

CHAPTER VII

Profits and Piety

Christianity is the greatest Enforcement & Security possible, of due Subjection & obedience to all just & rightful Authority; to all that power & the Exercises thereof, which any ways contribute to the good Order, & well-being of Society.

Jonathan Mayhew, 1759 [1]

JONATHAN MAYHEW'S ministry at the West Church coincided almost exactly with the period in which the economic growth of the American colonies was most conspicuous.[2] By 1748 "the tempest of enthusiasm" was over in Boston. Increased trade following the Peace of Aix-la-Chapelle, the government's new sound-money policy, and an expanding economy throughout all the British colonies in North America brought unparalleled prosperity to the town. A tidal wave of materialism submerged New Lights as well as Old Lights. When in 1754 Whitefield made one of his return trips to the community, he was sent on his way with the complaint that one week of his preaching had cost Boston £10,000 in time lost from work in addition to the large offerings the evangelist repeatedly carried away with him, a complaint echoed by many a citizen who had eagerly joined the throngs that heard Whitefield in the early 1740's. Increased prosperity was reflected in a higher standard of living for the commercial classes, who found revivals less attractive now than Mr. Draper's vocal and instrumental performances at the Concert Hall, or such diversions as "That Elaborate and Matchless Pile of ART, called The MICROCOSM, or The WORLD in MINIATURE," which William Fletcher, a member of Mayhew's parish, exhibited for a price in his West Boston mansion. Merchants, sea captains, ship owners, enterprising men of all descriptions, rubbed elbows at the Bunch of Grapes on King's Street, near the Long Wharf. After a few glasses at this "Best Punch House in Boston," saints and sinners, Puritans and Anglicans discovered no social or religious barriers to conviviality and planning together new ventures in pursuit of greater profits.[3]

One of the most conspicuous concomitants of this materialistic spirit was the slackening of the strict Puritan observance of the Sabbath. In 1746 "His Majesty's Justices of the Peace in the Town of Boston" served notice that they were going to patrol the streets on the Lord's Day to enforce the laws against unnecessary walking or loitering in public places. As late as 1766 these notices were still appearing in the newspapers, but to no avail. It was impossible to force soldiers and sailors to observe the blue laws, and Sabbath laxity was contagious. Mayhew observed in 1763 that from a fifth to a quarter of Boston's citizens almost never entered a church.[4] Merchant John (?) Green was typical of an increasing proportion of Mayhew's Sunday audience. Green attended the West Church when he was not wandering among various other meetings, including the Anglican, according to the dictates of his fancy. Equally prominent among Green's religious habits was his reluctance to attend services when he could muster any excuse, such as inclement weather, but his Puritan conscience still compelled him to record dutifully these excuses in his diary.[5] The magistrates made sporadic efforts to enforce other seventeenth-century laws. In 1757 Samuel Rhodes was convicted of blasphemy and forced to sit for one hour in the gallows with the noose around his neck, after which he was given twenty-five lashes and sent back to jail. The fine for profanity was still one crown per oath, *if* one was caught in the act. But no amount of vestigial observance could disguise the acquisitive society developing on the ruins of the Wilderness Zion.[6]

This society sustained a series of traumatic shocks from

1755 to 1760. At 4:30 a.m. on November 18, 1755, an earthquake sent most of the town's 15,500 residents running into
the streets in terror. A number of substantial brick buildings
collapsed, and there was considerable damage in general, although by good fortune no lives were lost. The renewal of
the war with France and Pitt's boycott made trade extremely
hazardous. By the end of 1758 seven of the West Church's
most prominent merchants, distillers, and shipbuilders had
declared themselves bankrupt. Finally, in 1760, just as the
expulsion of the hated Romanists from North America made
it seem that God was smiling on New England again, the
most disastrous of a series of fires consumed over three hundred buildings and left nearly as many families homeless.
The clergy agreed that it was a propitious time to call Boston
to repentance and to decry the sins for which God had declared war on the community.[7]

It was not an easy task. The Puritan divines of the colony
had from the beginning blessed trade, manufacturing, and
land development while at the same time they had warned
against the corrupting effects of wealth on vital piety. In the
eighteenth century the clergy were forced to recognize that
few if any of the saints could remain untarnished while they
amassed wealth. There is no better example of what had
happened to the Puritan doctrine that all wealth was a gift
from God and to be regarded as such than Thomas Foxcroft's
funeral sermon for John Coney in 1722: "Indeed his moral
Defects I have not mentioned, for they were only such as are
consistent with a good Estate, and small in comparison of his
Virtues, and therefore to be charitably cover'd in sacred
Silence." [8] Such sacred silence also covered the materialism
that was invading even the parsonages of the clergy. The
family of Cotton Mather's disappointing son, Samuel, now
ensconced in Boston's Tenth Congregational Church, seemed
to spend as much time trying to win at lotteries as they did

in family devotions and other exercises of Christian nurture. The Reverend Mr. Mather urged Samuel, Jr., to be "on the gaining Hand" and not to waste money in mourning for his brother, recently killed in battle. Coxcomb was the word Boston applied to "a reverend orator, with a diamond ring and a white handkerchief, exclaiming against the pomps and vanities of this wicked world, and desiring you to take heed for neither food nor raiment." [9]

Jonathan Mayhew's sermons during the second half of the 1750's have received scant attention from historians. But here is to be found his primary motivation, the headwaters of all he did or said—a strong, unwavering faith in his God, a faith that dominated and directed his entire being. Out of this faith came an intense, burning desire to strip religion of all superstition and sham so that men might serve the true God better, not less. The religious freedom he preached with such zeal was the freedom of the individual to live in harmony with the laws of "pure and undefiled" Christianity, a freedom acquired when the Christian answered the call to duty. When he saw that prosperous Boston was flirting with a pernicious materialism and secularism, he also decided it was high time to call his people back to God. The Sabbath after the earthquake in November 1755 he took his text from II Peter iii, 11: "Seeing then that all these things shall be dissolved, what manner of persons ought ye to be?" [10]

Although Mayhew tried to avoid "a common-place invective against the times" such as his pulpit contemporaries were pouring forth upon their congregations, he could not escape the conclusion that earthquakes, hard times, and fires were related to the lack of "pure and undefiled religion amongst us" and the presence of so much "flagrant immorality, profaneness and irreligion throughout these colonies." Such events do not just happen; they are acts of God. It is true that God no longer intervenes in human affairs by miraculous or preternatural methods as he did in Biblical times. Today the Almighty does not set aside the laws of nature, but He uses natural phenomena to turn the attention of men toward Him.[11] This was essentially the view held by his friend, John Winthrop of Harvard, who taught that earthquakes had natural causes and were not special acts of divine judgment, but rather phenomena with the "grand moral purpose" of developing in men "a reverent sense of the Deity." To his congregation the pastor praised Winthrop for a forthright stand against the absurd sermons on the earthquake by Thomas Prince and other local divines, but he was careful not to throw away the opportunity presented by the disasters of 1755–1760. Even of such a man-made event as the great Boston fire of 1760, Mayhew could say that "This evil, this great evil, has not surely come upon us, but by his appointment, and according to his sovereign pleasure. . . . We may assure ourselves, it is not without just and sufficient provocation, that he has appeared thus against us." [12]

Like his Puritan ancestors, Jonathan Mayhew had no fault to find with material things in themselves—a man can be rich and pious simultaneously. Religion allows one, he told the West Church, "while we live here, to be conversant about our secular affairs," and some good men often spend most of their time in worldly activities. At the same time, there can be no genuine pleasure in the material, for the most excellent part of human nature can enjoy only those objects of an intellectual or moral nature: a society that is primarily materialistic can never be truly happy. God is not angry with New England because it is prosperous, but rather because its prosperity has led to luxury, pride, selfishness, and formality in religion.[13]

New England, and particularly Boston, was unusually susceptible to such heinous sins because its religious theory and practice were so widely divergent. The Reformation doctrine of justification by faith alone had been perverted into an easy path to eternal life, a means that absolved one from obedience to Christian precepts. The land was full of hearers who were not doers of the Word, men whose lives were no better for their faith. Although he did not deprecate the role of faith in salvation, he was convinced that genuine internal faith "diffuses itself into the actions and lives of men, regulating and animating all their outward deportment." How did men excuse and justify their failure to accept practical as well as theoretical Christianity? Mayhew's answer would delight a modern psychologist. One person, for example, who is so orthodox "that he abhors the very name of *Arminianism*," may be substituting his orthodoxy for a real reformation of his life. Another may be extremely punctual in the performance of his religious duties or freely give alms to "cover a multitude of Sins." Or some may rationalize that Satan is powerful and subtle, or that good men in former times were also negligent in certain points of conduct.[14]

To awaken Boston from its apathy over this glaring discrepancy between religious theory and practice, Mayhew preached hellfire and damnation. There is, he reminded his parishioners after the great earthquake, "but an hand's or hair's-breadth," between man and "eternal perdition." If we "die in our sins, we shall incur the wrath of God, we shall lose our souls, and have our portion with the devil and his angels in outer darkness." Nothing can give us an idea "sufficiently strong and affecting" of hell, "unless perhaps it were, the groans, and fruitless lamentations of the damned, who have been already thus deluded to their perdition!" He did not doubt "but that both the bodies and souls of the wicked will together suffer that amazing punishment which the scriptures express by the second death." Mayhew's purpose was not to frighten sinners into a hasty repentance that at best would be superficial. Too many such conversions had failed to stand the test of prosperity in recent times. His plea was rather that if a man runs the risk of going to hell and losing his soul, it is only reasonable—common sense—for him to take the proper steps to avoid such a disastrous conclusion to his life. In religion as in trade and other occupations, "Prudent forethought is the parent of plenty and prosperity; delay is the mother of want, shame and wretchedness." [15]

The pastor of a middle-class congregation could not confine his arguments for the necessity of obeying the precepts of the gospel to the threat of eternal damnation. No Christian, Mayhew entreated, can be excused from the duty of attending church services, even if he cannot entirely agree with any one branch of the Christian church. Such is particularly the case for influential citizens, "the more knowing part of Christians," who must set an example for those who need the influence of the church, "the *common* people." If only the lower classes go to church, that institution will fall into disrepute, and society will lose its greatest stabilizing influence. Such an appeal was not lost on the West Church merchants. Their pastor was no advocate of levelism, no democrat in the modern definition of the term. They agreed with his dictum that "There is, as there ought to be, a wide difference of rank and circumstance amongst mankind, in this world." He saw no prospect of making the lot of the poor any more comfortable or any less burdensome. In his sermons are numerous examples that even Mayhew's "true primitive" Christianity functioned to keep all except the enterprising minority of men contented with their stations in life.[16]

But rich or poor, high or low, there is one truly happy life, the life of religion and virtue. Contrary to what many people believe, Mayhew told his congregation, "religion is so far from abridging us of the natural pleasures of life, which are worthy of our pursuit, that it refines and exalts them all." What does religion do for a man? It increases his temporal happiness by improving his health and lengthening his life.

It brings him to the esteem and respect of his neighbors. And, most important of all, religion gives one the prospect of eternal happiness. Reason, experience, and scripture all point to "sober religion and virtue" as being the only course that will bring you the long life and happiness you desire so much. The good life is the religious life.[17]

Every minister is faced with the obligation of maintaining in his personal life the standards he has set for others from his pulpit. In Mayhew's case this was a particularly onerous task, for the eyes of the town were upon him, watching and waiting for one breach of conduct that would confirm what many wanted to believe about the disturber of the religious peace. His exemplary conduct and modest standard of living failed to reward the vigilance of his critics.

He was afflicted with a long series of illnesses which began during his second year at Harvard, at which time gratitude to God for a rapid recovery inclined him toward the ministry as a career. When he wrote to his father in 1751 that "My Health is as usual," he was referring to his unsettled physical condition. The following year he fell victim to the smallpox epidemic that killed nearly six hundred of Boston's inhabitants and brought all life in the town to a standstill during the summer months. He survived the smallpox only to be stricken during convalescence with a siege of kidney stones and "Pleurisy-Fever" that threatened his life for the second time in a month. After this summer of misery, he appears to have been free from major ailments until his final illness in 1766, though in this period he sometimes gave poor health as an explanation for delays in correspondence and publication. As he explained to a friend, "I am better qualified to sympathize with the unhealthy than most People would chuse to be."[18]

The Massachusetts clergy of the eighteenth century were

confronted with the perennial professional-class problem of maintaining a gentleman's standard of living on an income far below that of their more prosperous peers. During Mayhew's years at West Church, some impoverished clergymen took to the newspapers as the only means of bringing their plight before the public.[19] In most cases, the Boston clergy, supported by a voluntary system of maintenance, received larger salaries than their country colleagues, whose compensation usually came from the tax rates. For his part, Mayhew was as well paid as any Congregational minister in Boston. Without a family to support and with many a sumptuous dinner from the tables of his parishioners, he was comfortably situated during his early years at the West Church. For the first time in his life he could buy a book or a new suit of clothes without sacrificing a necessity, and he could also support a wife. Yet for more than nine years after his ordination, the minister's pew remained empty of wife and family. A combination of poor health and concentration on studies appears responsible for the delay, but the records are silent as to whether there had been any previous affairs of the heart before Mayhew became an earnest suitor in the spring of 1756.

Elizabeth Clarke was twenty-two in 1756, and by all contemporary accounts she was one of the most beautiful young ladies to be seen in the town.[20] The Clarkes were a notable family; they boasted descent from Sir Richard Saltonstall and other worthies of Massachusetts Bay history. William Clarke, Elizabeth's uncle, had made a fortune in shipping, and then had attempted to outdo another of Boston's first families, the Hutchinsons, by building in the North End a brick mansion of twenty-six rooms and three stories that looked down in contempt on the two-story Hutchinson house. Uncle William had died in 1742 after suffering financial losses that eventually forced the family to sell his mansion. Elizabeth's father was

Sir—

Boston, Feb. 21. 1756.—

I presume it will be needless for me par:
ticularly to inform you, with what View I have
repeated my Visits at your House, so soon one
after another, as I have lately done. If you will
only please to reflect, what an agreeable Daugh
:ter you are bless'd with, and that I am still
a Bachelor you can, I think Sir, be at no
Loss for the Reason. I would also hope, that
both my Station & Character in the World
are such, as will leave you no Room to doubt
but that my Intentions are sincere & honon.
:rable. And having so far succeeded in them as
to obtain Miss Betty's Permission to visit her
again, I thought my self bound by the Rules of
Decency & Propriety, in the next Place to acquaint
you & your Lady herewith; and to crave your
Leave to prosecute a Design which I have so much
at Heart. This, Sir, I accordingly now do; hoping
that I shall not find either you or your Lady
averse to what I propose. Please to communicate
this Letter, or at least the Contents of it, to your
Lady, together with my very respectful Compli:
ments. I intend, with Submission to Providence,
to be at your House, on Monday Evening next:
When, unless you or Mrs Clarke should signify to
me your Disapprobation, I shall take it for
granted, that I have your Allowance to frequent
your House with the View I have intimated; which
will give me a very particular Satisfaction.

. I am, Sir, with great Respect,

Your, and your Lady's,

Most Obedt. Humble Servt.

J. Clarke Esq;

Jonathan Mayhew

Jonathan Mayhew seeks permission to court Elizabeth Clarke

the fourth Dr. John Clarke to practice medicine in Boston. Physicians in colonial New England faced uncertain and sporadic incomes, but the family still owned a collection of small houses and other properties near Clarke's Wharf and a farm in Waltham, where the Clarkes preferred to spend the summer. In addition to his medical practice, Dr. Clarke kept busy as a justice of the peace for Boston, and he made an occasional sally into Massachusetts politics. He had been elected to the Massachusetts Council in 1741, but his election had been vetoed by Governor Belcher, who objected to the physician's support of the loose-money principles of the Land Bank. Betty Clarke had been brought up in Boston's version of the genteel tradition. Her mother, of the same name, combined the practical arts with the more fashionable: such skills as sewing, japanning, and waxwork were as proudly displayed by the Clarke ladies as their pretty dresses. Betty knew what it meant to keep up appearances on a dwindling income— excellent schooling for life in a parsonage.[21]

Jonathan made repeated visits to the Clarke home in the beginning of 1756, and by the middle of February he had won Betty's approval to continue his calling. Now the thirty-five-year-old suitor thought himself "bound by the Rules of Decency & Propriety" to acquaint her father with the purpose of his visits, and to "crave" his "Leave to prosecute a Design" very close to the ministerial heart.[22] The "Design" seems to have met with no serious parental objections, although it was rumored around Boston that pressure was exerted on the parents to guard their daughter from such a heretical suitor. These rumors were plausible, for the Clarkes attended the New Brick Church, where the elegant Ebenezer Pemberton, Jr., waged war against theological liberalism. A contemporary story describes how this reverend gentleman exploded with anger one day while being shaved because the barber expressed a desire to hear Mayhew preach. Fortunately, few of

Pemberton's parishioners were in the habit of following their pastor's counsel.

Jonathan had become an intimate friend of William Clarke, Betty's older brother, who may have subverted the campaign to save his sister from theological contamination. In March the suitor invited the brother to a stag dinner featuring "Turtle-Food," a delicacy prized by the social avant-garde of the day. A postscript to the invitation indicated the progress of the courtship and illuminated a side of Mayhew's nature that only his few close friends were permitted to see: "I was going to request you to present my *Compliments* to Miss Betty: But I do not like the formality of that word—I desire you would, in plain Old English, give my *hearty Love to her:* but do not for the World let her know a Syllable what I have said about *Turtle-Food:* For you know ministers ought in Conscience to be very grave & stupid: And that for them to jest about such Things is almost as bad as Heresy." [23]

William kept the secret and Jonathan won his lady. The following September the couple filed intentions of marriage, and on a rainy Thursday evening, November 11, 1756, they were married. The bride did not appear to mind the reproach of heresy. There is every reason to believe their close friend, Harrison Gray, when he reported that "there never was a more happy Match upon Earth," and that "their Obliging behaviour to each Other . . . did Honour to the Marriage State." Jonathan's letters to his "Dear Bessey" reveal a passionate and tender marital relation. The West Church heartily approved the match that provided such a charming occupant of the minister's pew.[24]

There is no record of where the newlyweds first lived, and they did not purchase a home of their own. In 1763 they were renting a "Handsome well finished" house "pleasantly situated on a good Street at New Boston." There were two rooms and a kitchen on the first floor, a large yard with a

well and pump, a "good Garden Spot," and another building
fifty feet long that served as a barn and carriage house. Here
the Doctor and his bride lived comfortably without ostenta-
tion. The inventory of his estate made shortly after his death
in 1766 reveals a few items of luxury—a silver tea service, an
expensive clock, and "a large Sconce Glass with gilt Orna-
ments"—but most of the household equipment was designed
for everyday living. The lady of the house found sufficient
housewifely tasks to keep her capable hands occupied, and customarily she had a servant or two to direct. In 1761 a maid
and an indentured servant, an Indian boy from Martha's
Vineyard, were at work in the household.[25]

Mayhew retained his ministerial reserve with diligent care,
a policy dictated by his impetuosity. As a result, he often
struck his casual friends as a man of serious and grave deportment, who even in company was sometimes lost in contem-
plation. Only around the dinner table with his wife and a
few intimates could he throw off the ministerial role and once
again be the buoyant, mirthful undergraduate. Now the wine
glasses could be filled and filled again without fear of a pry-
ing tutor. There were other dinners with more formality.
Judges, lawyers, merchants, clergymen found an invitation
to the Mayhew home hard on their reputations in certain
quarters, but never dull or unrewarding. Aside from such
social life, there was little time for recreation. The three guns
listed in the inventory of his personal effects suggest that he
was fond of hunting, a carry-over from a boyhood on the
Vineyard. He refused to condemn young people who occasionally attended a dance or a concert, but he himself had
no "taste" for such diversions. The theater he labeled "im-
moral and profane," and he gave full support to the government's ban on theatrical performances in Massachusetts. In
his opinion, the blue laws involved no hardship. On one occasion he took even John Calvin to task for countenancing
recreation on the Sabbath.[26]

On May 1, 1759, Elizabeth bore her first child, a girl who was promptly named Elizabeth after mother and grandmother. A few months later, during his wife's absence to care for her ailing mother in Waltham, Jonathan revealed how much he had come to love family life. He wrote to Elizabeth: "This is to inform you that we are all very well; at least as well as could be expected when you are absent. I now hear your Daughter talking pretty fast, only I cannot understand her. I suppose she is calling her Mamma, and wants her to come home. . . . your ever loving and *TENDER* Husband, who longs to see you." The next child was a boy, born in March 1763. As the first girl was named after the mother, so the first boy was named for the father. Jonathan Mayhew, Jr., did not survive his second summer. With his death on July 15, 1764, died, as it turned out, the only hope of perpetuating the name the senior Jonathan had made famous on both sides of the Atlantic. Another daughter, Sarah, born in October 1765, also died in infancy. Daughter Elizabeth did her part to carry on the name of the father. She married Peter Wainwright, an Englishman, and their first child was named Jonathan Mayhew Wainwright. Since then the oldest son of the oldest son in the family has carried the name. The hero of Corregidor, General Jonathan Mayhew Wainwright, was the fourth in straight line of descent to be so-named, and his son is the fifth.[27]

The added financial responsibilities of a family did not appear to tax Jonathan's resources, although Elizabeth's father may have lent a helping hand. His own father had died in 1759 at eighty-five, after finally persuading Zachariah to continue the Indian mission; but Experience Mayhew was too poor to leave his youngest son anything more than a few books and a tract of land that had no immediate cash value. By the end of 1765, Jonathan Mayhew had accumulated more than £200, which he had invested in trade and from which he was beginning to receive profits by the time of his death the following year. Had he lived longer, his estate would possibly have been worth more than the £800 he left his widow. Even so, he had moved far from the days when he had been a charity student at Harvard.[28]

Jonathan Mayhew never doubted that he held his material interests in a proper relation to his prospects of eternal happiness, for him the ultimate goal of life. Two years before his death, he exclaimed to his congregation, "How contemptible all earthly pleasures, riches & glory, in comparison of those which are reserved in heaven for the faithful!" Such concern for the "due subordination" of profits to piety was not cant. He was fully aware that a people "called unto liberty" would be prone to forget their calling in a materialistic atmosphere. Unlike Samuel Adams, who feared that the decline of Puritanism would leave New England's free institutions too weak to withstand the corrupting influence of commercialism, Mayhew saw a rational Christianity, stripped of hypocrisy, as the only hope of keeping alive the spirit of liberty in a prosperous and increasingly secular society.[29]

EBENEZER GAY   CHARLES CHAUNCY

SAMUEL COOPER   ROBERT TREAT PAINE

SEVEN SERMONS

Upon The

Following Subjects;

viz.

The Difference betwixt Truth and Falfhood, Right and Wrong.	Objections confidered:
	The Love of God.
	The Love of our Neighbour.
The natural Abilities of Men for difcerning thefe Differences.	The firft and great Command: ment, &c.
The Right and Duty of private Judgment.	

Preached

At a LECTURE in the Weft Meeting-Houfe In BOSTON,

Begun the firft Thurfday in *June*, and ended the laft Thurfday In *Auguft*, 1748.

By JONATHAN MAYHEW, A. M.

Paftor of the Weft Church in *Bofton*.

BOSTON, N. E.

Printed and Sold by ROGERS and FOWLE in Queen-ftreet.

MDCCXLIX.

Mayhew's first volume of sermons

OBSERVATIONS

ON THE

CHARTER and CONDUCT

OF THE

SOCIETY

For the Propagation of the Gofpel in Foreign Parts;

DESIGNED TO SHEW

Their NON-CONFORMITY to each other.

WITH

REMARKS on the MISTAKES of

EAST APTHORP, M.A. Miffionary at CAMBRIDGE, in Quoting, and Reprefenting the Senfe of faid Charter, &c.

AS ALSO

Various incidental Reflections relative to the CHURCH of ENGLAND, and the State of Religion in NORTH-AMERICA, particularly in NEW-ENGLAND.

BY

JONATHAN MAYHEW, D.D.

Paftor of the Weft-Church in BOSTON.

Brethren unawares brought in, who came in privily to fpy out our LIBERTY which we have in Chrift Jefus, that they might bring us into BONDAGE : To whom we gave place by fubjection, no not for an hour ; that the truth of the GOSPEL might CONTINUE WITH YOU.

AP. PAUL to the *Galatians*.

BOSTON, NEW-ENGLAND:

Printed by RICHARD and SAMUEL DRAPER, in Newbury-Street, EDES and GILL, in Queen-Street, and THOMAS and JOHN FLEET at the Heart and Crown in Cornhill.

M,DCC,LXIII.

Mayhew's major attack on the Church of England

CHAPTER VIII

Uproar in Zion

Zeal for *Athanasian* & *Calvinistic* Orthodoxy, burns very
furiously amongst most People here, both Clergy & Laiety.
. . . However I propose to persevere in the Method of
Preaching I am now in, as long as I can, leaving the Event
to Providence, and taking no Thought for the Morrow.

Jonathan Mayhew, 1754[1]

THE LAST decade of Mayhew's life was a period of seeth-
ing controversy. There was seldom a moment from 1755 until
his death in 1766 in which he was not involved in one or more
theological, ecclesiastical, or political quarrels. To the bewilderment of both friend and foe he could in the same sermon plead for broad-minded toleration and denounce in
scathing invective those who refused to accept his views. A
sense of mission increased his natural belligerency. He had
concluded that the propagation of uncorrupted Christianity
depended on a handful of scattered individuals still loyal
to the true faith, whose task was to cut away the debris that
ignorant, irrational, or hypocritical men had piled on the
gospel. As his English friend George Benson wrote, "A few
such, in every country, firm & faithful to one another, would
shake the foundations of orthodoxy, & make primitive christianity to arise, in it's genuine purity." Certain that God and
reason were on his side, Mayhew found it more difficult to be
tolerant in practice than in theory. He defiantly declared in
1755, "I will not be, even *religiously* scolded, nor pitied, nor
wept and lamented, out of any principles which I believe
upon the authority of Scripture, in the exercise of that small
share of reason which God has given me: Nor will I postpone

this authority, to that of all the good *Fathers* of the Church, even with that of the good *Mothers* added to it!" New England was prone to attribute such an attitude to "haughty spirits and vanity." Pride was the epithet most often hurled toward the West Church study.[2]

Although Mayhew was keenly sensitive to the abuse and scurrility heaped upon him for his frankness in expressing his views, he was not surprised that the cause of true religion should require martyrs in his age as well as in the first centuries of the Christian church. In his case martyrdom would mean being driven from the ministry, a possibility of which he never lost sight. Opposition and ostracism only confirmed his consciousness of being right and increased the difficulty of tolerating error. He was fond of pointing out how much he differed from "our *Pulpit-Performers*," a practice that made it unlikely his brethren in the ministry would display "the spirit of charity and meekness" he demanded of those who dared to correct his errors.[3]

In his polemics Mayhew displayed a measure of the intellectual arrogance typical of eighteenth-century European rationalists. He shared their enthusiastic confidence that man's use of his rational faculties was opening door after door leading to new truths to replace the superstitions and ignorance of the past. Although this optimistic outlook rested on conclusions drawn from the work of Newton in science and Locke in philosophy, its immediate impact was nowhere more evident than in theology. Locke himself had pointed the way with *The Reasonableness of Christianity*, a book which indicated that the Enlightenment did not lead Christian thinkers inevitably into Deism or skepticism. Locke was followed by a group of Christian rationalists who were convinced that God and revelation could meet the most critical rational test. Their most influential representative was Samuel Clarke, the Anglican philosopher and theologian. Not only had Dr. Clarke

translated Newton's *Optics* in a manner that won the approval
of the great scientist, he had also engaged Leibnitz, the Ger-
man philosopher and mathematician, in a celebrated controversy. Even without the mathematics necessary to understand Newton's *Principia,* Mayhew could imbibe the spirit
of the Enlightenment directly from the works of Locke and
Clarke. These Christian rationalists agreed that Christianity
was a rational religion, its truths simple and nonspeculative,
and its chief aim the promotion of virtue. Mayhew's own
theology had developed along these lines. It was difficult for
him to understand why so many of his countrymen still preferred the monkish speculations of the past to this pure and
simple religion of the Age of Reason.[4]

Even the most orthodox of the Congregational clergy had
been reluctant to challenge openly West Boston's heretical
voice during the first eight years of his ministry. To extirpate
Arminianism by a frontal attack from pulpit and press appeared to be a hopeless task; it had seemed wiser to isolate
the disease in the hope it would die out before reaching the
epidemic stage. The bulk of the clergy were moderate Calvinists who feared Arminianism more for what they regarded as
its fatal consequence—an anchorless drift into Deism—than
for its immediate errors. For example, Thomas Foxcroft had
stood firm against radical Andrew Croswell's contention that
all Arminians were certain to go to hell. This uneasy ecclesiastical peace was broken in the middle 1750's by the appearance of a new heresy. It had been rumored that there were
Arians in Massachusetts, and these suspicions were seemingly
confirmed in 1755 by Mayhew's remarks on the Trinity in a
volume of sermons and by the republication in Boston the
following year of Thomas Emlyn's *Humble Inquiry,* an anti-
Trinitarian work published a half-century earlier in England.[5]

An ancient heresy, Arianism was a term now used loosely,

often in conjunction with Socinianism, to describe the views of Christians who doubted the traditional doctrine of the Trinity. The orthodox clung to the Athanasian Creed, which taught that the three persons of the Trinity were all "coeternal and coequal." Arians maintained that the Son was subordinate to the Father, yet had existed before the creation and the incarnation. Socinians rejected the idea that Christ had existed before His birth and made Him merely a man especially created by God. Both Arians and Socinians, however, insisted that God was *one* supreme being. They regarded the Athanasian Trinity as a metaphysical abstraction without the slightest basis in Scripture.[6]

Christian rationalists in England after Locke were almost inevitably drawn to an examination of the mysterious doctrine of the Trinity. But for the majority, Socinianism was too sharp a blow at their faith, too long a step toward Deism. They had a greater affinity with the Arian position, which included an expressed desire to accept whatever was demonstrable from the New Testament concerning the nature of the Godhead. Writing in this spirit, Dr. Samuel Clarke shook English Christendom in 1712 with his *The Scripture-Doctrine of the Trinity*. After a thorough study of all pertinent texts, this eminent scholar concluded that the Athanasian Trinity had little scriptural foundation. On the contrary, the Bible taught that the Father was the only supreme God and ultimate object of worship and that Christ was a subordinate being, to be worshiped only as a mediator between God and man. Characteristic of Clarke's insistence on adherence to a Biblical rather than a creedal position was his refusal to accept the Arian teaching that there had been a time when the Son had not existed. Such willingness to be satisfied with the language of Scripture was typical of the so-called Arian movement of eighteenth-century England. Clarke's influence was widespread, not only in Anglican ranks but also among the Dissenters of the next generation. Mayhew's clerical friends in England all exhibited various degrees of anti-Trinitarianism. Their letters to Boston contain no new theories of the Trinity but do reveal a determination to hear "every honest & free inquiry." [7]

In step with the English Christian rationalists, Mayhew began criticizing the Athanasian Trinity early in the 1750's, but his first clear public statement came in a volume of sermons published in 1755. "With the metaphysical abstract nature, or essence of the Deity," he wrote in a footnote, "I am not bold enough to meddle." He was willing to leave such questions "to the unaccountable Temerity of the *Athanasians.*" Yet of one thing he was certain—there is only one God. "Christians ought not, surely, to pay any such obedience or homage to the Son, as has a tendency to eclipse the Glory of God the Father; who is without Rival or Competitor. The Dominion and Sovereignty of the universe *is* necessarily *one,* and in ONE;—the *only* living and true GOD, who delegates such measures of power and authority to other Beings, as seemeth good in his sight; but 'will not give his [peculiar] glory to another.'" [8]

The Son, he continued, "claims no authority, besides what he claims by virtue of the *Father's* grant, and the commission which he received from *Him.*" Christ's role was that of a mediator between God and man, so "the mediatorial authority of Christ, being derived from HIM," is subordinate to the authority of God the Father. The Christian faith does not consist of a reliance on Christ for salvation, but rather of a faith and hope in God through Christ, who is *"the image of the invisible God."* A Christian owes immediate obedience to Christ, but that obedience "is *ultimately* referred to *His Father and our Father, to His God and our God."* [9]

Mayhew never progressed far toward any theory of the Trinity. He was certain that his Bible did not teach a personal union of a human soul with the deity. Later he asserted that "it was not some other divine Being, agent or person, distinct from the FATHER, that dwelt in the man Christ Jesus, as some have imagined, . . . but the Father himself." Mayhew's negative approach to the doctrine is evident in his objection to an unscriptural perversion of the title "The Son of God" into "God the Son." Such nonsense and contradiction could never be "too *sacred* to be ridiculous." He regarded disputes on the Trinity as a major source of Christian disunity and a barrier to the conversion of Jews and Mohammedans. "Some," he observed, "contend, and foam, and curse their brethren, for the sake of the *Athanasian Trinity,* 'till 'tis evident they do not love and fear the ONE living and true God as they ought to do." 10

A cry of shock and protest greeted the publication of Mayhew's remarks on the Trinity. Horror took hold of Andrew Croswell, pastor of Boston's schismatic Eleventh Congregational Church and self-appointed guardian of the heavenly gates against Arminians, when he read such "horrible Talk about the Trinity." As an antidote to this new heresy, Croswell and his friends hastened to republish an English discourse on *The Insufficience of Natural Religion.* One clergyman told young John Adams "That he could bear with an Arminian, but when, with Dr. Mayhew, they denied the Divinity and Satisfaction of J[esus] C[hrist] he had no more to do with them." The *Boston News-Letter* advertised the republication of a *Defence* of the deity of Christ that had just gone through two editions in England and was designed to subvert "by conclusive Scripture Arguments" the Arian doctrine which "seems of late to be creeping in among us." 11

In 1750 New England had exiled its best mind to the Indian mission at Stockbridge, but Jonathan Edwards was not so far removed from Boston that he could miss the impact of what he termed "Dr. Mayhew's late book, . . . wherein he ridicules

the doctrine of the Trinity." Nor could he regard the name
Mayhew with equanimity. Edwards' recent ouster from his
pastorate at Northampton had been spearheaded by his
cousin, Joseph Hawley, who had become an Arminian after
reading Experience Mayhew's *Grace Defended* in an atmosphere congenial to heresy at Harvard in 1744. Furthermore,
the elder Mayhew had voiced his objections to some points
of Edwards' doctrine. Only the infirmities of old age—a shaking hand and failing eyesight—had prevented Experience
Mayhew from publicly challenging this "precious servant of
God" who had "fallen into so wrong a way of thinking." [12]

Edwards wrote Thomas Foxcroft of the First Church to
emphasize the necessity of countering Mayhew's footnote.
Foxcroft replied that the question had been considered by
the Harvard Board of Overseers, but no action had been
taken.[13] It was rumored that Joseph Sewall and Thomas
Prince together with two members of the Massachusetts
Council signed a petition to have the heretic expelled from
the Board of Overseers, of which he was ex officio a member.
This was the matter to which Foxcroft referred, but no notice
of the action ever appeared in the Overseers records. Sewall
also failed in an attempt to discipline Mayhew by defeating
him for reëlection to the post of clerk of the Massachusetts
Congregational clergy, a position to which he had first been
elected in 1755 before the offensive remarks on the Trinity
appeared in print.[14]

Edwards' "uneasiness" was increased when Emlyn's *Humble Inquiry* was republished in Boston the year following
Mayhew's remarks on the Trinity with a preface that challenged scholars to refute its Arian views with scriptural evidence, *if* they were able. This time he wrote to Professor
Wigglesworth to express his fear that unless someone answered Mayhew and whoever republished Emlyn, it would
appear that the clergy were silent out of inability to defend

the doctrine of the Trinity. Edwards pleaded for Wigglesworth to accept the challenge himself, for an answer from the theology professor at Harvard would do more to aid the cause than the efforts of any other man. "I think Zion calls for help," he concluded. "If nothing be done, I dread the consequences." [15]

This appeal placed Wigglesworth in a difficult position. Hollis Professor of Divinity since 1722, he had developed a reputation for moderation and conciliation. Though not as liberal in his personal views as his students Mayhew and Chauncy, he had always taught respect for any honest expression of opinion. In reply, Wigglesworth sympathized with Edwards' objectives but proposed an oblique attack. He wrote that he also had found objectionable material in the recent volume of sermons. For one thing, he thought Mayhew had insinuated "that the canon of the Old Testament was compiled according to the humor and caprice of the people; that some books were admitted and others left out of the canon, according as the people relished or disrelished the contents of them." To refute this insinuation, Wigglesworth had lectured to Harvard students and had since published the lecture.[16]

Wigglesworth added that the ministers were vindicating the divinity of Christ in the Boston Thursday lecture, and now Ebenezer Pemberton had published "a catholic and judicious discourse" on the same topic, with a preface by Sewall and Prince.[17] It was best to do nothing more until an answer to Pemberton appeared. Wigglesworth blamed the printers for the republication of Emlyn's book: "But the printers, who live very much by disputes, observing that the people's passions were up, that any thing on that subject would fetch a penny, and that every thing was supposed to be pointed at Dr. Mayhew, continued printing little things with pompous advertisements about them in the newspapers,

week after week. If it had not been for these repeated and
long continued provocations, I don't think we should ever
have seen the 'Layman's' new edition of 'Emlyn's Inquiry.'"
The Professor hoped Emlyn's volume would attract little
attention; but, if it became popular, he promised to shield
the undergraduates from its pernicious teachings. The best
strategy in answering Emlyn would be to reissue an able
English answer to him. A controversy should be avoided at
all costs, for the resulting zeal, acrimony, and sarcasm "would
be a great disservice to the interests of religion." In a remarkably prophetic sentence, Wigglesworth told Edwards, "And
if the controversy be once begun, perhaps neither I nor you,
sir, who are much younger, will live to see the end of it." [18]

Edwards' son-in-law, President Aaron Burr of the College
of New Jersey (Princeton), took up the challenge Professor
Wigglesworth had declined. Burr's *The Supreme Deity of
Our Lord Jesus Christ, Maintained* appeared in Boston in
1757. Joseph Bellamy of Bethlehem, Connecticut, also close
to Edwards, preached and printed a masterful sermon in
1758 on *The Divinity of Jesus Christ*. Bellamy had predicted
in 1750 that those who denied original sin would soon be
tampering with the nature of Christ. Now he asserted that
there was a large party in Boston headed by a celebrated
D.D. who "boldly ridicules the doctrine of the Trinity." [19]

As always, New England preserved its sense of humor during this contest. The *Boston Gazette* in 1757 published "A
Letter of Thanks" from Beelzebub thanking the Rev. Mr.
Jonathan Parsons of Newburyport for a volume of sermons
in which he had assured his readers that Arminians and Arians
would burn in hell. A wag replied that although the devil
had not personally written the letter, he had a hand in it,
since the author was obviously an Arminian, and likely "a
Doctor of Arminian Divinity." Similarly, Mayhew has been
saddled with responsibility for nearly every anonymous

Arminian or Arian piece published from 1747–1766, including Emlyn's *Humble Inquiry*. Unfortunately, no evidence accompanied these charges.[20]

Jonathan Mayhew's criticism of the Athanasian Trinity occupied a peripheral location in his thinking. After his first printed remarks in 1755, he held fast to the position that the Athanasian Creed was an unscriptural and illogical invention of Roman Catholic theologians; a creed that had proved unacceptable to the majority of Christians in the past; and an affront to Jewish and Moslem believers in one God. Publicly he said little more except to reaffirm occasionally his faith that there can be only one God. As for the mystery of the Trinity, he was content with Biblical terminology. He took pains to point out the lack of scriptural evidence for the Socinian as well as the Athanasian theory, but he saw no need to identify himself with any particular position between the two.[21] His own words, written in 1763, offer the best summary of his thinking on this topic:

That I ever denied, or treated in a bold or ludicrous manner, the divinity of the Son of God, as revealed in scripture, I absolutely deny. My soul loves and adores him. Of his great salvation I have a good hope thro' grace; more prized by me than many, than all worlds: . . . I have indeed expressed my disbelief, and even contempt of certain metaphysical and scolastic, unscriptural and ridiculous definitions or explications of the *trinity*, which some men have given.[22]

The same 1755 volume of sermons brought the charge that the author had also denied the doctrine of justification by faith. Andrew Croswell accused Mayhew of adopting "the old Popish Doctrine of Justification by Works." The Doctor's sermons on justification, protested the angry Croswell, are as "*wretched Nonsense* as ever was printed." Bellamy was among those who saw heresy here as well as on the Trinity.

These criticisms struck at the most vulnerable spot in the bold minister's theological development. Having rejected the Calvinistic doctrines of original sin and election as well as the practice of revivalism, he was faced with the necessity of working out an explanation of the process of conversion that would fit his Arminian theology. He was spurred on by a pressing conviction that the Puritan separation of piety and ethics was foreign to the true purpose of Christianity.[23]

Mayhew had no fault to find with the central Reformation motif of justification by faith alone, but he had concluded that an emphasis on this idea was the source of a moral laxity that often seemed to excuse the conspicuous absence of those good works which should appear as evidence of a change of heart. This was exactly the point the unfortunate Lemuel Briant had made in his famous sermon on *The Absurdity and Blasphemy of depretiating Moral Virtue.* In his 1755 sermons Mayhew had attempted to explain that faith without works was just as dead as works without faith, but his statement that no man can prove he is possessed of saving faith without works sounded like salvation by works alone to a Reformation-minded New England. His insistence that a sinner must think on his sinful ways as a preliminary to his conversion struck hard at the Puritan emphasis upon the sovereignty of God. Critics demanded to know how at the same time he could maintain that salvation is always the work of God.[24]

Six years later Mayhew sought to clarify his position on justification in two published sermons entitled *Striving to enter in at the strait Gate . . .; And the Connexion of Salvation therewith, Proved From the Holy Scriptures.* "However free the grace of God is," he insisted, "it is manifest that he has required something of us in order to our salvation." Our part is an earnest striving to enter the strait gate "of eternal life and happiness." This striving necessarily involves a belief in the gospel; a consciousness of one's sinful condition; a desire

for salvation through Christ; a prayer to God for guidance,
pardon, and "newness of life"; an opposition to sinful practices; and a "real endeavour" to obey all the known commandments of God. One must strive with perseverance "as long
as it shall please God to continue us in the world." May an
unregenerate sinner strive? Yes, "at least in general," after
he has felt some "influence or operation of the good spirit of
God upon his heart," for the actions of the unregenerate are
not "*wholly* unpleasing to God." It is certain that "any sinner
who is willing and desirous, and strives, to obtain the salvation thus revealed" will not be rejected. From these two sermons it is evident that Mayhew found himself unable to
distinguish sharply between the regenerate and the unregenerate. Man does not merit salvation, and his good works cannot save him; still, thanks to God's free grace, the man who
is striving is on the road to heaven.[25]

The major answer to *Striving* came from the pen of Samuel
Hopkins, the ablest of the New Divinity men who, after the
death of Jonathan Edwards, endeavored to carry on his
theological work. Hopkins agreed with Mayhew that "The
promises of the gospel are beyond question made to all who
heartily desire the things promised," but he challenged his
antagonist to prove that the unregenerate have any desire to
be righteous. Well aware that Mayhew was attempting to
encourage weak men to live better lives, Hopkins answered
the practical objections so often raised against the Calvinist
emphasis on the sovereignty of God. No instances have been
produced, he wrote, of persons leaving the means of grace
because of discouragement over the lack of a certain relation
between their actions and salvation. He cited the frequent
soul-stirring revivals among Calvinists as evidence of this
statement. Furthermore, the necessity of always striving was
discouraging to weak believers and held out to them the false

hope that "the convinced and externally reformed sinner" was
on his way to joining the ranks of the regenerate.[26]

Apparently Mayhew had no intention of answering Hopkins; in any case, he did not live to do so. But in his sermons
at the West Church he continued to explore this theme. It
must be remembered that the Arminian definition of sin was
willful transgression of law. A perfectly righteous person—
one who had never broken a law of God—would have no need
of repentance. Since there are no such persons on earth, repentance is required of everyone who desires to be righteous.
The first step in repentance is for one to become conscious of
his error (his sin against God) and to feel personal remorse
coupled with an apprehension of God's "righteous displeas-
ure." Then, with his hope in Christ, the sinner develops a
horror and hatred of sin, which he resolves to forsake, and
he determines to live in harmony with God's known commandments. These steps of repentance, "being united together, constitute that change of temper, or renewed state of
mind, which the scriptures express by a new heart, the new
man, the new creature, and the like. . . . And, this repentance
is properly the Gift of God; not, indeed immediately, but
mediately by the Ministry of the Gospel, under the conduct
& influence of his holy & good Spirit." [27]

This penitent sinner is the "New Man" and has the "true
Temper & spirit of a Christian." Evidence of the change will
not be the ecstasy of a crisis experience but such internal
fruits of repentance as a sense of peace and pardon, love of
God, joy, charity and goodwill to all men, victory over the
world, and a desire to glorify God in the world and to serve
one's generation according to His will. There are also external
fruits of repentance: the forsaking of all the ways of sin, vice,
and folly; reparation for past wrongs; a proper regard for
prayer, public worship, and the ordinances of the Gospel;

and in general, "an holy and good life." It is not essential, he reminded the timid members of his parish, to make a public testimony to this change. A profession of Christianity may be effectually made without writing or speaking, for the fruits of repentance are self-evident.[28]

Christians are in "a state of trial, and conflict" and have enemies to combat during all of life in this "evil world." The Christian who fights to the end, he hopefully added, will not be deprived of his victory because he occasionally lapses into sin: "A good man may, thro' the malice, subtlety and power of his spiritual enemies, lose ground for a time, fall into grievous sins, and, to appearance almost become a prey to them; and yet, by the grace of God, recover new strength & resolution; and finally overcome." Mayhew's endeavor to bridge the gulf between Puritan piety and ethics left him open to the charge that he could not draw a dividing line between the work of man and the work of God in conversion and, hence, that he was preaching nothing more than natural morality. For him, nevertheless, God's role was no less necessary than man's striving.[29]

Mayhew's circle of Arminians in America and England feared a godless, Christless morality fully as much as a stupefying orthodoxy. He was alert to the danger that those who accept the principles of rational religion may easily degenerate into "mere Deism & Scepticism." Christian sobriety (the happy life of the righteous man) "is evidently such a sobriety of mind, not as Socrates or Plato, not as Cicero or Seneca taught, tho' in some respects truly excellent; nor yet merely such as Moses and the prophets taught; much less still, such as Lord *Shaftsbury* and Lord *Bollingbroke* taught: But such as the Lord from Heaven, and his inspired apostles taught; and such as all are to practice, who hope to ascend thither where he is, to behold, and to partake of his glory." He warned against "the fatal principles of our modern deists,"

such irreligious men as Collins, Woolston, Tindal, Shaftes-
bury, Chubb, and Bolingbroke. He identified Voltaire's design as "the intire subversion of *Revelation.*" All of these
"emissaries and apostles" of the devil will delude you to your
ruin, he cautioned his congregation.[30]

Modern scholars have found it easy to dismiss Mayhew's
warning against Deists and his insistence that divine aid was
ultimately necessary in conversion as only "a half-hearted
concession to the sentiments of his orthodox public."[31] It is
difficult to determine the vintage of new wine in old bottles.
In Jonathan Mayhew's image of himself, however, he was
battling to save and not to destroy the Christian hope of
salvation through Jesus Christ. For too long, in his opinion,
New England had substituted the legalism and pious hypocrisy of covenant theology for the "living, operative principle
of love and obedience," which never fails in time "to produce
good works, or a virtuous, holy and godly life." To make matters worse, the disciples of Jonathan Edwards were refurbish-
ing the rigid, unenlightened theology of original Calvinism,
including the notion that a sinner must love God so much as
to be willing to suffer eternal damnation for His glory. This
is "the height of absurdity," Mayhew exclaimed to his people!
Strive to enter the strait gate, "the gate of eternal life and
happiness," and be confident that a just and loving God will
reward your sincere efforts.[32]

Not all religious controversies in New England were con-
ducted in a scholarly vein. The clergy were usually careful
that any publications appearing under their names maintained
at least a semblance of dignity. But no such reserve was necessary in the newspapers, where the use of pseudonyms made
it possible to be plain-spoken. All the pent-up bitterness and
enmity between Mayhew and the clerical "old guard" of Boston erupted in the newspaper battle over the Cumming ordi-

nation in 1761. Alexander Cumming came to Boston to serve
as associate pastor of the Old South Church with the aging
Joseph Sewall. An unbending Calvinist, Cumming was welcomed as a reinforcement for the beleaguered forces of orthodoxy. When his ordination on February 25 was followed by
one of the most elaborate ordination celebrations Boston had
witnessed, Mayhew could not resist the temptation to point
to this event, held in Sewall's house, as evidence of the de-
generacy of his religious foes.[33]

Soon after the ordination, the *Boston Gazette* published a
letter from a man "some miles from Boston" who protested
the extravagance of the festivity of February 25. Evidently
written by Mayhew or a friend, the letter facetiously charged
that food had been purchased for the feast in such quantities
as to force a 25 percent increase in grocery prices. The writer
accused the Boston ministers of not observing the resolution
against "Feasting, Jollity and Revelling at ordinations"
adopted by the Massachusetts Congregational convention in
1759. Although Joseph Sewall had been the moderator of the
convention that had passed the resolution and voted that
it should be read from the pulpits the week before an ordination was to take place in the vicinity, the Boston churches
had failed to comply on the Sunday preceding Cumming's
installation.[34]

The next *News-Letter* carried an advertisement signed by
Mayhew. Whatever the other ministers had done, he had
read the resolution to his congregation and had declined an
invitation to the entertainment as inconsistent with his principles and engagements. As a result, the advertisement concluded, "he is entirely innocent of the heavy charges contained in that *public indictment*." These two pieces were
promptly answered by "A layman in the country," who stated
that the first letter had been written by Mayhew out of envy
at not having been invited to participate in the ordination.

Nothing more extravagant was served at the feast than enough "decent food" to feed the invited guests. The ministers were not obligated by the convention to read the resolution, and to have done so would have been "a gross affront" to one's congregation. Since when, the "layman" asked, did the heretical Doctor "pay a greater regard to the judgment of a convention than his *own?*" [35]

The first writer replied that attempting to fix the authorship of his letter on Mayhew, who "lies under a popular odium," was a stratagem to discredit the charges by attributing them to a "graceless Arminian" whose opinions of the feasting of "sound Calvinists" would not be accepted by the orthodox. In turn he suggested that the defense of the ordination festivity had been written by a Boston minister, "a certain thick, corpulent gentleman, noted for his turgid, declamatory stile, and his boisterous, affected zeal; for the shallowness of his reasoning, the emptiness of his harrangues, and his eternally putting his emphasis upon some insignificant monosyllable, to prove himself an accomplished orator." No Bostonian could mistake this description of Pemberton.[36]

The clerics who had attended the dinner were challenged to publish the menu as evidence of their "decent food." When no one responded, the writer of the original letter supplied the menu for the *Gazette:*

There were six tables, that held one with another 18 persons, upon each table a good rich plum pudding, a dish of boil'd pork and fowle, and a corn'd leg of pork, with sauce proper for it, a leg of bacon, a piece of alamode beef, a leg of mutton with caper sauce, a piece of roast beef, a roast line of veal, a roast turkey, a venison pastie, besides chefs cakes and tarts, cheese and butter. Half a dozen cooks were employed upon this occasion, upwards of twenty tenders to wait upon tables; they had the best of old cyder, one barrel of Lisbon wine, punch in plenty before and after dinner, made of old Barbados spirit. The cost of this moderate dinner was upwards of fifty pounds lawful money.[37]

Mayhew had won his point—this was hardly a "common dinner"—but he was not to have the last word. He was issued a public challenge to declare that he had not written the letters attacking the ministers who attended the feast. No such declaration was made, and Boston chuckled over its two "countrymen," Mayhew and Pemberton.[38]

Mayhew's excursion into "heresy" had a definite boundary beyond which he could not go. That boundary was an unshakable faith in the validity of the Holy Scriptures. His repudiation of the doctrines of original sin and predestination as well as his doubts on the Athanasian Trinity had resulted from rigorous study of the Bible. Even his severest critics recognized the scholarly diligence that continued from undergraduate days until death. In common with his English friends, all of whom owed something to the method developed by Samuel Clarke, Mayhew insisted that religious dogma stand the test of what he regarded as the only rational method of Biblical interpretation. First, the doctrine must be agreeable to the language and "Obvious Sense" of Scripture—"You should always interpret the more obscure and difficult parts of scripture, in consistence with those that are plain." Next, there must be no "insuperable Objections from Reason." Finally, the doctrine must not contradict principles of natural law, such as "our natural Notions" of justice and mercy. Using this method, by 1754 Mayhew had concluded that the doctrine of Christ's atonement for the sins of man was valid. In that year he voiced strong objections to the view of the atonement held by John Taylor of Norwich, his mentor on original sin: "The N. Testament both countenances & requires, an Explanation of this Doctrine, something more remote from the Socinian, than Mr. Taylor's appears to me to be." Mayhew was not blindly following the English Arminians.[39]

From the beginning of his ministry, he had taught that God was "a merciful and faithful Creator; a compassionate Parent;

a gentle Master, a righteous Judge." At the same time he had
preached the necessity of eternal punishment for those who
stubbornly refused to heed the admonitions of this kindly
Deity. The difficulty of reconciling a benevolent God with
the damnation of sinners left a chink in his armor which John
Cleaveland, a Separatist minister of Ipswich, Massachusetts,
sought to exploit. In 1763 Mayhew published *Two Sermons
On the Nature, Extent and Perfection of the Divine Goodness.*
There was little in this volume he had not said before, but
the title itself was another challenge to Calvinists. Cleaveland
charged in a lengthy *Essay* that the Boston heretic had pictured the divine goodness in such a light as to make Christ's
atoning sacrifice unnecessary. Even before Cleaveland's *Essay*
appeared, extracts from the sermons on *Divine Goodness* were
published in a newspaper to furnish evidence of Mayhew's
belief in the doctrine of the atonement.[40]

Cleaveland had struck at a logical weakness in Mayhew's
theology, but he gained little support. His reputation as a wild
and unstable New Light was widespread in New England,
thanks to his arbitrary expulsion from Yale without his degree
during the Great Awakening. He was held in such low esteem
in Boston that during the present controversy one anonymous
newspaper writer dared say of him, "the higher a Monkey
climbs the more he shews his backside." In addition, Mayhew's view of the atonement was so far from being heretical
that it was held by such staunch Calvinists as Joseph Bellamy
and Samuel Hopkins. Cleaveland insisted that only the An-
selmic or "satisfaction" theory provided a genuine atonement,
while in the sermons under attack Mayhew had expounded
the Grotian or "governmental" theory. God punishes sinners
solely to maintain His own glory, Cleaveland wrote. No, said
Mayhew, "a perfectly good and merciful" God punishes men
only to uphold His moral government in the universe and
to preserve "the common felicity of his intelligent creatures."[41]

Refusing to accept the Ipswich preacher as an equal, May-

hew published *A Letter of Reproof* only to correct the "rude-
ness and insolence, . . . misrepresentation and slander, falsehood and forgery" of Cleaveland's "libel." My principal aim
is "not to dispute with, but to chastize and admonish you, for
your real good; and to make you an example and warning to
others." To climax these insults, he offered to translate Latin
for one "so unletter'd . . . so raw and unstudied in divinity,"
who had made this vicious attack to gain a reputation and his
Yale degree (belatedly bestowed in 1763). Cleaveland answered in a mild *Reply* that dealt with theological issues and
avoided further vituperation. In spite of its mildness, the
Reply struck the most telling blow of the controversy by suggesting that Dr. Mayhew had not written in the spirit of the
Gospel.[42]

Jonathan Edwards, Aaron Burr, Joseph Bellamy, Samuel
Hopkins, Ebenezer Pemberton, John Cleaveland, Andrew
Croswell, Thomas Foxcroft—Calvinists of all shades—had
taken up arms against the man they considered to be the
Goliath of heresy. For opposite reasons, later historians of
Unitarianism hailed the herald of a liberal faith. In stressing
the discards, both groups neglected the remaining contents
of Mayhew's theology: the validity of Holy Scripture, as interpreted by human reason; God the Creator and the atonement of His Son, Jesus Christ; a final judgment with rewards
and punishments; and the second coming of Christ. Far from
having departed from what New England's "pious fore-fathers
considered as the *most essential* branches of christianity,"
he thought of himself as the guardian of that faith, which
shone more brightly now that he and his like-minded friends
had chipped off the surface corrosion to expose the real nature
of "pure and undefiled" religion. He could boast in 1763 that
"There is no such monster as an *Atheist* known amongst us;
hardly any such person as a *Deist*." [43]

CHAPTER IX

Real Whiggery

And tho' he [Cicero] did not fall at last as a martyr directly
for true religion; yet he fell as one of the most glorious
advocates for LIBERTY, that the world ever saw: An honor
next to that of suffering martyrdom for religion; and, in
some sort, the same thing; true religion comprising in it the
love of liberty, and of One's country; and the hatred of all
tyranny and oppression.

Jonathan Mayhew, 1763[1]

JONATHAN MAYHEW lived in a world at war. During
nearly the entire span of his maturity the British and French
empires were locked in a death struggle for possession of the
vast North American continent. While he studied for the ministry after graduation, a force from New England captured
the French stronghold at Louisburg, whose commanding position in the North Atlantic had posed a threat to British trade.
The year following his ordination, a European peace confer-
ence handed Louisburg back to the enemy, much to the disappointment of the provincials, who were now forced to conclude that the contest could never permanently end until one
side or the other had achieved a complete victory. In the
uneasy years between 1748 and 1754, the colonists awaited
the renewal of hostilities.

The spring of 1754 saw young George Washington set out
from Virginia for the Ohio River to strike a blow that would
inaugurate the final phase of the Anglo-French battle for
North America, "The Great War for Empire." Before Washington reached the Ohio, Mayhew, in his election sermon of
1754, warned that a showdown with the French was inevitable. "Peace is a great blessing," he told the governor and

legislators; "peace is what we would chuse; peace is the desire of all who deserve the name of Christians." But when the glory of God, the honor of the king, the good of the country, and the liberties of Europe and America are at stake, peace is impossible for honorable, God-fearing men:

And I am sure there is not a true New-England-Man, whose heart is not already engaged in this contest; and whose purse, and his arm also, if need be, is not ready to be employed in it; in a cause so just in the sight of God and man; a cause so necessary for our own self-defense; a cause wherein our liberties, our religion, our lives, our bodies, our souls, are all so nearly concerned. . . . We have *put our hand to the plough;* and he that *looks back,* is so far from being worthy the privileges of a *citizen of Heaven,* that he is not worthy to enjoy the rights of an *Englishman.*[2]

During the darkest days of the war in 1757, the *Boston Gazette* reprinted a portion of this plea for effective opposition to French expansion.[3] In the years before final victory, Mayhew threw the entire weight of his pulpit into what for him was a holy war against French tyranny and Romish superstition. He never doubted that Protestantism and British liberty were inseparably allied in a sacred union fighting for God against the forces of the devil, who sought to enslave men both religiously and politically. The present struggle was one phase "of the final triumph of the church of Christ over all its enemies." Britain's continental ally, Frederick the Great of Prussia, a monarch noted for his indifference to religion, was extolled in the West Church as "a Prince, so visibly upheld up by providence, to vindicate the rights of mankind against the invasions of tyranny, and the usurpations of the papal see . . . a Prince, whom God seems to have raised up, on purpose that in him he 'might make his power known, and that his name might be declared thro-out all the earth.' " Frederick's support of "true religion, or christian liberty, against the antichristian persecutors of the church of God," merited him a place, at least in Boston, among "such renowned warriors" of God as Gideon, Samson, and David.⁴

In sermons preached on the public days of thanksgiving which Massachusetts observed during the years of victory, 1758–1760, Mayhew not only justified the war to his congregation but also gave them dramatic reviews of the action in the various theaters. His comments on the fall of Quebec were particularly vivid. Did the "Unhappy Montcalm" not know "that those who fight for a Tyrant, will not fight like free-born Britons?" Did he think his relics, crosses, and saints would make him victorious against *"that* little host" who worshiped the true God? The fall of Quebec, "my brethren, is the Lord's doing; a great thing which he has performed for us, for our country and nation, whereof we are glad; and it may justly be wonderful in our eyes." ⁵

There were more material aspects of war. "A just and necessary war" furnishes employment for many. Manufacturing and commerce, Mayhew reminded his mercantile congregation, had never flourished so much in Great Britain and in America as during the present conflict. Nor did he neglect to point out the increased demand for British manufactures and the expansion of commerce that were certain to follow the conquest of Canada. Seldom in the annals of Christendom had righteousness and profits seemed so indissolubly wedded.⁶

The fall of Quebec presaged to Mayhew the eventual subjection of all Canada to British rule, and he could envision a new and more glorious role for America:

Yea, we may reasonably expect that this country, which has in a short time, and under many disadvantages, become so populous and flourishing, will, by the continued blessing of heaven, in another century or two become a mighty empire (I do not mean an independent one) in numbers little inferior perhaps to the greatest in Europe, and in felicity to none. . . . I cannot forbear fancying that I see a great and flourishing kingdom in these parts of America, peopled by our posterity. Methinks I see mighty cities rising on every hill, and by the side of every commodious port; mighty fleets alternately sailing out and returning, laden with the produce of this, and every other country under heaven; happy fields and villages wherever I turn my eyes, thro' a vastly extended territory; there the pastures cloathed with flocks, and here the vallies cover'd with corn, while the little hills rejoice on every side! And do I not there behold the savage nations, no longer our enemies, bowing the knee to Jesus Christ, and with joy confessing him to be "Lord, to the glory of God the Father!" Methinks I see religion professed and practised throughout this spacious kingdom, in far greater purity and perfection, than since the times of the apostles; the Lord being still as a wall of fire round about, and the glory in the midst of her! O happy country! happy kingdom! [7]

There is little evidence that this vision unearthed a vein of incipient American nationalism. Far from finding the connection with Britain burdensome, during the crisis of 1754–1760 the colonies realized as never before their complete dependence on the might and wealth of the mother country. In the beginning Mayhew understood the dire plight of the colonists; he knew that the outcome of the contest was by no means certain. When the tide turned in favor of the English, he congratulated his friends "on the happy Success of the British arms in America." He fully recognized the benefits Americans had received as a result of British protection, and he told his countrymen that they could hope for continued favors "if we persevere in our accustomed loyalty, and still conduct ourselves as dutiful subjects." In 1760 his dreams of the American future were part of a larger vision, shared by British subjects on both shores of the Atlantic, which saw a new era of peace, prosperity, and righteousness dating from the defeat of France.[8]

When George III ascended the throne toward the end of 1760, he had no more loyal or enthusiastic subject than the pastor of Boston's West Congregational Church. This loyalty rested on the confident assumption that the new monarch would reign over a British Empire much like that of the previous century, during which a colonial policy of benevolent neglect had permitted the Americans to enjoy liberty and prosperity hard to equal even in the mother country.[9] "So good a King" as George II had deserved law-abiding subjects who honored their sovereign and prayed "for the continuance of so good a government." At the same time Mayhew reminded his people that their blessings came from God, not the king, and that the proper way to express gratitude to Him for the recent victory over the French was by a renewed defense against tyranny:

. . . the privileges we enjoy under the British government, being so precious and invaluable, we are bound in reason and duty, if there should ever be occasion, to stand up in defence of them against any illegal encroachments or usurpations, whether as to things spiritual or temporal: for our legal privileges extend to both. It would be highly criminal in us tamely to suffer them to be wrested from us, if it was in our power to prevent it; or to give place, even "for an hour," to them who should have the hardness to attempt it. This would infer a contempt of God's goodness in giving, and preserving to us, these privileges, amidst so many perils and dangers as they have been in, first and last; particularly under the several inglorious, not to say infamous reigns of the Stewarts. In short, we cannot be true, hearty friends to the free English government, to the principles of the revolution, to the present Royal Family, or to the protestant religion, without detesting tyranny; and opposing in our several places, and to the utmost of our power, if ever there should be occasion given for it, all arbitrary, illegal proceedings, whether in church or state, whether of great men or little ones. This is scarce less the duty of every British subject, than submission to the legal commands of their political superiours.[10]

In 1760 Mayhew's nationalism was still British, or pan-English, even though the last two colonial wars had brought a recognition that the interests of all the American colonies might not always be identical with the objectives of the home government. In the elation of victory he spoke of "Great-

Britain and her American colonies, whose true interests are absolutely inseparable." With the French knife now withdrawn from their backs, the colonies were in a better position to insist upon their own definition of "true interests," a definition that the bold and articulate Boston preacher was helping to formulate at the very moment he was issuing a warning to stand guard against tyrants—just in case.[11]

The promise of the reign of George III seemed even brighter when viewed against the backdrop of the political and religious institutions of the recently defeated enemy. F-R-A-N-C-E spelled tyranny for Mayhew. The French people, he concluded, had been careless of their natural rights, and consequently they had been enslaved by their kings and priests. History was chiefly valuable for the lessons it held for the present, and to him the most significant historical truth was unmistakably clear:

Those nations who are now groaning under the iron scepter of tyranny, were once free. So they might, probably, have remained, by a seasonable precaution against despotic measures. Civil tyranny is usually small in its beginning, like "the drop of a bucket," till at length, like a mighty torrent, or the raging waves of the sea, it bears down all before it, and deluges whole countries and empires. Thus it is as to ecclesiastical tyranny also,—the most cruel, intolerable and impious, of any. From small beginnings, "it exalts itself above all that is called GOD and that is worshipped." [12]

It followed from this interpretation of history that the most effective opposition to tyranny was to be made at the level of "small beginnings." For Jonathan Mayhew, such opposition was a sacred duty: "it becomes every friend to truth and human kind; every lover of God and the Christian religion, to bear a part in opposing this hateful monster." The Christian is enjoined to resist equally the satanic powers who seek to damn his soul in the next world and the evil men who plot to deprive him of his liberty on earth. The pastor of the West Church had suggested this concept of liberty as early as 1750 in *Un-*

limited Submission. For the remainder of his life he retained the firm conviction that one of his most important duties as a minister of the gospel was to warn his unsuspecting countrymen of attempts to usurp their hard-won liberties. He was not alone, for his view that liberty was continually threatened by conspiracies of depraved and corrupt men was shared by most of the leaders who prepared the ground for the Revolution in Massachusetts: Samuel Adams, John Adams, James Otis, Oxenbridge Thacher, and others.[13] But from England, not Massachusetts, came the main source of inspiration for Mayhew's fight against tyranny, as he saw it, in his later years.

In the spring of 1755, Mayhew received a surprising letter from Jasper Mauduit, a member of George Benson's Dissenting congregation in London. The letter informed him that he should expect soon a box containing several copies of a book by that "great Statesman," Algernon Sidney. One copy he was requested to keep, one to give to Harvard College, and the others to forward as directed. The gift was from an anonymous English gentleman who had recently returned from an European tour with a "confirm'd Sence of English Liberty." He had been led to send the books after reading *Unlimited Submission.*[14]

Mayhew responded by sending his unknown admirer, through Mauduit, the volume of his sermons that had just come from the press. The following summer another letter from Mauduit announced that "our Mutual friend" was now sending a work by John Milton. A whole box of books sent by the same intermediary toward the end of 1757 was lost by shipwreck, and in sending a replacement, the benefactor revealed himself for the first time. By comparing handwriting Mayhew discovered that the books had been the gift of Thomas Hollis of London.[15]

Hollis was not a new name to a son of Harvard. Another Thomas Hollis, a great-uncle of Mayhew's new friend, was well known in New England as the "generous and catholic-spirited Gentleman" who had made several large donations to the college, including the endowment of the Hollis professorships of Divinity and of Mathematics and Natural Philosophy. The present Thomas Hollis had been born in 1720, a few months before Jonathan. From his great uncle, grandfather, and father he had inherited a fortune that by 1738 made him financially independent for life, whereupon he abandoned plans for a mercantile career in order to study the liberal arts. From 1740 to 1748 he resided at Lincoln's Inn, London and apparently studied law, but without any evident interest in the law as a profession.[16]

In 1748 Hollis embarked on a tour of the Continent that was to last, with one brief return to England, until 1753. His business on these trips was "to see the world, and converse at large." Throughout Western Europe he made observations and formed friendships that were to last a lifetime. Most of all, he compared English institutions with those he saw in Europe and came home obsessed with the idea that England's traditional liberties were a priceless treasure to be guarded at all costs. He returned to his homeland with an eye on a seat in Parliament, but politics in the age of the Pelhams was so repulsive to his political ideals that he soon gave up his hopes for public service. Although "I would give almost my right hand to be chosen into Parliament," he once wrote, "I could not give a single crown for it by way of BRIBE." For the remainder of his life he studiously avoided any public connection with political affairs, yet, by retreating into a carefully planned anonymity, Thomas Hollis found a role that in the long run proved nearly as rewarding as any parliamentary or other public career he might have followed. In so doing he sank into an obscurity that for two centuries has concealed his position as a figure of importance in British-American relations of the 1760's and early 1770's.[17]

The plan Hollis developed for his life was not an easy one; it demanded all his time and much of his fortune. From 1754 on he devoted himself completely to the preservation and propagation of liberty. His methods varied: he republished and distributed widely in Europe and America the writings of the great defenders of liberty; he collected and displayed medals and prints commemorating significant men and events in the growth of liberty; he encouraged and supported contemporary champions of liberty (such as Pitt and Mayhew); and he issued warnings to his countrymen when he saw their liberty in danger. "In this manner," he wrote to his Boston friend about 1762, "has T.H. passed the last eight Years of his life, the flower of his life, working *almost* incessantly Day, Week, Month, & Year, successive to each other." [18]

It was his original intention to distribute his efforts on behalf of liberty equally throughout the European world, but his close friendship with Mayhew and the mounting tension in American affairs after 1760 led him to give his main energies to the American colonies. He became, almost against his wishes, Massachusetts' most effective agent in England. In the words of Benjamin Franklin, who knew Hollis in London and found him "shy of my acquaintance," he "loved to do his good alone and secretly." Cut off from many of the social amenities of the day by his passion for anonymity, his time-consuming activities, and his frankness of expression, Hollis was often misunderstood. Dr. Samuel Johnson, who at first thought this "dull poor creature" to be quite harmless, later realized his mistake and blamed him for the entire American Revolution. Hollis had the satisfaction of believing that he was serving his generation as best he could under the circumstances, that he had not "refused sulkily these games tho' small" when "cut off by the Times from greater & more manly." [19]

Hollis regarded the seventeenth century as the most important period of English history, for it was in this eventful era that the British constitution had been restored to its pristine purity by those lovers of liberty, the original Whigs. Unfortunately, in the present age most of the Whigs had forsaken seventeenth-century principles as no longer appropriate to happy, prosperous, middle-class England. Only Hollis and a few other Real Whigs—as they often called themselves— had remained true. He had dedicated his life and fortune to the rejuvenation and dissemination of the political creed of the Puritan and Glorious Revolutions.[20]

Particularly important in his plan was the education of youth in the principles of liberty, "for Nations rise and fall by Individuals not Numbers, as I think all History proveth." He was appalled to discover that English university students did not read the works of such seventeenth-century martyrs for liberty as Algernon Sidney. To correct this condition he republished the works of Sidney, Locke, Neville, and other champions of the war against tyranny. These, along with works still in print which he purchased in quantity, he sent to universities and individuals in Europe, Asia, and America. Frequently he bound his books in rich Russian leathers of bright shades and stamped their covers with devices of some special significance—a figure of Britannia, a dagger, an owl, an olive branch were some of his favorites. On the flyleaves he penned inscriptions expressing his devotion to the principles contained within, and he was fond of annotating significant passages lest the reader miss the full impact.[21]

When asked concerning his political views, Hollis was in the habit of citing his favorite books, especially the works of "the matchless" John Milton. "It is to Milton, the divine Milton, and such as him, in the struggles of the civil wars and the Revolution, that we are beholden for all the manifold & unexampled Blessings which we now every where enjoy." In a letter to Mayhew, Hollis summarized Milton's and consequently his own political principles: "That government, at least our government, is by compact. That a King becoming a Tyrant, and the compact thereby broken, the Power reverts again to the Constituents, the People, who may punish such Tyrant as they see fit, and constitute such a new form of government as shall then appear to them to be most expedient." In this scheme of government Hollis had assigned himself the task of eternal vigilance against the possibility that the compact might be broken by tyranny without the people realizing that power was once again in their hands.[22]

One must accept Hollis at his own word when he told Mauduit that it was *Unlimited Submission* that had first turned his eyes toward Massachusetts. He later wrote Mayhew, "It was the excellence of your character, & the noble spirit of Liberty & of Truth which appeared in Your Writings" that motivated the initial shipment of books. A possible connection between them was Richard Baron, who republished *Unlimited Submission* in England and also worked on several editorial projects for Hollis. Mayhew had a natural religious affinity with Hollis, who came from a Dissenting Baptist family and shared the liberal views of Foster, Harris, and Benson. But Hollis, who never attended church or held membership in a religious body and whose religion was little more than piously phrased patriotism, seemed incapable of understanding the intensity of the Boston minister's religious convictions.[23]

The stream of books which had begun in 1755 with Sidney's *Discourses* continued unabated throughout Mayhew's lifetime. As only an occasional title is mentioned in their correspondence, it is impossible to estimate the number of Hollis books that were stacked in Mayhew's study from 1755 to 1766. Two or three times a year from 1759 on, he received boxes containing books, tracts, prints, newspapers, medals, and various odd or interesting items described by the donor

as "trifles." Seldom did a box arrive that did not contain dupli-
cate books or other gifts which the minister was requested to
distribute. In some cases the distribution was left to his dis-
cretion; in others specific recipients were mentioned: Andrew
Oliver, Thomas Hutchinson, Governor Bernard, General Amherst, James Otis, and others. Almost without exception each
box contained something for what Hollis once called "the
dissenting Academy of Harvard in New England." [24]

Harvard College was the special object of Hollis' benefactions. It is estimated that altogether he gave more than 1300
volumes to the college library, which in the past had contained
few, if any, books on government. No more than a tiny frac-
tion of these could have passed directly through Mayhew's
hands, but he was responsible for Hollis' maintaining a lively
interest in the college. When once President Holyoke acknowledged the receipt of Milton's prose works by writing, "we
have a very high Regard for that great Man, Whom (his
Political Principles not at all withstanding) We esteem a great
Honour to the British Name," Hollis complained in exaspera-
tion that without Milton and those like him Holyoke would
not have the liberties presently enjoyed by him and the college. The pastor diplomatically replied that Holyoke was "a
well-disposed, worthy gentleman" whose "political notions,
and sentiments concerning Milton . . . are not materially
different from your own." [25]

Hollis expected Mayhew, a member of the Board of Overseers, to prevent Harvard's annoying him with public expressions of gratitude or requests for additional benefactions. In
January 1764, the outbreak of smallpox in Boston forced the
Massachusetts General Court to transfer its meeting to the
library of Harvard Hall in Cambridge. On a cold night during
the session, a disastrous fire consumed the building and the
five thousand volumes in the library, including all the books
sent by Hollis except for a few cases as yet unpacked. When
the Board of Overseers requested Hollis to meet with certain

THOMAS HOLLIS

TWO TREATISES OF GOVERNMENT

BY IOHN LOCKE

SALUS POPULI SUPREMA LEX ESTO

LONDON PRINTED MDCLXXXVIIII
REPRINTED, THE SIXTH TIME, BY A. MILLAR, H.
WOODFALL, I. WHISTON AND B. WHITE, I. RI-
VINGTON, L. DAVIS AND C. REYMERS, R. BALD-
WIN, HAWES CLARKE AND COLLINS; W. IOHN-
STON, W. OWEN, I. RICHARDSON, S. CROWDER,
T. LONGMAN, B. LAW, C. RIVINGTON, E.
DILLY, R. WITHY, C. AND R. WARE, S. BAKER,
T. PAYNE, A. SHUCKBURGH, I. HINXMAN
MDCCLXIIII

Hollis edition of Locke, presented to Harvard College in
1764

IONATHAN MAYHEW, D·D·PASTOR OF THE WEST CHVRCH
IN BOSTON, IN NEW ENGLAND, AN ASSERTOR OF THE CIVIL
AND RELIGIOVS LIBERTIES OF HIS COVNTRY AND MANKIND,
WHO, OVERPLIED BY PVBLIC ENERGIES, DIED OF A NERVOVS FEVER,
IVLY VIIII, MDCCLXVI, AGED XXXXV

Etching commemorating Mayhew's death

The West Church in 1775

other gentlemen in London to confer on means of making up the loss sustained in the fire, he most emphatically refused. Mayhew quickly apologized for this unwelcome intrusion, accounting for it by his absence from the meeting where the Overseers had considered the matter. Although Hollis was disgruntled that a college library should be degraded into a council room, he spared no private efforts in replacing and enlarging the lost collection.[26]

To Mayhew and to Harvard, Hollis sent "canonical" works—those books he deemed essential to a proper understanding of his political principles. Some of these were editions of his own, including Toland's *Life of John Milton*, Sidney's *Discourses*, Locke's *Two Treatises of Government* and *Letters Concerning Toleration*, and Nedham's *The Excellencie of a Free State*. Among the other "canonical" books were Goodman's *How Superior Powers Ought to be Obeyd of Their Subjects*, Harrington's *Common-Wealth of Oceana*, and Trenchard's *Short History of Standing Armies in England*.[27] "Books of Government I have delighted most to send," Hollis wrote to Holyoke, "for if Government goes right all goes right." After ten years of stocking the Harvard library, he confided to his Boston correspondent, "More Books, especially on *Government*, are going for N.E. Should those go safe, it is hoped no principal Books on that *first* Subject, will be wanting in Harvard College, from the Days of Moses to these times. Men of New England, Bretheren, Use them for Yourselves & for others, & God bless You!"[28]

Hollis sometimes sent along the opposites to his "canonical" books so that New Englanders might discover the truth of the position maintained by the Whig writers, although he frequently inverted the marking device on the cover to indicate his disapproval of the contents. Nor was he "without digression to other Subjects either useful or ingenious," for he also gave Harvard works on science, language, aesthetics, travel, religion, economics, and education, in keeping with his belief "that liberty admits, seeks, professes every refinement of civil life; nor indeed can those refinements exist, for any time, without her." The religious volumes that were placed in the special Hollis alcove in the new Harvard library were by no means all orthodox. Here the undergraduate could find books by the skeptic Bayle, the Deists Anthony Collins and Lord Herbert of Cherbury, and the master of all critics of organized religion, Voltaire. Such titles were also included in the packages addressed to West Boston, but there is no reason to think that Mayhew moved toward further heresy as a result of Hollis' refusal to confine his selections to the tomes of orthodoxy. The chief effects of this stream of literature into the pastor's study were a confirmation of Real Whig political tenets already adopted and a renewal in mature years of a youthful passion to hunt out and destroy tyranny in both church and state.[29]

It required several years for Mayhew to understand the exact nature of his relation with Hollis. When in the beginning he attempted to lead the philanthropist into active public roles in behalf of New England causes, Hollis replied frankly that their correspondence would have to continue "as it began, in a literate manner *only*, without intermixture of business of any kind public or private; much less charges, or leads of business." He later added, "Little can I serve Your Cause, the Cause of Liberty in New England; but what I can I will serve it, tho' by ways, at times, unknown to any one."[30] Notwithstanding such gentle reproofs, so great was the affection he felt for the author of *Unlimited Submission* that Hollis granted him favors he seldom gave to others, not the least of which was a warm welcome to the Massachusetts gentlemen who called on him in London to present letters of recommendation from Dr. Mayhew and often to solicit aid in business enterprises.[31]

Hollis was not always satisfied with the minister's responses to his suggestions. A member of the Royal Society, the Society for Promoting Arts and Commerce, and other similar societies, Hollis devoted much time to such organizations, which he considered essential to the progress of civilization. Once he attempted to transform the British diplomatic service into a world-wide learned society. In 1760 he informed Mayhew that it was high time some societies were formed in the American colonies on the model of those in England. When his Massachusetts correspondent suggested in reply that New England in its present state of development could not support such an effort, Hollis furiously rebuked Mayhew and his friends for their diffidence and laziness. On another occasion he scolded him for being careless with postage, reminding him of the good that might have been accomplished with the wasted money.[32]

The knowledge that Mayhew had acquired a wealthy and influential connection in London soon spread throughout Boston. It is possible that he was not reticent in telling of his benefactor, just as he boasted to Hollis of the wealth of his mercantile acquaintances. As Hollis' fame grew in Massachusetts, he was plagued with unwelcome attempts to initiate correspondence. The result was invariably a polite but firm rebuff, even to Samuel Mather, for Hollis chose his friends with extreme care, usually preferring to work through only one individual in each country. From them he gleaned the news of science, government, and the arts that made him one of the best informed men in England.[33]

Hollis was willing to go to almost any length to secure the republication of Mayhew's works in the mother country. In 1760 he persuaded his favorite printer to bring out a London edition of *Two Discourses Delivered October 25th. 1759,* which Hollis described as "a very able summary of our successes in N. America, & a fair representation of the importance of Canada to our Colonies."[34] In the ensuing years he was responsible for London editions of four more works by the West Church minister.

Friendship with Hollis greatly extended the horizons of one who, as far as the record shows, never traveled more than a hundred miles in any direction from Boston. Through his London friend he began correspondences with Francis Blackburne, soon to be the author of a famous non-Trinitarian *Confessional*, and with William Harris, a liberal Dissenting minister of whom Hollis was extremely fond. The same agent introduced Mayhew to Mrs. Catherine Macaulay, to whose Whig *History of England* Hollis had made significant contributions. The pastor sent books to Benjamin Franklin by way of Hollis, and through the same source a correspondence developed with Caleb Fleming, the noted Arian minister of Hoxton Square. An early death deprived the Boston divine of the full benefit of this widened circle of contacts, but he did live long enough to become one of the best-known Americans in England by his death in 1766, thanks in a large measure to the work of this "strenuous Whig," as James Boswell had dubbed Hollis.[35]

CHAPTER X

Governor Bernard

It is said, there are some of these dirty, abandon'd fellows, who run about from place to place, and into every corner, to pimp, to hear, & to smell out, whatever they can; impudently assuming to themselves the *important air of friends to the Governor.*

Jonathan Mayhew, 1762[1]

MAYHEW'S VISION of the future greatness of America did not seem so unduly optimistic to his townsmen when the news of the fall of Montreal and the resulting surrender of Canada reached Boston on September 23, 1760. With a continent to be exploited without interference from the French and their Indian allies and with increased profits to be made on seas virtually cleared of French ships, as it celebrated victory in America New England soon forgot the war still raging in Europe. September 26 was appointed as a day of rejoicing. Boston harbor resounded with salutes from the harbor batteries and the ships at anchor there. A military parade was followed by a dinner at Faneuil Hall for 150 of the town's first citizens. In the evening all of Boston was illuminated— five-story bonfires on the hilltops could be seen for miles. Between blasts of fireworks one could hear incessant rounds of toasts to "His Majesty's Health and many other loyal Healths." As the *News-Letter* summed up the events of the day, "there were all possible Expressions of that universal Joy which this happy and glorious Event has diffused through this loyal and grateful People." [2]

Far from inaugurating a new era of peace and prosperity, this joyful day marked the beginning of fifteen years of misunderstanding, blundering, and increasing tension that were to culminate in the final break with Great Britain. There were already discordant notes. The previous August, the capable but petulant and ambitious Francis Bernard had arrived in Boston to replace Governor Thomas Pownall, whose vigorous executive leadership and exceptional political skills had produced a favorable image of the royal government in the minds of the citizens of Massachusetts during the last three years. Pownall's popularity, nevertheless, had been on the wane when news of his transfer arrived. "We have not made a bad exchange," wrote Lieutenant Governor Thomas Hutchinson, who disliked the former governor; "People that know Mr. Bernard say he is not a Man of Intrigue, that he loves to be quiet himself & is willing other People should be so too." [3]

It was to prove unfortunate for the peace of the Empire that the new governor did not understand that the moments of popularity and success enjoyed by the last two governors, Shirley and Pownall, had been the result of personal desire to win friends among all elements of the province and to serve and, where possible, identify the interests of both the colonial and imperial governments.[4] The future would require still greater tact and diplomacy, for Bernard had brought with him royal instructions mandating enforcement of the acts of trade, some of which had been openly violated for as long as anyone could remember, often with the collusion of the British customs officers. During the wars with France, New England skippers had enjoyed a profitable market for supplies in the French colonies in the New World, temporarily cut off from their normal sources of supply by the British Navy's control of the seas. A few weeks after Bernard arrived, William Pitt issued orders to the American governors that this "illegal & most pernicious Trade" with the enemy must be stopped without delay. When the new governor reminded the General Court of the blessings they had received as a result of their *"subjection* to Great Britain," the Council substituted the word *"relation"* for *"subjection,"* and the Assembly replied that Englishmen should not forget the blessings they derived from the loyalty of the colonies.[5]

On September 10, Chief Justice Stephen Sewall died in Boston. A jolly bachelor of fifty-eight, Sewall had been one of the most popular and important men in Massachusetts. Just before his death, a group of Boston merchants had attempted to enlist the Chief Justice in their campaign against the peacetime use of writs of assistance—court orders implementing the authority of customs officers to search for illegal goods. The merchants charged that the use of the writs by royal officers was a violation of fundamental property rights. Sewall apparently sympathized with the cause of the merchants and was reported to have expressed some doubt as to the legality of the writs. It is possible that his influence on the side of the merchants might have made a significant difference in the outcome of this case, but death relieved him of the necessity of making his position clear.[6]

As early as 1752, Jonathan Mayhew could write of "My good & Honoured Friend, Judge Sewall." The Chief Justice had regularly attended the West Church, and he was regarded by some as the pastor's patron. It was later suggested that the older man had exerted a moderating influence on the young firebrand, who himself admitted that their relation had been that of father and son.[7] On the Sunday afternoon following Sewall's death, Mayhew delivered a memorial discourse which was rushed to the press—a sixty-page recital of virtues and noble deeds that characterized the late Chief Justice as "a true patriot; a lover of his country, its laws and liberties; and an enemy to all tyranny and tyrants." With the new governor in mind, the preacher reminded his congregation that Sewall, also a member of the Governor's Council, had faithfully carried out his oath "to the best of his judgment at all times, freely to give his advice to the governor, for the good management of the public affairs of this government." [8]

Governor Bernard appointed Thomas Hutchinson to fill the vacancy created by Sewall's death, although James Otis of Barnstable, the Speaker of the House of Representatives, had expected to receive the appointment. In February 1761, the legality of the writs of assistance was argued before the new Chief Justice and his colleagues. James Otis, Jr., son of the disappointed officeseeker, resigned his position in the royal government to represent the merchants opposed to the issuance of the writs. After hearing the arguments, among them the fiery diatribes of the younger Otis, Hutchinson delayed his decision for several months while he awaited word from England as to whether the writs were still issued there. Being advised that they were, he ruled that they must also be legal in America. The efforts of Otis to demonstrate that the writs violated the natural rights of Englishmen had failed to win the legal argument, but he had easily convinced those who wanted to believe that here was clearly one of the "instruments of slavery" used by the Stuart monarchs of the past century.[9]

This case marked the origins of two gradually distinguishable parties in Massachusetts politics. One, headed by Thomas Hutchinson, tended increasingly to support the royal government of the colony. The other, led at first by James Otis, Jr., who had been elected to the House of Representatives on the strength of the reputation he had won in the writs case, became an opposition party seeking to unite the discontented elements of the province.[10] Party lines were not fixed, and few if any of Otis' friends shared his neurotic hatred of Bernard and Hutchinson. Mayhew and Otis had known each other since the time when both were undergraduates together at Harvard, but there is little direct evidence to indicate that any great intimacy had developed between the two. The minister remained on good terms with both Hutchinson and Otis, but the course of events from 1760 until his death led him, unavoidably he thought, into opposition to Governor Bernard and the royal party. He personally was drawn into a series of controversies that left him convinced that the Governor and his coterie were enemies to the cause of New England political and ecclesiastical liberty.

On November 17, 1761, two Indians from Martha's Vineyard, James Tallman and Judah Ossoort, walked up Boston's Marlborough Street and turned into the courtyard of the Province House, which stood nearly opposite the Old South Church. They were bringing a petition from the Vineyard Indians to the Governor.[11] At the door of the Province House they left the papers with a servant whose elegant livery so awed the Indians that they departed with the impression that they had talked with Bernard. After being told to return the following day to learn what action might be expected on the petition, they went to spend the night at the Mayhew home, where Tallman's son was an indentured servant. While there, Tallman told his host that he had wrapped two dollars in the petition and that the Governor had pocketed the money as soon as he opened the papers. The next day the Indians saw Bernard personally and realized that it was the Governor's servant who had taken the money; unfortunately, they left town without informing Mayhew of the mistaken identity. The story was too good to keep, and in time he let it slip to some friends, from whom it made its way back to the Province House. Bernard was furious, and summoned the minister to appear before him.

The only record of this seemingly trivial incident is Mayhew's lengthy manuscript entitled "A circumstantial Narrative."[12] This document is largely unsubstantiated, but its significance does not lie in the reliability of its facts. Frank, detailed, and off-the-record, the "circumstantial Narrative" provides dramatic evidence of the way in which enmity toward Governor Bernard and royal government in Massachusetts developed rapidly in the first years of his administration. Here also is found as nowhere else the Mayhew temperament so familiar to friends and enemies but missing from the more formal papers he and they left behind.

Mayhew began his "Narrative" by explaining that he was writing to acquaint his friends with the facts in the case, particularly in view of the rumor that the Governor was about to prosecute him for slander.[13] The Indians, he recalled, had repeatedly told him the story in response to careful questioning. Even then he had said nothing concerning the incident until early in December, when he had confided in two of his most intimate friends.

He did not realize that the news had spread beyond these two friends until on December 11, William Story, deputy register of the vice-admiralty court, called at his home to say that he had heard the bribe story and had made a large wager that it had not originated with the West Church pastor. When Story heard Tallman's version of the incident, he expressed concern for the honor of the Governor. He assured Mayhew, however, that he had called purely out of his own curiosity and not at Bernard's request. Not likely by coincidence, early the next day, Secretary Andrew Oliver came to inform Mayhew that the Governor would expect him to call at the Province House that same morning. Complying with the summons, the pastor found Bernard "not a little discomposed in mind." The Governor refused to discuss the source of his "uneasiness" until Oliver and Lieutenant Governor Thomas Hutchinson could be present to serve as witnesses, a step which in Mayhew's eyes changed a private interview into an illegal court hearing.

Bernard repeated the story, as he had heard it, to Hutchinson and Oliver and expressed his bewilderment that anyone could believe such a tale on the word of an Indian, especially when it concerned an official with a spotless record. The spread of such a story, he added, "convinced him more fully of the diabolical spirit of slander & defamation in the town . . . of which he had had great experience since coming to this government." It was likely that the preacher "had reported this story in some 'club' of scandal . . . when every one had some slander or tale to tell." Mayhew replied that he had said nothing slanderous or defamatory of the Governor—and that he "had no concern with *any* club whatsoever; especially, not with any such scandalous one as his Excellency had spoken of." Bernard now became vehement: "His Excellency then said . . . That the story was a *lye;* that I had *reported* it; that the spreader of a *lye* was equally obnoxious in law, with the *author* of it; and that he expected *satisfaction* of me. His Excellency added that it was indeed very probable, that those who could think *him* capable of taking the dollars, might not *believe him* in the denial of it; or, that they would not be willing to take *his bare word for it.* (Which I could not but think a very judicious observation of his Excellency.)"

Mayhew admitted that he now doubted the Indian's story. He excused his not coming to the Governor with the accusation before relating it elsewhere by his lack of an acquaintance with that gentleman and by his scorn of those who "run about tale-bearing." At this point Bernard "enlarged on his own easiness of access; his courtesy & affability, even to the *meannest persons*" (a statement Mayhew "did by no means *think proper to deny*"), and he admitted that since coming to Massachusetts he had treated no one "so harshly & angrily" as he had on this occasion. Was it not reasonable to expect that, if the minister did not feel free to come to him personally with what he had heard concerning the bribe, he would at least have kept the story to himself? Mayhew replied "That the

English government allow'd of great freedom of speech and writing. That much greater liberties, as his Excellency well knew, were taken in Britain with *greater men* than any in America. . . . That this freedom of speech and writing, tho' doubtless often abused, was sound, and acknowledged to be, of the utmost importance to the public welfare, & safety; and that our free constitution of government could not be secured without it, &c." "His Excellency's patience seem'd to be much lessen'd at this," and he charged that the minister was guilty before the law for having propagated a falsehood. Such liberties of speech had never been permitted, "even in the Oliverian times." The Governor declared that he knew the laws well, and that had anyone in London spoken of a minister of state in such a fashion, "he would have been *sent for,* or *taken up.*" Bernard believed the story had been spread "out of some personal dislike, or resentment," but he could think of no offence he had given, unless it was some remarks he had made on the pastor's writings.

In response to the Governor's insistence on having satisfaction, Mayhew offered to run a notice of the affair in the newspapers and include "That I *now* believed, the Indian had told me a *lye,*" although he also determined inwardly to clear the Indian's name should it turn out to be only a case of mistaken identity. As this proposal was unsatisfactory to Bernard, who refused to state at this time exactly the nature of the satisfaction he sought, the interview ended, after nearly one and one-half hours, with both parties resolved to seek legal counsel. Mayhew complained in the "Narrative" that he had been under a handicap during the confrontation, partially because of his "natural self-diffidence" in the presence of a royal governor, but even more because Bernard had showered him with crude and abusive language.

After taking legal advice, Mayhew was more determined than before to maintain the stand he had taken. One of the lawyers he consulted blamed him "for submitting to such an extrajudicial & unfair examination: which was as remote from the nature of an arbitration, or mutual reference, as it was from a legal trial." On Wednesday, December 16, Hutchinson called on the minister to express his wish "that the affair might be compromised." The Lieutenant Governor intimated that Bernard was now ready to drop the entire matter if Mayhew would acknowledge his wrong or ask the Governor's pardon. But the minister replied that he "was fully determined to ask no pardon, nor make any sort of acknowledgment," although he "was willing to do any thing I could in honor, and justice to myself, to give ease to his Excellency's mind." Hutchinson reported this conversation to his superior, who "remained quite dissatisfied" and threatened to lay the case before the Council, until some "wise friends" dissuaded him. A member of the Council then informed Mayhew that the Governor was willing to have five members of the Council consider the case "in a private way." The minister wrote a letter to Bernard to explain his reasons for declining this offer. He pointed out again that the two persons to whom he had confided the story were his "particular, intimate friends," one a member of the Council and the other a deacon in the West Church. He did not associate with scandalmongers: "And your Excellency may be pleased farther to know, that those persons, whom I make my particular friends and companions, are of such an irreproachable character, that it would be no disgrace even to your Excellency to be sometimes, or indeed often, seen, in such *honest* company." [14]

When there was still no answer from Bernard by Christmas, Mayhew went to Hutchinson and Oliver individually and offered to let them read a copy of his letter to the Governor so that each might judge the accuracy of its contents. One of these gentlemen refused, but the other had no objections. After reading it, he admitted that the letter contained no misrepresentation of what had taken place at the hearing, although he was not fully in accord with the opinions expressed. After another week without a reply, Mayhew prepared a second letter in which he intimated that he "thought himself not well-used" by the Governor's neglect of the first letter, but he decided not to send it when he remembered that Bernard was probably absorbed in the celebration of Christmas, a holiday which New England Congregationalists still regarded as pagan. Another fortnight of waiting exhausted Mayhew's patience. If Bernard was satisfied, he should have let him know in some manner and possibly have softened some of the unkind remarks he had made about the minister and townspeople.

By now, according to the "Narrative," the affair had become common gossip throughout Boston and was being discussed in such places as barber shops. It had been "spread abroad chiefly thro' the indiscretion of some of the Governor's over-zealous & officious friends." The story, often "grosly misrepresented," had reached the ears of the "good people" of the West Church, and Mayhew was afraid that common people would conclude that any reprimand of a man of the cloth by the Governor must be for good reasons, hence placing him "in danger of losing his influence." And there were suggestions that he had made privately an "acknowledgment & submission" to the Governor—a rumor at which he was "justly displeased," both because it was false and because it would have amounted to a confession of a crime of which he was innocent. He had contemplated giving the public an account of the whole affair; but, thinking better of it, he limited himself to providing a correct version to interested persons.

The remainder of the "circumstantial Narrative" analyzed Bernard's motives in handling the divine so roughly and contrasted their political philosophies. Since the Governor's anger and the grounds he gave for it were disproportionate, Mayhew concluded that the incident had been only an excuse to let loose "a huge mass of water, which had been long collecting from different springs & sources." The real causes were the minister's religious and political views. Opposition to some of the Thirty-Nine Articles, to the Anglican liturgy, and to the establishment of a bishop in America had not been pleasing to "a true son" of the Church of England. Furthermore, Bernard was a member of the Anglican Society for the Propagation of the Gospel in Foreign Parts, an organization that Mayhew had repeatedly charged with misapplying its funds.

The "Narrative" suggested three of Mayhew's political views to which the Governor might have taken exception: his remarks on Charles I and the other Stuarts in *Unlimited Submission;* his frequent praise of civil liberty; and his commendation of the late Chief Justice for having "ever given advice *freely* to the Governor." Once in a certain gathering Bernard had spoken of Oliver Cromwell as a *"coward* or at least a man whose courage was problematical." Mayhew had answered that he "had never met with any historians of credit and impartiality who had spoken of Cromwell as such a man." Bernard's reaction was surprise at such "*ignorance* of history," and he had seemed "a little displeased." The Governor's loyalty to the infamous Stuarts had been manifested in his order to hang large portraits of Charles II and James II in the Council Chamber, a situation that should be remedied: "Either . . . some proper means ought to be used to make James II *abdicate* the council chamber; of which the best I can think of, is to *introduce* William III. Or else, if the said James must continue there, . . . a *painter* should be speedily employed *to clap a good halter about his neck.*" Mayhew suspected that Bernard drew his political ideas from such writers as Hobbes, Filmer, and Sacheverell, and so considered him "a man of *bad* principles, relative to civil government." He was certain that the Governor had a "particular aversion" to him, "on

account of my notions of civil liberty; which he might possibly
think incompatible with his own, respecting power and prerogative; not to say, *with some of his practices upon them.*"

After receiving a letter from his brother, who had inter-
viewed Tallman on his return to the Vineyard and exacted
from him the story of the mistaken identity, Mayhew admitted
privately that there had been no bribe involved in the case.[15]
Bernard took no further action. Apparently he understood the
difficulty of clearing himself, whatever the facts, with those
Bostonians who wanted to believe the worst of him. It was a
topic that no one could discuss publicly with immunity. The
Boston Gazette came as close as it dared to a reference to the
case on February 8, 1762, when it published some "Miscellaneous Thoughts extracted from some of the most celebrated
Writers, ancient and modern." Without mentioning a name,
this piece made its point clear: "The Author whose Writings
tend to abridge the Authority of an imperious Dictator . . .
will unavoidably be the Object of furious Malediction, as well
as of Praise and Commendation." Furthermore, "That the
People have no Right to inspect into, or animadvert upon,
the Actions of their Superiors, is a Doctrine fit only for a Tyrant to enjoin, and Slaves to obey."

Exactly one month after "Thoughts" were published in the
Gazette, Bernard and Mayhew came face to face at the meeting of the Harvard Overseers.[16] Regrettably, the records of
the Overseers contain only the official business transacted on
that occasion. Even if one accepts the "Narrative" as a full
and accurate record of the incident, it is difficult to exonerate
the minister for his refusal to seek Bernard's pardon after
learning of the mistaken identity. Mayhew's zeal for liberty
and his concern for the constitutional principles and rights of
the subject potentially involved in this affair blinded him to
what ordinarily he would have considered a Christian duty.
More significant, Bernard's conduct in this case, which came

at the very beginning of his administration, convinced Mayhew that the royal government of Massachusetts was in the
hands of a would-be tyrant. While the present governor remained in office, the guardians of liberty must exercise unusual diligence.

An occasion for such diligence arose while Mayhew's close
friends were still reading the "circumstantial Narrative."
This time it was a public encounter and the minister did not
stand alone. The New Lights of the Great Awakening had
been severely critical of "ungodly" Harvard, and their criticisms had seemed confirmed more recently by the prominence
of Mayhew and other heretical alumni. It was believed in
some quarters that to send a boy to Cambridge for four years
was to expose him to evil doctrines that would threaten his
soul's welfare. The people of the Connecticut Valley in western Massachusetts had additional complaints against President Holyoke's institution. Tuition fees were high and Cambridge was a considerable journey from the valley towns,
"by reason of which many good natural genius's are prevented
a Liberal Education." Even those families who could afford
to send their sons to Harvard protested that social discrimina-
tion was practiced against students from the western part
of the province. The most powerful man in Hampshire
County, which after 1761 comprised the section of Massachusetts along the Connecticut River, was Israel Williams of
Hatfield, dubbed the "King of Hampshire County." Williams
had felt chagrin when his son was placed lower in the Class
of 1751 "than befitted the son of a King." [17]

Early in 1762 a group of Hampshire men, led by Israel
Williams, petitioned Governor Bernard for a charter establishing Queen's College in one of the Hampshire towns. Harvard interests countered by proposing that as an alternative
the government build an additional dormitory at Cambridge.

Bernard thought that he alone, as the King's representative, had the authority to issue charters; but to avoid raising an issue he permitted the question to be referred to the General Court. The House of Representatives, where western influence was strong, voted to grant the charter, which was then rejected by the Council, whose members were also ex officio members of the Harvard Board of Overseers. Israel Williams was not to be put aside so easily. He persuaded the Governor to issue the charter on his own authority, although the document was made as unobjectionable as possible to the friends of Harvard. Bernard's action joined the issue of whether Massachusetts needed another college with the constitutional question of the governor's right to issue charters without legislative approval. A delegation from the Board of Overseers requested the Governor to take no action until they could meet, and he agreed to recall the charter temporarily. After James Otis, Jr., had declared that Bernard's action in issuing the charter was a violation of the constitution, the House reversed its position and also requested the Governor to withhold the document.[18]

The Overseers met on March 8 to strike the charter a death blow. Thomas Hutchinson sought to delay any action for fear of further alienation of the Hampshire interests, but after five hours of debate the Overseers voted to request the Governor to withdraw permanently the charter as "greatly prejudicial to Harvard College," and a committee was appointed to draw up arguments against the charter.[19] Mayhew was given the job of drafting the committee's "Remonstrance against the Establishment of a College in Hampshire County." This document ignored the question of the governor's right to grant a charter, for Bernard had told the Overseers that, whatever their opinions on this point, it was no concern of theirs as a governing body of Harvard College. Rather, Mayhew confined his arguments to the traditional relation between the provincial government and Harvard and the certain weakening of that cherished institution should the Hampshire college be established. He stressed the point that one strong college was better than two weak schools. His answer to the complaint that few boys in western Massachusetts could afford to travel to Cambridge and were thus deprived of an education provides a striking example of his social outlook:

For although more of our youth might by this means receive what is usually called a liberal education, and which might pass for a very good one with many, yet we apprehend this would be rather a disadvantage than the contrary, as it would prevent a sufficient, though smaller number of our youth, being sent to Cambridge, where they would unquestionably be much more thoroughly instructed and far better qualified for doing service to their country. And the natural consequence hereof would be, not only the filling too many important civil offices, but a great part of our pulpits, with comparatively unlettered persons, at once to the detriment both of the Commonwealth, and of the churches here established.[20]

The Overseers adopted the "Remonstrance" and appointed a committee to wait on the Governor with it. Mayhew was not a member of this committee, presumably because of his poor standing with Bernard. On this occasion Bernard proved conciliatory. He promised to withdraw the charter and to refrain from aiding any attempt to secure another directly from the King, as the Hampshire people were now threatening to do. To guard further against this possibility, Mayhew drafted a letter which the Overseers sent to several influential people in England. Hollis, as usual, refused to cooperate in such "public business," although he did agree with the "Remonstrance" and recommended Jasper Mauduit as the best person in the mother country to head off any attempt to go to the King. The General Court stood firm with the Overseers, and the solidarity of the Massachusetts government doomed any efforts to have the charter issued in England.[21]

Harvard was safe, but Bernard's original popularity had

been dissipated. He had lost the opportunity to secure the gratitude of Williams and other Hampshire leaders. By insisting on his right to issue a charter, he had raised a constitutional storm that put Mayhew, Otis, and others more on their guard than ever. As Charles Chauncy explained, "The more we think of it, the more we are convinced, it will be ruinous to the Province, in a religious as well as civil respect, should the Governor be allowed to grant charters by his own single power." [22]

To those more concerned with heresy than with constitutional issues, the failure of the Hampshire college effort was further evidence of how deeply the forces of liberalism were entrenched in the province. There was one example of renewed bitterness toward the West Church pastor. The Ancient and Honorable Artillery Company had long since ceased to be the defenders of the realm, but its members still retained the traditional military pomp of the early years of the colony. On the first Monday of June each year the company elected its officers in an elaborate ceremony, including an election sermon in which, as a critic remarked, the members were "addressed from the pulpit as the peculiar guardians of the people, and only bulwark of the country." When, in April 1762, the company voted on a minister for the coming election, it was discovered that Mayhew had received a majority. A few of the members who had not troubled to vote heard the results with amazement and hastened to voice some "indecent reflections" upon the choice. After a display of "party spirit" a new election was held and another minister selected. The newspaper controversy that followed proved once again that the name Mayhew was a fighting word in Boston. [23]

Jonathan Mayhew had been drawn into opposition to the royal government of Massachusetts because he believed it threatened the political and ecclesiastical liberty of the province. This was not yet a controversy between the mother country and her American colonies. To his dying day he thought of himself as a true Englishman, loyal—certainly more loyal than Governor Bernard—to the beloved though nebulous English constitution. As the *Boston Gazette* commented in a veiled reference to Mayhew, "A Man may in general account himself happy in Proportion as he has given those Reason to hate him, who hate their Country." [24]

What was needed was not a revolution but a general reform in the home government that would replace the present timeservers with men devoted to the principles of the Puritan and Glorious Revolutions. Return a few men such as William Pitt to office, and "a truly British spirit" would again prevail. "If England cannot at this day be justly called the *Land of Patriots,* it is not destitute of some glorious ones." In these times he drew closer to his friend Thomas Hollis, who was, in Mayhew's opinion, the foremost of English patriots. [25]

CHAPTER XI

Deep in the Plot

. . . the common people in New England, by means of our
schools, and the instructions of our "able, learned, orthodox ministers," are, and have all along been, philosophers
and divines in comparison of the common people in England, of the communion of the church there established.

Jonathan Mayhew, 1763[1]

A PHILADELPHIA hospital confined in 1760 a demented
Congregational clergyman who had become obsessed with the
conviction that he must earn his way to heaven by murdering
a minister of the Church of England.[2] In the eyes of many
Anglicans on both sides of the Atlantic, the only difference
between this unfortunate inmate and the pastor of Boston's
West Church was that the latter was still at large and thus
more dangerous—both were madmen. After occasional as-
saults upon the Church of England during his first fifteen years
in the ministry, Jonathan Mayhew began an all-out attack in
1763. The more the Anglicans in the northern colonies
screamed in protest at the "foul libels" hurled in their direction by this "very dirty Fellow," the more his Congregational
brethren forgot that he was a dangerous heretic and rallied
to his support. It was a pleasant reversal of roles, and he made
the most of his new-found popularity.

Puritan tradition in America had carefully preserved and
developed the saga of the flight of the Puritan fathers from
the England of tyrannical King Charles I and his persecuting
archbishop, Williad Laud. The clergy had never tired of ex-
horting new generations to "Let all mankind know that we
came into the *Wilderness,* because we would worship God

without that *Episcopacy,* that *Common Prayer,* and those unwarrantable *Ceremonies,* with which the *Land* of our *Fore Fathers' Sepulchres* has been defiled; we came hither because we would have our Posterity settled under the pure and full *Dispensations* of the Gospel; defended by *Rulers, that should be of our selves."*[3] For half a century after its founding, Massachusetts did not see a surpliced minister, but as the colony came more directly under royal control in the 1680's, one of the first acts of the royal authorities had been the establishment of King's Chapel in Boston. By 1734 Boston Anglicans were worshiping in three churches of their own. Friction was only sporadic until the 1720's when a notable series of conversions to the Church of England at Yale College shocked New England into a new awareness of its origins. One of the apostates, Timothy Cutler, was soon settled as rector of Christ's Church in Boston. The native Anglican clergy were much more vociferous and impolitic in advancing their cause than their English-born predecessors had been. They did not hesitate to appeal to the ecclesiastical and political authorities in England for aid in maintaining their foothold in New England.[4]

The main source of such aid from the mother country was the Society for the Propagation of the Gospel in Foreign Parts. Established by royal charter in 1701, the society maintained missionaries in most of the English colonies on the North American continent. The charter was vague as to the objectives of the S.P.G., as it was usually called. In practice the main goal had been the establishment of the Church of England in the colonies, and work among the Indians and Negro slaves had been regarded as a secondary objective to be pursued only after the primary objective had been at least partially achieved. The S.P.G. traditionally elected the Archbishop of Canterbury to its presidency, leaving no doubt in the minds of Dissenters that it was an Anglican institution, although the charter contained no denominational limitations. It was difficult for the S.P.G. to hide the fact that it spent a large proportion of the funds it raised by subscriptions and voluntary contributions on the maintenance of Anglican clergymen in New England.[5]

New England Congregationalists did not relish being regarded as fit subjects for missionary endeavors and resented the accounts S.P.G. missionaries sent home of their exploits in the Wilderness Zion. The missionaries were accused of exaggerating the results they achieved in the hope of obtaining more generous support. It was pointed out that they seldom boasted of the conversions of Indians or Roman Catholics, but rather emphasized the number of Dissenters won back to the Mother Church. The main design of the S.P.G., wrote an anonymous newspaper correspondent in a sentence that summarized the attitude of the Congregationalists, was "to proselyte *Protestant Dissenters to the Church of England!* as if they imagine there can be *no Salvation* out of that Church." Anglican clergymen made themselves particularly obnoxious to the Congregationalists during the Great Awakening by their reports that a "multitude" of sensible people had seen the folly of Dissenter enthusiasm and had hastened to the Church of England "as their only Ark of Safety." One Anglican dared to prophesy publicly in 1747 "that in a few Years Time *Episcopacy* will generally prevail in this Part of the World." [6]

In Boston, where the clergy of all churches were supported by voluntary contributions, relations betwen the laity of the two communions were generally friendly. Since the beginning of the century the town's clergy had noted with alarm that the wealthier members of their parishes were sometimes moving in Anglican social circles and losing their hostility toward the Prayer Book. The Brattle Street Church had been founded in 1699 just in time to include a group with Episcopal sympathies who might otherwise have turned Anglican. By the middle of the century the problem had become more acute. King's Chapel's "exceedingly elegant" new edifice was opened in 1754 after its construction had been partially financed by contributions and loans from Congregationalists. More serious than such expressions of goodwill was the tendency of some leading members of the community to attend Anglican services on occasion. An interesting example was Robert Treat Paine, Mayhew's close friend and ardent admirer, who recorded in his diary the many Sundays when he deserted the West Church for King's Chapel or Trinity Church. In this atmosphere of social intercourse and religious tolerance, the Boston Congregational clergy feared their flocks would forget the reasons that had impelled the fathers of New England to leave the homeland.[7]

In the country districts, where the clergy were paid from the tax rates, the strife between the two groups was endless. Here Episcopacy often became a convenient refuge for those who for any reason were unhappy with the local church or minister. Anglicans complained of being taxed to support Congregational clergy, and not until 1742 was a permanent law enacted in Massachusetts to permit the tax of Anglicans to be applied toward the support of their own ministers. This law, however, provided no relief for those without an Anglican church in the immediate vicinity, a loophole which Congregationalists sometimes exploited by finding devious means to block the erection of new Anglican sanctuaries. Yet, even in the country areas, time usually dissipated the initial hostility that was sure to follow the establishment of an Anglican congregation in a new locality, and there were often evidences of friendship and cooperation. In Cambridge friction resulted from the requirement that all Harvard students must attend services at Mr. Appleton's church. Finally, in 1760 the Overseers agreed to permit Anglican scholars to go to their own services, but not without a written application to the president and faculty.[8]

Shortly after its founding, the S.P.G. had become the leading advocate of an American episcopate. From the beginning the missionaries had realized the difficulty of carrying on the work of an Episcopal-type church in the colonies without a resident bishop to ordain, confirm, supervise, and discipline. To receive ordination in the absence of a bishop in America, a ministerial candidate had to journey to England, a trip which required not only a relatively large expenditure of funds but also subjected the candidate to the rigors of an Atlantic crossing. By 1766 no fewer than nine New Englanders had been lost on voyages to England for ordination. The barriers to ordination were a major deterrent to the growth of the Church of England in the colonies. During the reign of Queen Anne, the S.P.G. had nearly succeeded in obtaining the American episcopate, only to have the death of the Queen and the subsequent fall of the Tory Party bring the plan to nought. After this setback the agitation for an American bishopric almost ceased until the conversion of Timothy Cutler and the other Yale men in 1722. The new converts were zealous advocates of the episcopate, even though they received no encouragement from southern Anglicans, who feared that Episcopal supervision would upset their easygoing pattern of ecclesiastical order.[9]

The fervent pleas for a bishop heard from New England and the middle colonies brought results in 1741, when Thomas Secker, Bishop of Oxford, revived the issue in a sermon before the S.P.G. The Bishop's sermon alarmed New Englanders who feared that a colonial bishop would be supported by a general tax levied on all the colonies, not excluding those where the Congregational Church was established by law. A celebrated court case in Rhode Island, which was eventually appealed to the Privy Council, together with the efforts of the Rev. Noah Hobart of Connecticut to demonstrate that an American bishopric was both unnecessary and dangerous kept the question before the public in the 1740's. Fearful of the consequences in New England, the British ministry in 1750 pressed the hierarchy into dropping, or at least postponing, their campaign.

When Secker became Archbishop of Canterbury in 1758, he cautioned the Anglican clergy in New England to act with moderation and to spread the idea that, whatever bishops had been in 1630, "those of the present age are, and have always been, most sincere patrons of extensive toleration," and desire supervision over only the Episcopal congregations in the colonies. At the same time, he pledged never to abandon his plans for an American episcopate. Born a Dissenter, Secker had discovered that his considerable talents for preaching, administration, and politics could be combined through a career in the Hanoverian Church of England. Although he remained personally tolerant toward nonconformists, he worked indefatigably to strengthen the political as well as religious position of the Church. His rapid rise in the Anglican hierarchy was a testimony to his artful management of political connections. By exactly the same maneuvering Hoadley and Clarke had won immunity from ecclesiastical discipline. In the reign of George III, however, such a man as Secker was naturally a Tory. As prelate he sought a closer relation between Church and Crown.[10]

To American Dissenters Secker's elevation meant only that the most unrelenting advocate of the scheme to establish bishops in America was now head of the Church of England and that the S.P.G. had been transformed from a missionary society into an agent of British imperial control. Such views were strengthened when a few of the American Anglican clergy openly advocated Episcopacy as a means of keeping the colonies loyal to the mother country. Dr. Samuel Johnson, one of the Yale apostates, had stated the Anglican position most succinctly in 1745: "It has always been Fact & is obvious in the nature of the thing, that antiepiscopal are, of course, antimonarchial principles." Although they still honored such great Anglican bishops of the past as Burnett, Tillotson, and Hoadley, Mayhew and his Congregational brethren saw themselves threatened in the 1760's by a new breed of American High Churchmen whose political as well as religious objectives were supported by the English hierarchy and the swelling corps of royal officials in New England.[11]

By April 1762 Mayhew had heard that new plans to establish an American bishopric were being formulated, and he was convinced that Governor Bernard, "a true churchman," was "deep in the *plot*."[12] Therefore, he considered it imperative that the province have sympathetic and vigorous representation in England during the coming years. William Bollan, the son-in-law of former Governor Shirley, had been the Massachusetts agent for many years and on several occasions had rendered excellent service. But Bollan was an Anglican, and a gentleman of the Church of England, as Mayhew put it, was unlikely "to serve the Province in its most essential Interests." There had been other complaints against Bollan. Otis regarded him as "little more than an agent for his father-in-law, and what is here called the Shirlean faction, a motley mixture of high church men, and dissenters who, for the sake of the offices they sustain, are full as high in their notions of prerogative as the churchmen." Furthermore, said Otis, the House of Representatives could never get any information from Bollan. Several members of the House had wanted to select a new agent toward the end of 1759, but action had been postponed until the crisis of the war with France was over.[13]

When Bollan was finally dismissed in April 1762, a spirited

contest to elect his successor ensued. In spite of Bernard's attempt to have his friend Richard Jackson selected, Jasper Mauduit won the job after "a great division in the assembly." A lay leader among English Dissenters and a successful woolen merchant, Mauduit had been well recommended by Hollis and seemed to Otis and Mayhew the ideal man for the task, though there was some doubt whether he would accept the agency. At the request of several interested persons, Mayhew wrote to Mauduit that "The most steady friends of Liberty amongst us, and all the Friends to the dissenting Interest . . . would be extremely sorry if you should decline this Service." Mauduit replied that his health would not permit his acceptance unless his brother and business partner, Israel Mauduit, was associated with him in the agency.[14]

Since Israel was by far the abler of the brothers, the House voted to permit him to act for the province when his brother was indisposed, as long as no extra expense was incurred. The Council refused to concur in this action, after heavy pressure from Bernard, who was afraid that the addition of Israel would make the new agency so satisfactory that it would be impossible to replace the Mauduit brothers with Jackson, as he hoped to do soon. As a result, Jasper Mauduit continued officially to act alone as agent for the next three years, despite his lack of the physical vigor and political skills demanded by the position. Mayhew gradually came to the conclusion that the choice had been an unwise one, although he continued to correspond with Israel Mauduit in a friendly spirit. Lieutenant Governor Hutchinson noticed that "Some of the friends of our New Agent seem to be cool & growing sensible of his insufficiency." Newspaper controversies kept Jasper Mauduit's inability before the public. In the beginning of 1765 the agent resigned, and Bernard and Hutchinson secured the election of Jackson, now also agent for Connecticut and Pennsylvania, over Israel Mauduit. When it was learned a few months later that Jackson was also the private secretary of George Grenville, author of the Stamp Act, Mayhew and his friends thought their worst suspicions of Governor Bernard had been confirmed.[15]

To Mayhew and to many of his fellow Congregationalists, the insincerity of the S.P.G.'s religious objectives was unmasked in 1762 and 1763 when that society opposed the plans of a Massachusetts group to organize an Indian missionary society. However discouraged he might be at times over the meager results of his father's work, no son of Experience Mayhew could ever lose interest in the task of Christianizing the Indians of New England. The defeat of France in North America revived New England's zeal for Indian missions by providing an opportunity to send Protestant missionaries to those tribes that had hitherto been under French and Catholic domination. It was believed that the natives on New England's borders could never be entirely pacified until they had been weaned from French religious as well as political control. Would this task fall to the lot of the Congregationalists or the Anglicans? Should the S.P.G. be entrusted with this assignment, the position of the Church of England in New England would be appreciably strengthened. One tribe of Massachusetts Indians, formerly allied with the French, had already requested a Catholic priest from Governor Bernard, but he hoped to send them an Episcopal clergyman, whose ritual, he believed, would impress the native minds fully as much as the Catholic Mass. Neither the New England Company nor a society in Scotland that had formerly carried on some missionary work in New England was equal to the task, so the opponents of Episcopacy in Massachusetts determined to act before the S.P.G. took the initiative.[16]

In January 1762, the Congregational clergy and a group of the most prominent men in Boston, including a number of

wealthy merchants, petitioned the General Court for a charter establishing a local society to sponsor Indian missions.
The following month the Court passed "An Act to Incorporate
Certain Persons by the Name of the Society for Propagating
Christian Knowledge among the Indians of North America."
The American Society, as the new organization was usually
known, was empowered by the act to raise and invest funds
for the fulfillment of its plans. Governor Bernard consented to
the act, although he had grave doubts about undermining
"the King's right to incorporate by Charter." The society
organized and elected James Bowdoin as the first president.
Within two months of the passage of the act, £2000 sterling
had been raised, but these funds could not be used until the
act had received the approbation of the Privy Council in
England.[17]

The members of the new society stated that their motives
were entirely nonpartisan, and they pointed with pride to the
cordial welcome extended to the only gentleman of the
Church of England who had applied for membership. To
New England Anglicans, however, it was plain that the
S.P.G. now faced an affluent local rival. Henry Caner of King's
Chapel urgently appealed to Archbishop Secker to work
against royal approval of the act because "the real design of
it is to frustrate the pious designs" of the S.P.G. Caner informed his superior that the Dissenters are not interested in
the Indians as much as they desire "to send missionaries to
interfere with those the Society has already placed upon our
Frontier settlements."[18]

Opponents of the American Society found a vigorous advocate in William Smith, provost of the College of Philadelphia,
who was then in London on a mission for his college. A controversial figure in Pennsylvania politics, Smith was a warm
friend to the proposed American episcopate and made no
effort to conceal his ambition to be one of the bishops ap-

pointed. He wrote to Secker that "Not only the Good of the Church in America, but the very Subsistence of the Society for Propagating the Gospel seem to be affected by this Law." The new organization, he warned the Archbishop, would enjoy advantages over the S.P.G. from the location of its headquarters in the colonies and would soon boast that its work had removed all excuse for the existence of a foreign society. As a result, many of the S.P.G.'s sources of income would dry up. Smith enclosed with his letter a list of political objections to the American venture, as he thought it best to avoid any appearance of opposition from a partisan religious position. One passage in Smith's objections indicates how widespread Mayhew's reputation as an opponent of Episcopacy had become by the end of 1762: "All of them [members], we may well believe, deny the King's supremacy in religious matters. Dr. Mayhew, one of the chief of them, sneering at our establishment, says 'In a certain Island the King is Head of the Church'; felicitating himself that this is not the case in New England." [19]

In London the Mauduit brothers encountered so much opposition to the American Society that Jasper Mauduit advised a postponement of the attempt to have the act confirmed. But from Boston came word that the agent should press for immediate approval so the society might begin its work before the initial burst of enthusiasm for the project had passed. To Mayhew the confirmation was "of great importance both to our civil & religious Welfare." Mauduit's efforts on behalf of the act were to no avail. Thomas Pownall, former Governor of Massachusetts, informed the agent that "something was under consideration for the whole of Indian affairs," with which it was feared the American Society might clash. In addition, said Pownall, there was a strong suspicion that the money raised would be used to counter the Church of England's missionaries. One of Mauduit's frequent attacks of gout kept him from attending the Board of Trade meeting in March 1763, where the matter was considered. The Board drew up its objections to the act, and on the strength of this recommendation the Privy Council officially disallowed the act in May.[20]

The Anglican bishops had absented themselves from all meetings that considered the proposal but had worked behind the scenes to defeat it. Both Archbishop Secker and the Archbishop of York had agreed that it would be dangerous for the S.P.G. to appear openly against the American Society: "It will be said we ought gladly to let others do what we confess we have not been able to do ourselves in any great Degree." Privately, Secker made it clear that one of his chief objections was the inclusion in the membership of so many Dissenting ministers, "and amongst them one Dr. Mayhew, who hath been a most foul-mouthed Bespatterer of our Church & our Missionaries in print." Perhaps influenced by Smith, Secker prepared a memorandum that stressed only the political objections to the project. The reasons advanced by the Privy Council for its action closely followed the Archbishop's arguments and gave little hint of the religious friction involved. According to the record, the act had been disallowed because it extended the operations of a provincial organization beyond the boundaries of the province; because such extensive power as the act granted to the society might interfere with any general plan for Indian affairs; and because there had been no provision for civil control and an audit of funds.[21]

The sponsors of the American Society experienced keen disappointment when news of the disallowance of the act reached Boston. Mayhew had anticipated heavy opposition from "our good *Friends*" of the Church of England, but James Bowdoin had been more optimistic. He wrote that "This opposition was least to be expected from a Society, the end of

whose institution so much coincided with that of ours." The
Boston Gazette continued the fight by printing letters concerning the affair from the London newspapers as well as from
local writers. Henry Caner stood guard lest the American
Society secure authorization to act under some existing charter, a move of which he had heard rumors. In the meantime,
the question of the proposed American Society merged with
a larger controversy involving the status of the S.P.G. in the
colonies and the revival of the movement for an American
episcopate.[22]

Jonathan Mayhew had contested the claims of the Church
of England from the time he first entered the West Church
pulpit. He frankly acknowledged his prejudice: "I own, that
early in life, I imbibed strong *prepossessions* against diocesan
bishops; *i.e.* if a full persuasion, the result of free enquiry
and reading, that their order itself is unscriptural, and that
they have generally been a pernicious set of men, both to
church and state, may properly be called *prepossession*." [23]

Much of this hostility came from two sources: his desire to
make clear his personal rejection of the traditional affinity
between Anglicanism and Arminianism, and the need to protect his congregation against the temptations of Anglican high
society in Boston. A third source was his inherited concern
for Indian missions, now heightened by the conclusion that
the S.P.G. would neither do the job itself nor allow anyone
else to do it. To these sources must be added in 1763 a more
intangible but nevertheless important motive—Mayhew never
turned away from a good fight in defense of liberty. It was
obvious that a battle was in the offing, a battle that might
determine whether the principle of religious dissent or the
principle of religious establishment would prevail in the
northern colonies, for both Anglicans and Congregationalists
expected that Secker would seek to have his episcopate

scheme and the establishment of the Church of England in the new Canadian territories included in the general settlement of colonial matters certain to follow the official end of the Seven Years' War.[24] It was possible that a new king and ministry, inexperienced in colonial affairs, might throw their weight behind the Archbishop's plans. In Massachusetts a recent flurry of Anglican activity could be observed. Most conspicuous was the construction of an Anglican church in Cambridge within sight of Harvard's halls, a step that immediately alerted the Congregational clergy.

Mayhew had been collecting published S.P.G. documents. By the beginning of 1763, he was ready to defend his land and church against "brethren unawares brought in, who came in privily to spy out our liberty which we have in Christ Jesus, that they might bring us into bondage."[25]

CHAPTER XII

No Bishop, No King

One of our Kings, it is well known, excited his Scotch subjects to take up arms against him, in a great measure, if not
chiefly, by attempting to force the English liturgy upon
them, at the instigation of the furious episcopal zealots of
that day; by whom he was wheedled and duped to his destruction. But GOD be praised, we have a KING, . . . too
wise, just and good to be put upon any violent measures,
to gratify men of such a depraved turn of mind.

Jonathan Mayhew, 1763[1]

IN FEBRUARY 1763, four months before the Privy Council
struck down the American Society, Dr. Ebenezer Miller died
in Braintree, a town on the shore a few miles south of Boston.
For thirty-six years Miller had labored faithfully as rector
of an Anglican church that was partially supported by the
S.P.G. In the weeks following his death, the *Boston Gazette*
published a satirical review of Miller's life and work, as communicated by "T.L." of Braintree. These letters to the editor
pointed out that Miller, born and educated in New England,
had gone to England for Episcopal ordination and then had
returned as a missionary "to Civilize and Christianize the poor
Natives and *Africans* of Braintree." Since his death, "T.L."
continued, the natives now fear they will not have another
missionary sent to them, "in which Case, they may perhaps,
in the Course of a few Years, relapse into the same *savage*
and *barbarous* State, in which they were before there was
an Episcopal Minister settled here." Incidentally, the writer
added, the natives of Braintree are so fair-skinned that they
are often mistaken for Englishmen until one converses with

them. Subsequent letters charged the S.P.G. with violating its charter by sending its missionaries to convert Dissenters rather than Indians and Negro slaves. There is no evidence as to the identity of "T.L.," although Mayhew was often accused of being responsible for these letters from Braintree, where he had friends and relatives.[2]

"T.L." was answered by a flood of newspaper obloquy, but the principal defense of Miller and the S.P.G. against the newspaper charges came from the pen of East Apthorp, who personally symbolized some of the most compelling reasons that motivated the Congregational struggle against Episcopacy. Fifth son of one of Boston's wealthiest merchants, Apthorp had been educated in England at Cambridge University. He returned to Massachusetts upon his father's death in 1758 and consented to head the new S.P.G. mission in the American Cambridge. Henry Caner of King's Chapel had persuaded him to accept this assignment not only to minister to Cambridge Anglicans, but also to prevent Socinianism, Deism, and other errors "from poysoning the Fountain of Education." Fearful that the establishment of an S.P.G. station within sight of Harvard College would raise "a great clamour," Archbishop Secker commanded a policy of prudence and caution. He had appraised the situation correctly. When Cambridge Anglicans opened their handsome new building in October 1761, it appeared in the eyes of the Congregational clergy to take the shape of a dagger aimed at the heart of the Puritan tradition in America. To make matters worse, East Apthorp used some of his newly inherited wealth to build a large and sumptuous residence (a "Bishop's Palace," Mayhew later called it) in Cambridge for himself and his new bride. Rich and scholarly, this young clergyman was a splendid advertisement of the genteel Anglican tradition that had proved so attractive to New England's *nouveau riche*.[3]

Apthorp published his short and mild *Considerations* in

March 1763. He argued that the S.P.G., according to its charter, had been established chiefly to support the cause of
religion among Englishmen in the colonies and that missionary work among the natives was only a subordinate objective.
The best way to convert the heathen was to start with the
English. New England needed the Anglican Church in its
midst to "hinder *corruptions* of Christianity from prevailing
there," especially since "Many pernicious errors took early
root in these provinces." Wherever practicable the society
had ministered to the Indians, although with discouraging
results. It should be remembered, he added, that missionaries
are never sent to a locality unless they are first requested by
some of the inhabitants, as had been the case in Cambridge.[4]

Boston soon heard that Mayhew was preparing to challenge
Apthorp. Meanwhile the newspaper scurrility continued. One
of the most original examples was the paper which "P.Q.R."
maintained he had picked up on a Boston street. After clean-
ing off the mud, he could make out a letter from "Pierre
Le Prenoque" of Boston to his brother in Quebec: "dare is
vun Toctur *Mayu,* I tink da cal him, ant he is a going to rite
acinst him [Apthorp] agin—ant peepel gesses he vil Nok him
up—Put I hop he vont, caus u no, teer broder Jon, dat ve
Roman Catliks all likes de Jurch ov *Hinclant,* caus tis so neer
kin tu owr one."[5]

Ezra Stiles, pastor at Newport, Rhode Island, and later
president of Yale College, had heard that Mayhew's plans to
reply to Apthorp had been sidetracked by "some Episcopalians
of the first Distinction & Power" who had reached the minister
through mutual friends. This was discouraging news to Stiles,
who two years before had published and sold over seven
thousand copies of *A Discourse on the Christian Union,* a
plea for Dissenter solidarity against the threat of Episcopacy.
Stiles wrote a long letter to Mayhew in which he pointed out
the serious consequences for New England religion that he

thought were certain to follow the establishment of an American episcopate. He praised Mayhew's earlier stand against Episcopacy and reminded him that the churches today "require as vigilant & Spirited Defence as the first hundred years of the Reformation." [6]

Stiles's fears were groundless. By the time his letter had reached Boston, Mayhew's *Observations on the Charter and Conduct of the Society for the Propagation of the Gospel . . . With Remarks on the Mistakes of East Apthorp* was off the press. Several times longer than Apthorp's *Considerations,* the *Observations* drove home the charge that the S.P.G. had violated its charter by directing its main efforts toward the development of the Church of England in the well-churched older settlements of New England rather than in more heathen areas where only meager religious facilities existed.[7] There was no question in Mayhew's mind that such a policy of "setting up altar against altar" was a departure from the society's charter, which had been granted for the express purpose of furnishing religious instruction and worship to those subjects, native and English, who lived in areas without normal religious facilities. Why had this perversion of the charter been permitted? Because, he answered, "the Society have long had a formal design to dissolve and root out all our New-England churches; or . . . to reduce them all to the episcopal form." At the same time the S.P.G. had turned a deaf ear to the pleas of the "heathenish colonies" for ministers, and it had neglected to evangelize the Indians, a work that promised not only great spiritual gain but economic and political benefits as well.[8]

After having long been regarded by many as a traitor to the New England Way, Mayhew now put on the mantle of Cotton Mather. He refuted Apthorp's charges of gravity, superstition, hypocrisy, and intolerance against the New England churches. He spoke for both Harvard and Yale. To

Apthorp's contention that the S.P.G. was bringing Americans back "to good manners and a christian life," he countered that the common people of New England are philosophers and divines in comparison to the English lower classes under the yoke of the Church of England.[9] The present friction was nothing new to Mayhew; it was a continuation of the persecutions that had driven the Puritans of the 1630's to Massachusetts Bay:

Will they never let us rest in peace, except *where all the weary are at rest?* Is it not enough, that they persecuted us out of the old world? Will they pursue us into the new to convert us here?— *compassing sea and land to make us proselytes,* while they neglect the heathen and heathenish plantations! What other new world remains as a sanctuary for us from their oppressions, in case of need? Where is the COLUMBUS to explore one for, and pilot us to it, before we are consumed by the flames, or deluged in a flood of episcopacy?[10]

The reception of the *Observations* followed a strictly partisan line. Harrison Gray wrote that "I never knew any performance of a Controversial nature [to] meet with so general approbation and applause, excepting among some bigoted high Churchmen, who most sincerely Curse it."[11] Stiles thought the work too mild: "he has not told half the invidious Truth nor developed half this Mystery of Iniquity."[12] To Caner the *Observations* had been written "in so dirty a manner, that it seems to be below the Character of a gentleman to enter into controversy with him." But Dr. Samuel Johnson, president of the recently founded King's College in New York, called for an answer from the mother country to this "rough, ludicrous, audacious & malicious man, equally disliked by most of the Dissenters & us, & equally an Enemy to the Trinity, to Royalty & Episcopacy." Admitting he was "an unequal antagonist" for Mayhew, Apthorp declined to continue the controversy in spite of Caner's urging.[13] Others proved less reluctant. Some *Verses on Doctor Mayhew's Book of Observations* appeared first in a Providence newspaper and then in a pamphlet with added remarks.[14] The *Verses* focused on the preacher's lack of gratitude for Britain's bounties to New England:

> Whilst *Britain* led by Royal George
>   New Blessings doth disperse;
> And where her Sword and Treasure sav'd,
>   Spreads Learning, Truth and Sense.

> Ungrateful *Mayhew's* desperate Hand,
>   Foul Libels dares to write,
> To prove her Charities are Crimes,
>   Her Favors all a Bite. . . .

> O *Mayhew!* hadst thou been reserv'd
>   To curse some future Day;
> We also might from *Britain's* Sun,
>   Have felt a gladd'ning Ray.

> By Nature vain, by Art made worse,
>   And greedy of false Fame;
> Thro' Truth disguis'd, and Mobs deceiv'd,
>   Thou fain woulds't get a Name.

The notes accompanying the anonymous *Verses* accused Mayhew of attempting to set up an inquisition against the national religion, a scheme that lacked only Oliver Cromwell and his "Forty Thousand Cut-throats" to be put into practice.

The Rev. Mr. Arthur Browne of Portsmouth, New Hampshire, now entered the controversy with a pamphlet entitled *Remarks on Dr. Mayhew's Incidental Reflections, Relative to the Church of England As contained in his Observations.* . . . Mayhew's "Reflections" on Episcopacy reminded Browne of the Oliverian writers "whose spittle he hath lick'd up, and cough'd it out again, with some addition of his own filth and phlegm." [15] Browne's personal attack did not, as his title indicates, attempt to deal with the charges against the S.P.G. Another attempt to blacken Mayhew's character was issued as a broadside that accused him of engineering the entire controversy to make himself more popular among the Congregationalists who hitherto had disliked his liberal theology. Mayhew, this *Advertisement* stated, had written many of the recent newspaper articles to inflame anew the Puritan hatred of their ancient Anglican enemies, and in so doing had dishonored his profession: "Are you not a very *dirty Fellow Jonathan*, for a Teacher? Are you not ashamed to publish such rag-mannerly stuff on Monday, after holding forth with solemn Hiccough on Sunday?" [16]

The *Observations* had raised real issues which could not be met with attacks on the character of the author. Mayhew had struck at the right hour, the very moment Secker was attempting to push his plans for an American episcopate to completion. Even some sincere Anglicans, including East Apthorp, had expressed doubts concerning the propriety of the S.P.G.'s sending its funds to New England's towns to the neglect of the natives. In the summer of 1763, the *Boston News-Letter* twice noticed reports from London that the appointment of a bishop for North America was imminent, and word arrived of a bequest of £1000 for the first bishop's support. Mayhew's scholarly English friend, Nathaniel Lardner, related the same dismal news in a letter. In Boston it was announced in September that a merchant had bequeathed £500 to support an assistant minister to William Hooper at Trinity Church. As Congregationalists became more and more alarmed at these reports of what they considered Anglican aggression, friends of Episcopacy realized they would have to counter Mayhew's charges with facts and logic rather than blasts at his character. One answer came from New England, another from the mother country.[17]

The New England answer came from the pen of Henry

Caner, whose anonymous *A Candid Examination of Dr. Mayhew's Observations* appeared in October 1763. Caner's opening lines set the tone for his polemic: "Every gentleman who has had a liberal and polite education, thinks it beneath his character to enter the lists with one who observes no measures of decency or good manners, nay who does not scruple to sacrifice the meek and gentle spirit of the Gospel to the gratification of a licentious and ungovern'd temper." Still, the job had to be done, and Caner thought he saw two fatal weaknesses in his opponent's position. First, he pointed out that Mayhew had become a threat to New England's civil liberties by devoting his career to stirring up needless controversy and engendering a party spirit against the royal church. Such action, if continued, might force the home government to curtail colonial liberties. Second, the rector attempted to drive a wedge between Mayhew and his more orthodox supporters in this struggle: "Can you, I say, cherish and flatter the man, who has been labouring from pulpit and press to demolish the doctrines which your fore-fathers have handed down to you? . . . How is it then that you have complimented the Dr. with your thanks . . . for his book of observations, who by his other writings, has been destroying the fundamentals of your faith?" [18]

Caner failed to win either point. The threat of royal action against the enemies of Episcopacy only confirmed the suspicion that bishops would use their political connections to crush Dissenters whenever possible. His fellow Congregationalists could not see that Mayhew's theological deviation made him any less capable of exposing the Church of England's plot to destroy the New England churches. As one commentator remarked, even a Deist could compare the conduct of the S.P.G. with its charter and point out "the manifest inconsistency of the one with the other." Two years later Samuel Hopkins prefaced his attack on Mayhew's theology with a statement of his pleasure and gratitude that a gentleman of such "abilities and advantages" had undertaken the defense of their common cause. Most gratifying of all, the Boston ministers voted their thanks for the *Observations*.[19]

More serious was Caner's attempt to prove that the Church of England had from the beginning been the established religion in New England. He further trespassed on Puritan tradition by suggesting that the founding fathers had left England to better their economic status and not for the pious motives assigned by their descendants. Whatever persecution the Puritans had suffered in England had been light compared to the religious intolerance that had been the rule in early New England. Mayhew's spirit in attacking the S.P.G. was to Caner a new eruption of the same persecuting zeal that had driven Anne Hutchinson into the wilderness to be murdered by Indians.[20]

Appended to Caner's *Candid Examination* was *a Letter to a Friend,* written anonymously by New England's most noted Anglican, Dr. Samuel Johnson.[21] After preparing a full-length reply to the *Observations,* Johnson had learned of Caner's efforts and decided to condense his own as an appendix to the other work. Johnson's *Letter* reiterated the familiar argument that an American bishop would have ecclesiastical jurisdiction over only Anglicans, and could in no way constitute a threat to New England's political or religious liberty.

Before the year was over, Mayhew published *A Defence of the Observations* in answer to both Caner and Johnson. At the outset he shamed the defenders of the S.P.G. for hiding in anonymity. Most of these writers, he noticed, "have discharged little besides mud and dirt at me; from which no execution could be expected; And accordingly, I find myself at last, not wounded, but only bespattered." To the argument that the S.P.G. charter did not list Indians as an objective of its missions, he countered that the design of the charter could not be fulfilled unless the main energies of the society were devoted to Indian work. For thirty pages he cited laws, proclamations, and precedents to disprove Caner's contention that the Church of England was established in all the English colonies. The crux of the case was that it is "only the *common law* at most, and those statutes that are made in affirmation or explanation of it, that English subjects carry with them when they emigrate into colonies, so as to be bound by them. And I conclude, it will not be said that the Church of England is established by common law, which had its origin among *heathen* nations; and was compleat as a system long before the reformation." Whatever the legal aspects of this case, Mayhew had New England history on his side. It was impossible to explain to the descendants of John Winthrop and John Cotton that the Congregational churches had not been established at least *de facto* since the founding of Massachusetts and Connecticut.[22]

Again Mayhew took his stand with the Puritan fathers: this time he utilized quotations from Cotton Mather and Thomas Prince. It is true, he admitted, that I differ in "religious sentiments" from the fathers, but that difference has been grossly exaggerated by those seeking to discredit my views on the S.P.G. Unaware of the eminence of its author, he dismissed Johnson's *Letter* with a curt sentence: "it bears the marks of age, with its usual infirmities, whoever was the author of it." [23] A sidelight to the exchange between Mayhew and Johnson was the latter's request of the Archbishop for an honorary doctorate for Caner to uphold the honor and prestige of the Church of England in Massachusetts, where there were three Doctors of Divinity among the Congregationalists. Two years later Oxford University did its part in this sheepskin war by holding a convocation to confer degrees upon Caner and two other important Anglicans in the northern colonies.[24]

The second answer to Mayhew's *Observations* came from London and from no less a person than Archbishop Secker. Aware of the close connection between the American and English Dissenters, the Archbishop could hardly have been surprised when the present controversy received almost as much attention in London as in Boston. Unlike most other American problems, the Episcopal question was a domestic as well as a colonial issue. Charges from a Boston preacher that the chief goal of the S.P.G. was to extirpate non-Anglicans seemed entirely logical to English Dissenters, who had not yet freed themselves from all the disadvantages of nonconformity. The dispute in America was zealously followed and extended in the English newspapers.[25]

Aside from this common interest of English and American Dissenters, the attention Mayhew's anti-Episcopal writings received in the mother country was largely the result of the work of Thomas Hollis. During a twenty-year friendship with the Archbishop, Hollis had made a concerted effort to win him over to the Whig cause, only to conclude at last that the prelate "shewed no hearty affection to Liberty of any sort, nor those men who loved it." After observing the current plans for an American episcopate, Hollis resolved "to drop him wholly." Unlike Mayhew's other English correspondents, he did not think there was any immediate danger of the erection of an episcopate in the colonies, but he warned that "You cannot be too much on your guard, in this so very important affair." The *Observations* so pleased him that he determined to have the tract reprinted in London. No ordinary printer would do. He persuaded Andrew Millar, who did the S.P.G.'s printing, to do the job. Millar approved the contents but thought the length would prevent a ready sale. Hollis insisted on a complete republication, and in the fall, just as summer vacationers were returning to London, the full text of the *Observations* appeared with Apthorp's *Considerations* an-

nexed to it. Likewise, Hollis induced Millar to reprint Mayhew's *Defence* in the spring of 1764, a project which he aided
by a contribution of six guineas.[26]

Secker could not ignore this challenge from his own doorstep.
Early in 1764 an anonymous *Answer to Dr. Mayhew's Observations* appeared in London. It was soon known on both sides
of the Atlantic that the London *Answer* was the Archbishop's
work. Except for a marked note of moderation and charity,
it contained little that was new. He was willing to concede
that S.P.G. funds had not always been wisely appropriated
in view of the needs of the remote sections of the North
American colonies, and he promised to rectify whatever
abuses he discovered in the future. Secker's aim was obviously
to advance his plan for the American episcopate by disarming
the Congregationalists with a tolerant and charitable spirit.[27]
Israel Mauduit wrote Mayhew that his *Observations* had induced the Archbishop to request the S.P.G. to send no more
missionaries to the settled parts of New England for fear of
prejudicing the inhabitants against Episcopacy. When Henry
Caner also heard this report, he filed a sharp protest: "If the
Society should be obliged to desert the Churches in New
England, Dr. Mayhew's malicious slander and falsehood will
have obtained its end, & truth and innocence must sink under
the weight of calumny and abuse." [28]

The London *Answer* appeared in a Boston edition in the
spring of 1764, and Mayhew advertised that he was preparing
a reply, which appeared in June under the title *Remarks on
an Anonymous Tract*. Although he reciprocated the prelate's
moderation, even paying a mild tribute to the author's freedom from bigotry, Mayhew lashed out at the proposed episcopate. He conceded that the *Answer* has "set this proposal
for American bishops in a more plausible, and less exceptional
point of view, than I have seen it placed before." But "The
declaration of an *anonymous* writer . . . is not, surely, sufficient

to satisfy us, that this is the *true* scheme planned." What if
the American bishop should be another Sacheverell?—"no
impossible supposition." The lesson of history was clear in
Boston's pure air if not in London's fog:

It is however, pretty evident from our history, that in arbitrary
reigns, and foolish and wicked administrations, the bishops have
commonly been *the most useful members, or instruments,* that
the crown or court had, in establishing a tyranny over the bodies
and souls of men. . . . "Our own bishops, for near an hundred
years before the revolution, were in every scheme for promoting
tyranny and bondage." . . . The old cry, *No bishop, no king* has
indeed been of mighty efficacy in times past.[29]

The great threat to our liberties, Mayhew concluded, is
that "Bishops being once fixed in America, pretexts might
easily be found, both for encreasing their number, and enlarging their powers." History was again clear on this point:
"People are not usually deprived of their liberties all at once,
but gradually." This "entering wedge" argument was the
heart of the entire case against the episcopate, and it was
so much a part of the vestigial Puritan mind that it blinded
non-Anglicans to the obvious logic of Secker's contention that
the reasons Mayhew and others advanced in this dispute
contradicted their own principles of liberty. The Archbishop
was willing to make almost any concession necessary to secure
bishops for the American Church, but each concession was
interpreted by the Congregational clergy as only a sharper
wedge.[30]

This ocean of history and suspicion that separated New
England Congregationalists from the Church of England was
brought into sharp focus in one exchange between Mayhew
and Secker. In his *Answer* the Archbishop ridiculed as only
"the poor Man's fears" the charge made in the *Observations*
that the proposed colonial episcopate constituted a threat to
American liberties. Mayhew's caustic reply contrasted the

spirituality of the Congregational clergy with the venality of Secker and his brethren:

I am indeed, even literally, a "poor man," as this gentleman calls me, I suppose, in another sense: . . . I had much rather be the *poor* son of a good man, who spent a long life and his patrimony in the humble and laborious, tho' apostolical employment of preaching the "unsearchable riches of Christ" to *poor Indians;* . . . than even the *rich* son and heir of One who had, by temporizing in religion, and tampering with politics, by flattering the Great, and prostituting his conscience, made his way to a bishoprick, and the worldly dignity of a peer; how large a *bag* soever he had carried with him thro' a life of idleness and pride, of intrigue and luxury, or left behind him at death, the *black period* of all his greatness and glory.[31]

To Hollis, the *Remarks* was "a valuable master tract." He was elated to read Mayhew's denunciation of Episcopal complacency at the growth of Catholicism in England, a situation reported at length in his letters to Boston. Millar was induced to reprint the *Remarks,* this time with a subsidy of only three guineas. The London edition was timed to appear at the opening of Parliament in October. Hollis sent copies to libraries and colleges in Scotland, and he distributed others to strategic persons at home. Moreover, he paid a guinea to have extracts from the *Remarks* concerning the close relation between popery and Episcopacy inserted in the *London Chronicle.* Mayhew's other friends in England were not as active as Hollis, but they sent encouraging letters of approbation. Michael Towgood of Exon spoke for this group when he wrote, "It is a Subject I have long wished to see examined & presented in a just light by so good an Hand." By the summer of 1764 the Boston minister was firmly established as the international champion of English nonconformity.[32]

In Boston the Anglicans were generally unwilling to believe that Secker had written the London *Answer.* Either they regarded Mayhew as too insignificant an opponent for an archbishop, or they thought it incredible that the prelate would have made so many concessions to Congregational opinion. The Boston newspapers had followed the contest in London as well as the local struggle, and they reprinted letters on both sides from the English press. Anglicans pointed with joy to the harsh notices of Mayhew's performances in the *Critical Review*, a London literary journal; and Congregationalists rejoined with extracts from the *Monthly Review*, a similar periodical that usually took a friendlier view of the same writings. Hollis sent newspaper clippings to Mayhew, who passed them on to local editors. Between the great military victories of 1759–1760 and the Stamp Act crisis of 1765–1766, no event in New England aroused so much general interest as the Mayhew controversy of 1763–1765. In Fairfield, Connecticut, Noah Hobart, who had engaged in a similar but less-known dispute twenty years before, followed every detail of the current campaign against bishops. His long letters of advice and encouragement to his fellow divine in Boston urged a severe chastisement of Episcopalians.[33]

Discouraged over the failure of his parish to grow and sensitive to his unwittingly having become the symbol of Anglican aggression in the Boston area, East Apthorp, whom Hollis called Secker's spy, returned to England permanently in 1764. Mayhew could not conceal his glee over the report that the Anglican church in Cambridge was closed and that some of its members were now attending Congregational meetings.[34] From London, Apthorp fired the last shot in this immediate controversy with *A Review of Dr. Mayhew's Remarks on the Answer.* (To Apthorp's credit, he was the only Anglican in this battle who wrote under his own name.) He denied that Secker had made any concessions, for all the previous proposals for American bishops had been equally mild. Only Mayhew's ignorance of earlier plans had led him to regard the present scheme as unusually temperate. By this time Apthorp had become disillusioned with American Angli-

cans, who, he said, displayed great zeal for their religion in
only one superfluous area, the construction of ornamental
church buildings. He remained as unwavering in his basic
position, however, as Mayhew did in his. His final word was,
"I cannot but be persuaded that the advancement of the Church
of *England* is for the interest of Truth, Order, and reasonable
Liberty." [35] Congregationalists had their own ideas about the
extent of Episcopal "reasonable Liberty." Mayhew saw nothing in Apthorp's work that demanded an answer, and he had
no desire to continue the controversy during the Stamp Act
turbulence.

To Hollis, who in his later years had delusions of being
pursued by Jesuits, the master stroke of the paper war had
been Mayhew's charge that the Anglican hierarchy, particularly Secker, was sympathetic to Catholicism. "I am of an
opinion," he wrote, "that You will never get another [answer],
a direct one, from him or any other Church leader, now that
you have touched on Popery; no ass in sand cast, skin-cut &
goaded, being more tender than the A.B., & his Bretheren
when touched on that Subject." The transition from Episcopacy to popery was an easy one for a people who still celebrated Pope's Day.[36] Hardly by coincidence, Mayhew was
invited in May 1765 to deliver Harvard's Dudleian Lecture,
founded by Judge Paul Dudley to refute errors in religion,
among them Catholicism. The lecture, printed as *Popish
Idolatry*, provided a medium to broadcast some of the material Hollis had been sending him for years. After the usual
attack on transubstantiation, saints, angels, pictures, and
images, he drew a conclusion for the present age: "Our controversy with her [Rome] is not merely a religious one: . . .
But a defence of our laws, liberties and civil rights as men,
in opposition to the proud claims of ecclesiastical persons,
who under the pretext of religion and saving mens souls,
would engross all power and property to themselves, and
reduce us to the most abject slavery. . . . Popery and liberty

are incompatible; at irreconcileable enmity with each other." [37]

Hollis was so delighted with *Popish Idolatry* that he rushed a copy to the British Museum "to gall Leviathan [Secker], President there by office" and to Archbishop Tennison's library "to gall him there too." During the fall of 1765 and the following year, the English newspapers published letter after letter written by correspondents who volunteered to assist in "galling" the hierarchy of the Church of England for an alleged softness toward Catholicism. [38]

After Mayhew's death in 1766, the struggle over an American episcopate continued with new antagonists until the outbreak of the American Revolution. Each party possessed an unique historical background that made it impossible to understand the arguments of the other. Mayhew's contacts abroad had all been with men of his own persuasion; thus he had not the cosmopolitan outlook that enabled other Americans—Benjamin Franklin, for example—to appreciate the fact that the bishopless Anglicans had a real grievance. [39] On the other hand, from the standpoint of the American Dissenters, opposition to the episcopate was historically correct, for the strength of the Church of England, with a few exceptions, was in the Tory Party. Secker wrote Johnson that George III "is thoroughly sensible that the Episcopalians are his best friends in America." Johnson earlier had pleaded with the Archbishop to demolish these "pernicious charter governments" and reduce them "all to one form, in immediate dependence on the King," if the episcopate could not be obtained otherwise. Mild as it was, Secker's proposal for an American episcopate was premised on the ground that it was essential "for the Cultivating Religion and Virtue, for the propagating Principles conducive to the quiet of the State and securing the Allegiance and Loyalty of his Majesty's Subjects in those parts." During the Stamp Act crisis Henry Caner wrote home reminding his ecclesiastical superiors that Anglicanism is "the only religious Profession among us that sincerely cultivates the Principles of Loyalty and Obedience to the British Crown and Government." [40]

In spite of this profusion of loyalty, the American Anglicans fought in a lost cause. Even in the first years of the reign of George III, the British ministry had little inclination to support Archbishop Secker's plans for an American episcopate in the face of the determined opposition of an overwhelming majority of American Dissenters, an opposition dramatized by the exchanges between Mayhew and his Episcopal foes. Secker may have regarded himself as an enlightened Archbishop Laud, but George III was in no position to play the role of Charles I. In the words of Horace Walpole, the prelate "rose in the Church without ever making a figure in the State." The home government had more important colonial problems to settle, of which the most urgent was the question of how to induce the Americans to pay their share of the cost of administering and defending the Empire.[41]

The Mayhew controversy merged with the revenue question. Emotions aroused in the one contest were redirected to the other. If Parliament could tax the colonies without the consent of their legislatures, what was to prevent it from appropriating the upkeep of a half dozen American bishops? Bishops and stamps, religious and political freedom, were thoroughly intertwined in the Dissenting mind of the northern American colonies by the end of 1764. When William Allen, Chief Justice of Pennsylvania, returned from a trip to England in 1764, he reported to Mayhew that "from what I could observe, the Bishops, nor their office have not many friends among the Nobility and Gentry: if ever they are sent among us it will be with Political views to make us more tame, and submissive to the Yoke intended to be laid on us." The episcopate controversy had increased the unwillingness of Mayhew and other key colonial spokesmen to carry even such a light British "yoke" as the Stamp Act.[42]

CHAPTER XIII

Slavery

Only slaves are bound to labor for the pleasure & profit of others; and to subsist merely on what their Masters are pleased to allow them; tho' they may possibly have kind masters, who treat them with tenderness & humanity, still they are as really in a state of slavery, as those who have hard & cruel masters.

Jonathan Mayhew, 1765[1]

IN ENGLISH eyes the revenue question was simple. The British debt was staggering; the American debt insignificant. Englishmen paid high taxes; Americans low taxes. Much of the British debt had been acquired defending the colonies from the French, and now the territory to guard and administer had been vastly enlarged by the recent war. Therefore, tax revenues from the colonies must be increased, said George Grenville, who in 1763 became head of a coalition British ministry. Such a conclusion in England raised momentous questions across the Atlantic: Since the mother country reaped the preponderance of the benefits and profits of the Empire, why should not she pay the imperial military and administrative expenses? Can Englishmen be taxed without the consent of their representatives? And does not the colonial legislature stand in the same relation to the people of its colony as Parliament to the people of England?

Whatever the merits of his cause, Grenville's financial measures seemed designed to produce the maximum amount of friction. The Sugar Act of 1764 threatened seriously to curtail the West Indian trade that the merchants regarded as the foundation of New England prosperity. In August 1764, a group of Boston merchants agreed to stop importing luxury items from Great Britain in the hope that such a move would produce unemployment in England and give the unemployed "Leisure to inquire into the Conduct of those who have deprived us of the Means to procure Luxury, and the Propriety of Measures Calculated to enlarge the Revenue at the Expence of Trade." [2]

Grenville's second revenue act, the Stamp Act of 1765, lifted the taxation issue out of the realm of profits and losses and made it a question of constitutional and natural rights. By levying stamp duties on most legal and commercial documents, playing cards, dice, pamphlets, newspapers and newspaper advertisements, almanacs, and even university degrees, the Stamp Act made British taxation obnoxious to many who hitherto had not been directly concerned with the merchant's cause. In the period of general economic depression that followed the close of the war, it was a simple matter to channel the accumulated discontent of all classes into opposition to what was presented as an unwarranted violation of the British constitution. Such was particularly the case in Boston, where the communication media of press, pulpit, town meeting, and caucus were more developed than in the other colonial centers of population. But sparks from Boston settled upon combustible material along the entire Atlantic coast. Whereas the Sugar Act contained many provisions for the regulation of trade that had all along been accepted as constitutional by the colonists, the Stamp Act could be pictured as a clear-cut disregard of the right of British subjects to tax themselves in their own legislatures. As a result, in the fall of 1765 and spring of 1766, American colonists exhibited greater unanimity and resolution in opposition to the British government than ever before or again. [3]

Mayhew had no difficulty in deciding that the Sugar and Stamp acts were "extremely hard and injurious" measures

which, "If long persisted in, . . . will at best greatly cramp,
and retard the population of, the Colonies, to the very essential detriment of the Mother country." Here was an act of
tyranny tailor-made to fit the warnings of the plot against
liberty he had been detailing from the West Church pulpit
for the past eighteen years. But his passion for liberty had
been highly academic. It was one thing to extol the revolu-
tionaries of 1649 and 1688; it was quite a different matter to
advocate revolution in one's own time. When on August 8,
the day before the names of the stamp distributors were to
be announced in Boston, Mayhew wrote Hollis "that no people are under a *religious obligation* to be slaves, if they are
able to set themselves at liberty," he was unaware that before
the end of the month his political principles would receive
their severest test.[4]

While Boston waited uneasily for November 1, the day
the Stamp Act was to go into effect, the enmity between
Hutchinson and the Otis faction reappeared. All Boston soon
heard the rumor that the Lieutenant Governor had sponsored
the Stamp Act "for the sake of recommending himself to his
Superiors in England." Hutchinson categorically denied that
he had possessed any advance knowledge of the Act other
than what he had read in the newspapers, but the appointment of his brother-in-law, Andrew Oliver, to the position of
stamp distributor for Massachusetts served to convict the
Lieutenant Governor in the eyes of those who were jealous
of his fortune and numerous offices in the government. Mayhew reported the rumor to Hollis without giving an opinion
of its validity, though he had learned from Chief Justice
William Allen that Hutchinson had sent to England a manuscript which so ably refuted the arguments for the Sugar and
Stamp acts that Allen thought a copy should be delivered to
every member of Parliament.[5]

Violent opposition to the Stamp Act broke out sooner than

Mayhew had expected. On the morning of August 14, Boston
awakened to the sight of Andrew Oliver hung in effigy. On
one arm was a paper bearing "A. O." in large letters, and on
the other arm was another paper containing the verse, "A
goodlier sight who e'er did see? A Stamp-Man hanging on
a tree!" At the side of the effigy hung an old boot—a jibe at
the unpopular Lord Bute—out of which protruded the head
and fork of the devil. The foot of the boot had a new green
sole, or as Boston punned, "a *Green-vile* sole." The effigy
remained on display all day and was viewed by thousands of
people. Let Mayhew finish the story in his own words:

At dusk of the evening it was cut down, and carried thro' the
Streets in Solemn form, by great Numbers (unarmed) and had
its head sawed off before Mr. Oliver's Door, and was then burnt
at a little distance, amidst loud Acclamations. A new Building
which Mr. O. had just erected, for a Stamp-Office, but unfinished
was intirely demolished, and part of the timber, &c. burnt with
the Effigies. That gentleman's Mansion House was also assaulted
& damaged the same Evening; And the next day he gave it under
his hand, that he would not serve as Stamp-Officer; which, it is
supposed, was the only thing that prevented his House being torn
down the Next Night.[6]

Governor Bernard issued a proclamation calling for the
arrest of the leaders of the mob, who were said to be persons
of quality. "But if any of them should be discovered & committed," Mayhew told Hollis, "I am confident the prison
would not hold them many hours. In this town, and within
20 miles of it, there are, I suppose, 10,000 men, who if need
be, could & would soon be collected together, on such an
Occasion." Two nights later the mob surrounded Hutchinson's
mansion, but he escaped and the crowd withdrew without
doing any serious damage. Such demonstrations convinced
Mayhew that the Stamp Act could be carried into execution
only at the point of a sword. Only such oppressive treatment
as this—Britain waging war against her American colonies—

could, he thought, create a desire for independence. "God forbid there should be an intire Breach between them, which might prove very fatal to both!" In such times he remembered an extract from the popular Whig political treatise, *Cato's Letters*, which now seemed to him almost a prophecy. It read, in part:

> It is not to be hoped, in the corrupt State of human Nature, that any Nation will be subject to another any longer than it finds its own Account in it, and cannot help itself. . . . All Nature points out that Course. No Creatures suck the Teats of their Dams longer than they can draw milk from thence, or can provide themselves with better Food: Nor will any Country continue their Subjection to another, only because their Great Grandmothers were acquainted.[7]

There are only two ways by which a mother country can hold its colonies, this passage continued: either by force or by good treatment. Mayhew recommended this extract from *Cato's Letters* to Hollis for publication in the London newspapers. In Boston it appeared, likely from the same source, in the *Evening-Post* of Monday, August 26, the day after the people of the West Church had heard what to the townsmen became the most famous—or infamous—sermon ever preached in that building.

No one will ever know exactly what Jonathan Mayhew said to his congregation on Sunday afternoon, August 25. More important, the inflections, attitude, and emphasis of this sermon have been lost forever, for what was said may not have been as significant as how it was said. His text was Galatians v, 12–13: "I would they were even cut off which trouble you. For, brethren, ye have been called unto liberty; only *use* not liberty for an occasion to the flesh, but by love serve one another." There are only three extant sources for what followed, all of them written by Mayhew after the sermon became the subject of heated controversy. From these biased sources it is possible to reconstruct much but not all of the contents.[8]

After beginning as usual by exploring the Biblical significance of his text, Mayhew launched into a discussion of what the Apostle Paul meant by "ye have been called unto liberty." Six varieties of liberty were described, but the longest exposition was reserved for the last of the six, civil liberty. Here he gave the congregation a succinct summation of the political philosophy of Locke, Milton, and Sidney. One passage in this section of the sermon had particular relevance to the contemporary situation:

Civil liberty also supposeth, that those laws, by which a nation is governed, are made by common consent & choice; that all have some hand in framing them, at least by their representatives, chosen to act for them, if not in their own persons. If a nation is governed according to laws made by a single person, only for his own interest or pleasure, and one whom they do not chuse or appoint to govern them, such nation is in a state of slavery. Nor does it make any material alteration in the case, if the laws by which they are governed, are made by a considerable number of persons instead of one, if they are thus governed, contrary to, or independently of, their own will & consent: . . .[9]

For the essence of slavery consists in being subjected to the arbitrary pleasure of others; whether many, few, or but one, it matters not. . . .

. . . people of the same Nation may be in very different circumstances with respect to civil liberty; some of them enjoying it in as high a degree as can be desired, while others are in a state little or nothing better than that of slavery: As, for example, a Mother-country & her Colonies. While she is free, it is supposeable that her colonies may be kept in a state of real slavery to her. For if they are to possess no property, nor to enjoy the fruits of their own labor, but by the mere precarious pleasure of the Mother, or of a distant legislature, in which they neither are, nor can be represented; this is really slavery, not civil liberty.[10]

Mayhew did not neglect the "use not liberty for an occasion to the flesh" section of his text. They use liberty for an occa-

sion to the flesh, he declared, "who under color of it disregard
the wholesome laws of Society," or "who causelessly &
maliciously speak evil of their rulers," or "who cause factions
or insurrections against the government," or "who rebel
against, or resist their lawful rulers, in the due discharge of
their offices." On the other hand, when a nation is unquestionably abused and mistreated by its rulers, opposition to
such rulers and to "the execution of unrighteous & oppressive
laws" could not properly be placed under the category of
using liberty for an occasion to the flesh.[11]

Somewhere in this exegesis of the gospel according to Saint
John Locke, Mayhew mentioned the Stamp Act by name. He
called it "a great grievance, likely to prove detrimental in a
high degree, both to the Colonies, and to the Mother Country." [12] Some people suspect "that persons in the colonies had
encouraged, and been instrumental of bringing upon us, so
great a burden & grievance, for the sake of present gain; . . .
But this I would charitably hope is not true." According to
Mayhew's account, the sermon ended on a note of caution:
"But let not us, my brethren, use liberty for an occasion to
the flesh, or use any method, for the defence of our rights
& privileges, besides those which are honest & honourable.
Within these restrictions & limitations let us do all in our
power." [13]

Monday evening the mob struck again. After attacking the
homes of two customs officials and burning the records of the
admiralty court, they once more surrounded Hutchinson's
house. This time the mob was not to be turned aside. The
jealousy and hatred of a dozen years were released in a single
night's rioting. By morning the Lieutenant Governor's house,
furnishings, books, papers, and wardrobe were destroyed or
in shambles. This night of violence produced an immediate
reaction among the upper classes of the town, who were
sickened by the fury of the unloosed mob. At the same time

it was apparent that the reaction was not sufficiently strong to permit the leaders to be held in jail, so Bernard dared not take further action.[14]

A few days earlier it had been voiced around town that Mayhew had justified and prayed for the success of the riot of August 14. Governor Bernard, complaining that he had become "a Prisoner at large," had already communicated this tale to his superiors in England.[15] Likewise, the story spread that the sermon in the West Church of August 25 had inspired the destruction of the 26th. On September 5 Henry Caner informed Archbishop Secker of what he had heard: "Dr. Mayhew has distinguished himself in the pulpit upon this Occasion (it is said) in One of the most seditious Sermons ever delivered, advising the people to stand up for their rights to the last drop of their Blood." Another version of the rumor contained the accusation that a leader of the mob had testified during a short stay in jail that the sermon had convinced him he was doing God's service in opposing the Stamp Act with violence. If such was the case, the individual was never identified nor was any affidavit taken. Andrew Eliot, an eyewitness to the destruction of Hutchinson's house, doubted that one of the rioters had ever heard of the sermon. It was true that two members of the Loyal Nine, soon to become the Sons of Liberty, were members of the West Church; but there is no record of who was in attendance at the afternoon service of August 25, and the names of the rioters was the town's best kept secret.[16]

No one exhibited more revulsion from the attack on Hutchinson's property than Mayhew, who appeared shocked and frightened that he should be accused of instigating this villainy. "Of the 14th of August, I choose to say nothing," he told Andrew Eliot; but "the proceedings of the 26th I abhor, from my very soul." On Tuesday he addressed a letter to the Lieutenant Governor in which he expressed his abhorrence of the violence and destruction and denied the charge that he had incited the riot. "I had rather lose my hand, than be an encourager of such outrages," Mayhew wrote. He blamed the rumors on "some of my numerous and causeless enemies." Far from believing or spreading the tale that Hutchinson had been responsible for the Stamp Act, he had often in private conversation attempted "to remove those prejudices" which some people possess on this point. The preacher flatly denied that he knew a single member of the mob or their advisors. On the contrary, he requested the Lieutenant Governor not to divulge the contents of this letter for fear that the rioters might seek "heavy vengeance" upon its writer. Hutchinson replied that he had never doubted Mayhew's friendship and that, having been often misunderstood himself, he could appreciate such a plight. Privately, the Lieutenant Governor seems to have concluded that the sermon had been inflammatory but directed toward the Governor and not himself. In his *History,* written years later, he was noncommittal: "The text alone, without a comment, delivered from the pulpit at that time, might be construed by some of the auditory into an approbation of the prevailing irregularities." He added in a footnote, "The verse which follows, . . . if properly enforced, would have been sufficient to have kept the people within bounds." [17]

At first Mayhew thought of trying to clear himself by publishing his side of the case in the newspapers, but he soon abandoned this move as too perilous. Instead, he preached the following Sunday against "abusing liberty to licentiousness." This sermon gave rise to a suspicion among the radicals that he favored the Stamp Act. Nor did it placate Richard Clarke, a Boston merchant who accepted the story of his pastor's responsibility for the riot and angrily withdrew himself and family from membership in the West Church. In a long letter to Clarke, Mayhew admitted "that it was a very

unfortunate time to preach a sermon, the chief aim of which
was to show the importance of Liberty, when people were
before so generally apprehensive of the danger of losing it."
At such a time the congregation should have been "moderated
and pacified," not excited. "I still love liberty as much as
ever," he added, "but have apprehensions of the greatest in-
conveniences likely to follow on a forceable [and] violent
opposition to an act of parliament." [18]

By the end of September, Mayhew was more certain than
ever that the Stamp Act would never be enforced "without
the effusion of much blood." At the same time he was convinced that "forcible, riotous & illegal proceedings, in opposition to parliamentary Authority" were dangerous and in-
expedient. There is no reason to doubt the sincerity of his
many statements to this effect. His radicalism was doctrinaire.
In spite of numerous generalizations to the contrary by nineteenth-century historians, not one scrap of evidence has been
produced to link him at this time with Samuel Adams, James
Otis, or the Loyal Nine. Benjamin Edes and John Gill, pub-
lishers of the notoriously radical *Boston Gazette*, attended the
West Church, but so did Richard Draper of the conservative
Boston News-Letter. Mayhew was opposed to the Stamp Act,
as was Hutchinson, and both denounced violence as an instrument of forcing Parliament to reconsider the law. Less than
one year before, Mayhew had praised the first two volumes
of Hutchinson's *History* as "very full in the principles of
liberty, civil and religious," except on the one issue of church
and state relations—a judgment in which Hollis concurred.
Mayhew's opposition to the Stamp Act reflected the attitude
of conservative, mercantile Boston, which in its efforts to
force a repeal of the revenue acts had unloosed the lower
classes and now feared the consequences of a rising moboc-
racy.[19]

The "dreaded never to be forgotten" 1st of November

arrived, but the Stamp Act did not go into operation. No one dared to touch the stamps, and Governor Bernard had retained the ship carrying them at the harbor fort for safekeeping. Within a few weeks most of the activities which required stamps were being carried on normally, although the question of whether the courts should accept unstamped documents dragged on endlessly. On December 17 Andrew Oliver was forced to resign again his office as stamp distributor, this time in the presence of an assembly around the Liberty Tree.[20]

Meanwhile in London, Hollis was proving himself a loyal and active friend to the American colonies. It is doubtful if any individual in England, except perhaps Benjamin Franklin, worked so assiduously to secure the repeal of the Stamp Act. On October 12 he received Mayhew's letter of August 19 in which the preacher had described the events of August 14, had given his opinion that the Stamp Act would never be carried into execution except by force, had doubted that the rioters could be held in jail, and had suggested the reprinting of the extract from *Cato's Letters*. Almost at once Hollis ran the extract in the *Saint James Chronicle*. His next step was to seek an appointment with the Marquis of Rockingham, who had just succeeded Grenville as head of the ministry. The interview was granted for October 21, and Hollis recorded the results:

Shewed him the letter received from Dr. Mayhew the twelfth, without acquainting him with the name of the Writer of it, which however, from some circumstances of our conversation, it is probable he guessed at. The Marquis treated me with great civility; read the letter attentively; but did by no means appear to feel the importance of it, nor the very imminent danger there is at this time of losing our Northern Colonies. That being the Case with respect to him; and also, as it should seem, by his talk, with his Brother Ministers; the meeting of Parliament for Business being put off effectively till after Christmass; and, and, and—[21]

Hollis had expected little better from this "poor dumb
creature," so he did not give up the fight. In the next few
weeks he went regularly to the New England Coffee House to
read the American papers, some of which he found "wonderfully spirited and free." Here he discussed the American crisis
with Jasper Mauduit, whom he had avoided up to now, with
Henry Bromfield, a Boston merchant who brought a letter
of recommendation from Mayhew, and with other Americans.
In his efforts to persuade editors to support the movement for
repeal of the Stamp Act, Hollis found that a few guineas
dropped here and there helped to keep the press "steady to
the Cause of Liberty & the Mother Country & Colonies."
He was responsible for the republication in a London newspaper of John Adams' defense of American politics and religion, "A Dissertation on the Canon and Feudal Law," which
had first appeared in the *Boston Gazette*. This was only one
of several significant pieces of American propaganda published through the exertions of Hollis just before and during
the parliamentary session that debated the question whether
to enforce or repeal the Stamp Act.[22]

Ministers of the Rockingham variety drew from Hollis the
comment that contemporary English politics was "Scrub and
all Scrub." Yet there was hope, for it was said that the new
administration sought only the mildest measures. Believing
history to be shaped largely by individual action, Hollis
turned to the only politician in whom he had implicit confidence, that "Chieftain of Liberty," William Pitt. For a number of years he had wooed the great war minister with favors
and gifts, including the standard list of Whig publications.
On January 20, 1766, he requested Pitt to read "A Dissertation
on the Canon and Feudal Law," and on the following day he
noted in his diary, "Received the very note I could have
wished from Mr. Pitt." There was no further elaboration, for
as usual Hollis was exerting his "*little* Energies . . . in good

offices betwixt the Mother Country & her Colonies" in obscurity.[23]

Returning home from the New England Coffee House on February 10, Hollis received assurances from a well-placed friend that the Stamp Act was to be repealed. Overjoyed at the news, he ran to the office of the *Saint James Chronicle* in the hope of getting the report inserted into that evening's edition. When Parliament finally completed action on March 18, he was ready with an advertisement for the *London Chronicle:* "Englishmen, Scottishmen, Irishmen, Colonial Bretheren, Rejoice in the Wisdom, Fortitude of *one* Man, which hath saved you from Civil War & Your Enemies! Erect a Statue to that Man in the Metropolis of your Dominions! Place a garland of Oak leaves on the Pedestal and grave in it Concord." That Parliament had received scores of petitions favoring repeal from British merchants threatened with the loss of their American accounts meant little to Hollis. One man, Pitt alone, had "saved Mother Country & Colonies, and Family upon the Throne." He discounted the efforts of Benjamin Franklin as those of a "Trimmer" who had not come forth in opposition to the Stamp Act until after the ministry was committed to repeal. As a reward to his champion, the Real Whig sent to Pitt's lodgings in Bond Street a hogshead of Lipari wine that had recently come from an Italian correspondent.[24]

It was rumored in London that Archbishop Secker was seeking to have Mayhew brought to England for a parliamentary inquiry into his responsibility for the Boston riots. Hollis reported this alarming news in a letter written in May, but he assured his Boston friend that the repeal had put aside any such plans that might have been on foot. Although Hollis wrote that he had heard this report whispered about more than once, he admitted he was never able to learn how much truth it contained. It was likely a twisted version of one feature of the debate in the House of Commons over repeal of the Stamp Act. A resolution to punish those responsible for the riots had been introduced by the ministry, then quickly withdrawn as being too severe. In any case, Archbishop Secker's policy of placating American Dissenters as a preliminary to securing their acquiescence to an American episcopate would hardly have been expedited by hailing the chief defender of New England Congregationalism to England for trial.[25]

Mayhew's reaction to the Hutchinson riot did not change his attitude toward the Stamp Act. "Great Britain has doubtless power to enforce it," he wrote in January, "but not without the destruction of the Colonies, or what is scarce better." He had no "great expectations" of the Rockingham ministry, although he failed to see how it could be worse than its predecessor. In April reports reached Boston that the Stamp Act had been repealed, and the Sugar Act modified, but not until Friday, May 16, did the official notice arrive. On Monday Boston threw the biggest celebration in its history—twenty-three continuous hours of rejoicing stimulated by joy and the madeira wine donated by John Hancock for the occasion. The same gentlemen and artisans who a few months before had been tearing down the homes of royal officials now marched behind a banner bearing the inscription "Stamp Act repeal'd, Liberty restored, all Trades flourishing, GOD save the King & bless the Parliament." No one worried about the constitutional statement that had accompanied the bill for repeal, the Declaratory Act which affirmed Parliament's right to legislate for the colonies. "All was Loyalty to the King, Blessings on the Parliament of Great Britain, Honour and Gratitude to the Present Ministry." [26]

Few Americans seemed mindful that the failure of the Stamp Act left unsolved, indeed more acute, the imperial problems that had occasioned the Act in the first place. At

the request of his congregation Mayhew prepared a thanksgiving message to be preached on Friday, May 23. Six days
after its delivery this sermon, entitled *The Snare Broken,* was
printed and ready for sale. This was his last published sermon,
and it became one of his most famous. Of several hundred
sermons on the repeal of the Stamp Act, Mayhew's was the
most widely circulated and read. By August a second Boston
edition was off the presses, and a London edition appeared
the same year. In America it was known as far south as Virginia. Accepting Hollis' version of repeal at its face value,
the author dedicated *The Snare Broken* to William Pitt, "who
hath twice at least been a principal Instrument in the hand
of GOD, of saving Great Britain and her Colonies from impend-
ing ruin." As soon as the sermon reached England, Hollis
hastened a copy to the Great Commoner.[27]

Mayhew's text expressed the joy Americans felt in their
hearts: "Our soul is escaped as a bird from the snare of the
fowlers; the snare is broken, and we are escaped. Our help is
in the name of the Lord, who made heaven and earth" (Psalms
cxxiv, 7–8). The colonies, he cried, are "emancipated from a
slavish, inglorious bondage; are re-instated in the enjoyment
of their ancient rights and privileges, and a foundation is laid
for lasting harmony between Great Britain and them, to their
mutual advantage." The Stamp Act had been a violation of
the rights of free men, rights confirmed by Magna Carta, the
colonial charters, and the entire British constitution. The
colonies are poor, and Great Britain enjoys substantial profits
from their commerce, so a denial of colonial liberties would
only discourage trade and act ultimately to the detriment of
the mother country. The minister seemed more aware than
Hollis that Parliament had repealed the act on economic and
not constitutional grounds, for in celebration of repeal he
reminded his hearers and readers that this economic weapon
was still loaded.[28]

In no other sermon does Mayhew reveal his political and
social position in language so unencumbered with the mis-
leading platitudes of eighteenth-century liberal thought.
Twice he praised the role of the merchants in opposing the
Stamp Act, but at the same time he forcefully condemned the
rioters, those "who had the effrontery to cloke their rapacious
violence with the pretext of zeal for liberty" or those who
seized an opportunity to gratify personal resentments or
greedy natures by perpetrating "abominable excesses and
outrages on the persons or property of others." As for the
populace, "Even the poor, and labouring part of the community, whom I am very far from despising, have had so
much to say about government and politics, in the late times
of danger, tumult, and confusion, that many of them seem to
forget, they had anything to *do*. Methinks, it would now be
expedient for *them*, and perhaps for most of us, to do something more, and talk something less." The point was clear: all
classes had done their duty to their country; it was time for
the merchant to return to his profits and the worker to his
labor.[29]

By blaming the Stamp Act on "some evil-minded individuals in Britain" who sought to serve the cause of the Pre-
tender to the Throne and the Court of France by bringing
about a rupture between Great Britain and her colonies,
The Snare Broken removed the burden of guilt from the
Protestant and Hanoverian George III. With unwarranted
optimism, Mayhew observed that King, Ministry, and Parliament seem ready to enlarge rather than to curtail American
liberties. It is time to repay the faith of Pitt and other English
friends of the colonies. "God forbid, my brethren, that any
one of them should ever have the least reason to blush for
his ill placed confidence in us."[30] He displayed his gratitude
by recommending a position on the question of parliamentary
authority over the colonies that, although equivocal, was

almost identical with the views of Pitt, who was much less liberal on this point than most Americans thought:

Let me farther exhort you to pay due respect in all things to the British Parliament; the Lords and Commons being the two branches of the supreme legislature over all his Majesty's dominions. The right of parliament to superintend the general affairs of the colonies, to direct, check or controul them, seems to be supposed in their charters; all which, I think, while they grant the power of legislation, limit the exercise of it to enacting such laws as are *not contrary* to the laws of England, or Great Britain; so that our several legislatures are subordinate to that of the mother-country, which extends to and over all the King's dominions: At least, so far as to prevent any parts of them from doing what would be either destructive to each other, or manifestly to the ruin of Britain. It might be of the most dangerous consequence to the mother-country, to relinquish this supposed authority or right, which, certainly, has all along been recognized by the colonies; or to leave them dependent on the crown *only,* since, probably, within a century, the subjects in them will be more than thrice as numerous as those of Great-Britain and Ireland. And, indeed, if the colonies are properly parts of the British empire, as it is both their interest and honor to be, it seems absurd to deny, that they are subject to the highest authority therein, or not bound to yield obedience to it. I hope there are very few people, if any, in the colonies, who have the least inclination to renounce the general jurisdiction of Parliament over them, whatever we may think of the particular right of taxation.[31]

Mayhew explained that the colonies had learned a lesson for the future. They must be watchful lest their liberties be taken away while they sleep. But the proper way to secure a redress of grievances will be by "joint, manly and spirited, but yet respectful and loyal petitioning." He failed to add what should be done in case such petitions were rejected, but presumably the right of revolution had not been repealed along with the Stamp Act. For the present, it was a time to forget the recent enmity toward Great Britain and those few

who had been suspected of aiding parliamentary interests—
"bury in oblivion what is past." [32]

One passage in *The Snare Broken* so well expresses Mayhew's commitment to liberty that it not only furnishes an
appropriate conclusion to his views on the Stamp Act but a
coda to his entire life:

Having been initiated, in youth, in the doctrines of civil liberty,
as they were taught by such men as Plato, Demosthenes, Cicero
and other renowned persons among the ancients; and such as
Sidney and Milton, Locke and Hoadley, among the moderns; I
liked them; they seemed rational. Having, earlier still learnt from
the holy scriptures, that wise, brave and virtuous men were always
friends to liberty; that God gave the Israelites a King (or absolute
Monarch) in his anger, because they had not sense and virtue
enough to like a free common-wealth, and to have himself for
their King; that the Son of God came down from heaven, to make
us "free indeed"; and that "where the Spirit of the Lord is, there
is liberty"; this made me conclude, that freedom was a great
blessing. Having, also, from my childhood up, by the kind providence of my God, and the tender care of a good parent now at
rest with Him, been educated to the love of liberty, tho' not of
licentiousness; which chaste and virtuous passion was still increased in me, as I advanced towards, and into, manhood; I would
not, I cannot now, tho' past middle age, relinquish the fair object
of my youthful affections, LIBERTY; whose charms, instead of
decaying with time in my eyes, have daily captivated me more
and more. I was, accordingly, penetrated with the most sensible
grief, when, about the *first of November last*, that day of darkness, a day hardly to be numbered with the other days of the year,
SHE seemed about to take her final departure from America, and
to leave that ugly Hag *Slavery*, the deformed child of Satan, in
her room. I am now filled with a proportionable degree of joy in
God, on occasion of HER speedy return, with new smiles on her
face, with augmented beauty and splendor—Once more then,
Hail! celestial Maid, the daughter of God, and, excepting his Son,
the first-born of heaven! Welcome to these shores again; welcome
to every expanding heart! Long mayest thou reside among us, the

delight of the wise, good and brave; the protectress of innocence from wrongs and oppression, the patroness of learning, arts, eloquence, virtue, rational loyalty, religion! And if any miserable people on the continent or isles of Europe, after being weakened by luxury, debauchery, venality, intestine quarrels, or other vices, should in the rude collisions, or now-uncertain revolutions of kingdoms, be driven, in their extremity, to seek a safe retreat from slavery in some far-distant climate; let them find, O let them find one in America under thy brooding, sacred wings; where *our* oppressed fathers once found it, and we now enjoy it, by the favor of Him, whose service is the most glorious freedom! Never, O never may He permit thee to forsake us, for our unworthiness to enjoy thy enlivening presence! By His high permission, attend us thro' life AND DEATH to the regions of the blessed, thy original abode, there to enjoy forever the "glorious liberty of the sons of God!" [33]

Once again Mayhew found himself tampering with the Christian Godhead, this time to make room for the Goddess of Liberty.

CHAPTER XIV

Even unto the Death

It is not safe for the colonies to *sleep*, since they will probably always have some *wakeful* enemies in Britain; & if
they should be such children as to do so, I hope there are
at least some persons too much of men, & friends to them,
to rock the cradle, or sing lullabie to them.

                              Jonathan Mayhew, 1766[1]

JONATHAN MAYHEW was forty-five years of age when
the Stamp Act was repealed. The gray hair beneath his clerical
wig and the knowledge that he was now passing what his
century called "middle age" brought moments of reflection
on the course of his life. At times he found himself "almost
sick of this World" which contains "so little sense & integrity,
so much folly & villainy." But if he was in a reflective mood
on April 26, 1766, he had reason to think of how far he had
traveled since that summer day in 1747 when the Boston
clergy boycotted his ordination. Evidence of his altered status
had arrived in a letter from Samuel Checkly of the New South
Church. Checkly had joined in Mayhew's ostracism, but now
he wrote to invite the West Church and its pastor to attend
the ordination of an associate minister at the New South.
This was Checkly's second letter concerning the ordination.
He had heard that the first letter was not fully understood,
and he was anxious that there should be no misunderstanding.
Mayhew was unaccustomed to such solicitous attention from
the Boston clergy. Of all his colleagues, only Chauncy had
been consistently friendly and sympathetic. Elizabeth Mayhew complained that even those who were not known enemies
to her husband's principles did not "speak in the softest terms"

of him. She understood more than anyone else the mixture of tragedy and irony in his dying at the time when his international reputation was beginning to demand that old clerical antagonists treat him openly at least with respect and civility.[2]

Outside Boston, Mayhew had enjoyed fellowship with far more of the clergy, some of whom wrote to him requesting advice and favors. His struggle against Episcopacy made him especially popular in those communities that had an "Anglican problem" of their own. The Congregational Church in Rutland (later Barre), Massachusetts seems to have been attracted by his prestige when it invited the West Church to send its pastor and one lay messenger to serve on an ecclesiastical council it was calling in June 1766 to hear charges against its minister, Thomas Frink. Massachusetts Congregationalists had avoided ecclesiastical organization and preserved the authority of the local congregation. In cases where a church could not settle its own differences, it had become customary to summon a council of five neighboring churches to give advice on the matter at hand. Such advice was not obligatory, but in practice it was usually accepted as such. The scene of the coming council was nearly sixty miles from Boston, but Mayhew accepted the invitation. He and Captain Andrew Cragie prepared to set out on Monday, June 9.[3]

The Sunday before, Mayhew awakened at dawn. As his mind wandered over the prospects of the week ahead and then to the Stamp Act crisis so recently passed, he saw a connection between these two lines of thought. If we can have a council or "communion of churches," why not also a "communion of Colonies"? The idea struck him so forcibly that he got out of bed and wrote a letter to James Otis. "Would it not be very proper & decorous," he asked, "for our assembly to send circular congratulatory Letters to all the rest without exception, on the repeal, and the present favorable aspect of Things?" These letters could be "conceived at once in terms of warm friendship & regard to them, of Loyalty to the king, of filial affection towards the mother country; and intimating a desire to cement & perpetuate union among ourselves, by all practicable & laudable methods." It is important to maintain and increase the spirit of unity that has brought the repeal of the Stamp Act. Such unity may be the only means of saving American liberties, "for what may be hereafter we cannot tell, how favorable soever the present appearances may be." [4]

There is no evidence that this letter to Otis produced any results.[5] Its importance lies instead in the revelation that less than one month after New England celebrated the repeal of the Stamp Act, Mayhew had recovered from the shock of his first encounter with mob violence and was again on guard against new infringements of American liberties. Written at the very moment the Massachusetts Whigs were taking advantage of the "retreat" of the imperial government to isolate Bernard and Hutchinson in the provincial government, the letter indicates where Mayhew's sympathies lay. Spiritually and intellectually, if not more directly, he was taking his place in the small group of New England men who were resolved not to let the easy victory in the Stamp Act crisis lull the colonies into a sense of security while their enemies in Britain continued to plot. The letter also reveals that recent events had left their mark on him. He cautioned Otis that it was not the time for "asperity in language," but for "firmness in adhering to our rights, in opposition to all encroachments."

The council at Rutland convened on Tuesday, June 10, and for six days heard complaints against the arbitrary conduct of Mr. Frink. Mayhew served as scribe, recording the charges against the pastor and the judgment of the council on each count. On June 18 the visiting clergy and laymen handed down a decision in which they unanimously recommended that Frink's relation with the Rutland church be terminated.

"This advice we give," the record read, "as we trust, in Simplicity and the Fear of God, to whom we Expect to give an Account." The scribe who wrote these lines was to give his account much sooner than he anticipated as he began the trip back to Boston.[6]

Mayhew returned home fatigued and weak. The difficult journey in addition to the arduous proceedings of the council had been too much for his poor health. He tried to ignore the severe headaches he suffered soon after his return, but within four days he was seized with a "violent nervous Disorder" (apparently a stroke or cerebral hemorrhage) that paralyzed his right side and left him in a stupor. During the next two weeks he had only occasional moments of lucidity. By July 3 recovery seemed impossible. The prospect of death was nothing new to one who had enjoyed few periods of health during his entire lifetime. Two years before he had told his congregation, "Merely to die once, is a small matter to those who are to die no more."[7]

Some of the town's clergy could not conceal their curiosity to see how such a notorious heretic would face his Creator. Was it true, as some of the orthodox maintained, that Arminians always repented on their death beds and chose to die Calvinists? Three years earlier, Mayhew had boasted, "I am certain, that in that great day, I shall not be condemned by him for any wilful perversion of his gospel, . . . in this respect at least, I am innocent; clear from the blood of you and all men, whether old or young." A story that cannot be traced to a contemporary source relates that Samuel Cooper asked the minister in his dying hours if he still held fast to the religious tenets he had maintained during his life. The answer was, "My integrity I hold fast, and will not let it go." On July 8 the clergy resigned him "to the Father and Redeemer of Spirits," and the following morning, Wednesday, July 9, he breathed his last between five and six o'clock, exactly three months before his forty-sixth birthday.[8]

On a very hot Friday the people of the West Church and a multitude of Boston citizenry gathered in the late afternoon to pay their last respects. Retaining some of the Puritan abhorrence of elaborate Anglican funerals and Roman Catholic prayers for the dead, Congregationalists customarily held no religious service over the deceased; but on this occasion Charles Chauncy prayed before the corpse was carried from the West Church. The procession to the grave was one of the longest Boston had ever seen. One hundred and fourteen men of the parish walked ahead of the casket, borne by six ministerial pallbearers, who were followed by the family, mourners, and women of the West Church. Then came the clergy and gentlemen of the town in their carriages and coaches, fifty-seven vehicles in all.[9]

The following Sunday the West Church gathered to hear Chauncy eulogize their departed pastor as "a friend to liberty both civil and religious." Although he was Mayhew's closest friend among the local clergy, Chauncy had often been abashed at the forthrightness of his colleague's sermons and polemical writing, a feeling which he did not attempt to hide in this eulogy: "And if his zeal, at any time, betrayed him into too great a severity of expression, it was against the attempts of those who would make slaves either of men's souls or bodies."[10] Professor John Winthrop's obituary notice in the Boston newspapers contained the same apologetic note:

If at any Time thro' the Warmth of his Imagination, his earnestness in the Cause of Religion and Truth, and his fixed aversion to Establishments of Men in the Church of Christ, he may, in some few Instances have been hurried beyond the Bounds of Moderation, his many Virtues, and great Services towards establishing Christianity on the most enlarged Foundation abundantly atone for such Foibles: Indeed the natural Keenness and Poignancy of his Wit, whetted often by cruel and unchristian Usage, *must* paliate his severest Strokes of Satire. Nor will these light Objections depreciate his general Reputation, if it be remembered, that in his most social Hours, he invariably sustained, the united character of the Christian and the Gentleman.[11]

Apologies for Mayhew's fervor were unnecessary. He had died almost immediately after championing his two most popular causes. Tributes in verse and prose came from every direction, often from persons who earlier had recoiled in horror from his theology. Whatever their source, the eulogies revealed a surge of New England pride at the sight of a boy from Martha's Vineyard speaking in a voice that carried all the way to Whitehall.

It was feared by the ultraorthodox that Dr. Mayhew's death at the peak of his popularity would popularize his religious as well as his political principles. Someone pointed out that several ministers who were not avowed Arians had preached funeral discourses extolling his virtues. Andrew Croswell, who had been so shocked at Mayhew's remarks on the Trinity, belatedly admitted that he esteemed him highly for many good qualities, "especially for his singular Integrity and Uprightness, wherein he was a shining Example for his Brethren in the Ministry to follow." Unfortunately, Croswell added, "since his Sickness and Death, the cause of Arianism hath been promoted among us." Mayhew's friends came out of mourning to answer the theological conservatives, but the battle continued at a slower pace without the bold proclamations from the West Church.[12]

Thomas Hollis did not learn of Mayhew's illness until he read of it in the Boston newspapers that reached London in the middle of August. As soon as he read that his friend was near death, he ran a notice in the *London Chronicle* of August 21: "The Rev. Dr. Mayhew now lies at the Point of Death, in a kind of Stupor, and it is thought, can survive, but a few hours. Reader, Persue his Plan, the Good of North America & of Mankind, live like him to great Ends, nor dread, from the excess of it, his Exit." Two weeks later Hollis paid the editor of the same newspaper to publish the complete obituary notice as it had appeared in the Boston newspapers. He had completed six years of spreading throughout England the fame of "JONATHAN MAYHEW D.D. an unswerving, magnanimous Assertor of Truth and Liberty, even unto the Death." [13]

Quirks of fate have a large place in the postscript to Jonathan Mayhew's life. The son of his only surviving child (daughter Elizabeth) entered the Anglican priesthood in 1817 and returned briefly to Boston in 1834 as rector of Trinity Episcopal Church. With all his grandfather's temerity the grandson proclaimed that "there cannot be a church, without a bishop." By the time of his death in 1854, Jonathan Mayhew Wainwright, perhaps America's most distinguished Episcopalian, had become Bishop of New York.[14]

In 1775, only nine years after Mayhew's death, the handsome steeple of the West Church was demolished by British soldiers, who suspected that it was being used to send signals to patriot forces stationed across the Charles River in Cambridge. Just after a copy of *The Snare Broken,* displaying its dedication to William Pitt, reached that Great Commoner, he accepted the title of Lord Chatham and fell temporarily from virtue in the eye of Hollis and his Real Whig circle. When the Revolution came, some of the close friends Mayhew left behind followed the course of loyalty to the mother country.[15]

No member of the congregation was more profoundly affected by Mayhew's death than Harrison Gray, the province treasurer. A charter member of the West Church, Gray had looked to his minister as a confidant and almost infallible mentor in politics and religion. When he became a widower later the same year, Gray was attracted to the still young and beautiful widow of his late pastor. Elizabeth Mayhew preferred a second husband nearer her own age and eventually married Jonathan's successor in the West Church pulpit, Simeon Howard. Disappointed and sensitive to his rejection, Harrison Gray and his children left the congregation in which he had been a major figure for thirty years.[16]

At the time of the Stamp Act, Gray had gone on record as being a Whig. After 1766 he drifted into the Tory camp, although his brother and only daughter had married into the Otis family. He never became an ardent Loyalist, but neither could he support armed opposition to Great Britain. When the hour of decision came, he chose the British side as the lesser of two evils and fled Boston at the time the royal troops evacuated the town in 1776. From London in 1783, Gray sent Elizabeth Mayhew, the daughter of his former pastor, a portrait of her father. For himself, he wrote, he was retaining a small picture, "which no consideration would tempt him to part with, as it serves to refresh his Memory with the Majesty and Dignity of the Doctor's Countenance." After a Revolution that had deprived him of homeland and property, Harrison Gray still cherished those nineteen years during which he sat under the ministry of Jonathan Mayhew.[17]

For the most part, Mayhew's West Boston moved on to the Revolution and to the American Unitarian movement. In Simeon Howard, Elizabeth Mayhew found another devoted husband and Jonathan Mayhew a successor with the same religious and political outlook. Howard guided the West Church through the difficult days of the Revolution and passed it on to the distinguished ministers who maintained its liberal traditions throughout the next century. As Massachusetts was debating the ratification of its new republican constitution in 1780, Howard was invited to preach the annual election sermon. His discourse was so full of the principles his predecessor had espoused that with a little imagination— and a dash of spirit added to the prose—one can picture a hoary Mayhew delivering the same sermon.[18]

Thomas Hollis dropped dead on January 1, 1774. The detailed instructions for burial contained in his will were followed. He was lowered into a grave dug ten feet deep in a meadow on his country estate in Dorset. As soon as the earth had been replaced, the field was plowed so that no trace of the site remained. By coincidence, the location of Mayhew's grave is also unknown today. Like Hollis, his monument is not in stone but in free institutions that reflect the ideas for which he contended.[19]

EPILOGUE

In his pulpit Mayhew expounded ideas gleaned from the Bible, the classics of Greece and Rome, the seventeenth-century Puritans and Whigs, the Anglican Latitudinarians, and the many voices of the Enlightenment. His problem had been to develop a religious pattern combining Puritan tradition, science and rationalism, and the enterprising, independent spirit of his townsmen. If religion was to retain its hold on the West Church sea captains, merchants, and shopkeepers, it must above all be pragmatic; it must work in an increasingly affluent and secular Boston. With this rationale built into his daily environment, he saw no problem in mixing the Reformation with the Enlightenment, revelation with rationalism, and individualism with deference to one's betters.

One who analyzes this mass of heterogeneous ideas today is likely to agree with the colonial Samuel Johnson that the Boston minister was a "loose" thinker. But Dr. Johnson did not make the mistake of concluding that Mayhew's importance in eighteenth-century New England could be understood from the study of his mind alone—nor did anyone else who had felt the power of his polemics.[1] In the present century, his works have been so readily available and so little has been known concerning his career and personality that it has been easy to overlook the spirit of the man that gave his ideas a vigor far beyond their logical merits. With the fervor of the original Puritan, with the enthusiasm of the New Light of the Great Awakening—he was in background and experience a little of each—Mayhew proclaimed the good news that Americans had been "called unto liberty." So intensely did he preach that his sermons evoked every extreme of anger and acclaim; and such reactions in turn spread his fame and ideas even farther. Without that overdose of zeal which regularly enraged his opponents and sometimes embarrassed his friends, Jonathan Mayhew would have had little influence on his generation. Almost without exception, the tributes paid to him in the quarter-century after his death by those who had first-hand knowledge of his work were full of words denoting vigorous action and unlimited courage. They make it clear that he was not just another scholarly New England minister, but a pulpit champion who had "preached what others only dared to think." [2]

Mayhew directed his fervor into important causes. From the West Church he launched a frontal attack on Puritan theology that helped to gain a foothold for Arminianism in eastern Massachusetts. As Conrad Wright has pointed out, the growth of Arminian theology in this area was by no means inevitable, for moderate Calvinism might have satisfied those persons with liberal religious tendencies here as it did in other sections of New England.[3] The leadership of Mayhew and the less belligerent Charles Chauncy of the First Church was largely responsible for the development of Arminianism from a soul-damning heresy to the religion of many well-educated and influential persons in Boston and nearby towns. As a way station between the Puritanism of John Cotton and the Unitarianism of William Ellery Channing, Arminian theology occupies a significant place in the history of American religious thought. Historians of Unitarianism have been right in hailing Mayhew as a pioneer of their movement, though they have been wrong in confusing his theology with their own.

Connecting Mayhew historically with nineteenth-century

Unitarianism, nevertheless, hides a major reason for his effectiveness in disseminating ideas. Most of the New Englanders to whom he spoke remained conservative Christians; very few would embrace his theology or follow his spiritual descendants into Unitarianism. It was precisely because his liberalism was grounded on much of the traditional faith, notably the authority of revelation, that he was so easily understood. He preached his message of human freedom with the assurance that it was taken directly from the Holy Scriptures with no more than occasional footnotes from uninspired writers. The new concepts of the Enlightenment were filtered through a Biblical mesh. He preached the Real Whig political philosophy as if it came from Jesus Christ and Saint Paul rather than Sidney and Locke. Even those who abominated his theology understood the divine sanction behind his call to liberty. It is not surprising that European Deism failed to find fertile soil in a society whose most famous religious liberal threatened his congregation with hellfire if they refused to follow his rationalistic precepts. Nor would this society a generation later encounter any difficulty in covering such a dubious Christian as George Washington with a blanket of evangelical religion. By helping to weld libertarian ideas to Christian tradition in America, Jonathan Mayhew made his spiritual zeal felt far beyond the limited geographical area in which his theology found acceptance. The study of his life makes it easier to understand how a nation of orthodox Christians, led by such near-Deists as Benjamin Franklin, John Adams, and Thomas Jefferson, could undertake a revolution justified by the theory that all men "are endowed by their Creator with certain unalienable rights."

These sacred and "unalienable rights" were the heart of the Real Whig ideology that reverberated from the large sounding board surmounting the West Church pulpit. They were an importation from England, where throughout the eighteenth century a small coterie of stubborn men held fast to the political principles of the seventeenth-century republicans. Thomas Hollis and the other Real Whigs realized scant success at home and had to be satisfied with the preservation of their heritage for nineteenth-century England. But in the American colonies, where their ideas received the environmental and spiritual support they lacked in the mother country, the Real Whigs found genuine fulfillment: the American Revolution was the completion of the unfinished business of the Puritan and Glorious Revolutions. Mayhew's contribution was to take the lead, although it was by no means a solitary effort, in giving a new spiritual vigor to this ideology that made it seem relevant to the colonial scene even at the beginning of the final Anglo-French war for possession of North America.

Historians are accustomed to think of the American Revolution as the aftermath of the Great War for Empire, for the glorious peace of 1763 brought with it new American problems that made a reorganization of the Empire appear necessary in British eyes. The sermons preached in New England from 1754 to 1760 suggest that the Revolution was also an intellectual and emotional aftermath of the war. With their sensitivity to arbitrary government increased from six years of preaching a holy war against French tyranny and Romish superstition, Mayhew and his Congregational colleagues turned to face the English Parliament and the Anglican Church. In this state of mind the constitutional principles that Hollis reiterated in his letters to Boston seemed applicable to a petty quarrel growing out of the false tale that Governor Bernard had accepted a two-dollar bribe from an Indian.

Now, too, Archbishop Secker's natural desire to send a bishop to the colonies and to advance the interests of his Church in Canada became one phase of a plot to enslave Americans. When all due allowance has been made for the

justice of the proposed colonial episcopate and the refusal
of the ministry to force its erection, it remains evident that
the fear of seeing a bishop's carriage drawn through the streets
of Boston, Newport, or New Haven hardened the attitude of
the Congregational clergy toward the mother country and
forced them to enlarge their own theories of religious freedom. In Mayhew's mind there could be no separation of civil
and religious liberty, nor could there be any concessions to
the enemies of either. As one turns the pages of the newspapers published in the northern colonies from 1760 to 1764,
it becomes obvious that Mayhew's inflexible attitude was
widely shared by his countrymen. The episcopate controversy was not responsible for this fear of compromise. Such
a spirit was in part a vestige of the Puritan unwillingness to
condone any form of sin. It arose also from an almost sub-
conscious awareness that colonial liberties, in practice more
extensive than anywhere in Europe, must be defended against
those who might seek to square practice with the still conservative social and political theory. But the episcopate question, reaching a new peak in Mayhew's attack on Anglican
"aggression" in 1763 and 1764, did provide a reaffirmation of
the no-compromise resolve at the very moment the revenue
acts were being proposed and enacted.

Could Mayhew, the Harvard graduate, the rationalist, the
intellectual offspring of the Enlightenment, really think that
George Grenville's mild Stamp Act fastened a slave's chains
on the colonies? His entire life had been preparation for an
affirmative answer to this question. There are no degrees of
slavery. Freedom, like a woman's virtue, is lost by the first
misstep. A Christian sins when he fails to resist any attempt
at the seduction of God-given liberties by actual or potential
tyrants.

George Bancroft so stressed the unfolding of divine providence in his nineteenth-century *History of the United States*

that modern scholars have usually discounted his references to religion. Yet, few historians have better understood the religious emotionalism with which the rank and file of Americans carried out the decision that George III, "whose character is . . . marked by every act which may define a Tyrant, is unfit to be the ruler of a free People." In one memorable passage Bancroft summarized the transfer of religious fervor into political channels:

Standing in manifold relations with the governments, the culture, and the experience of the past, the Americans seized as their peculiar inheritance the traditions of liberty. . . . The idea of freedom had always revealed itself at least to a few of the wise whose prophetic instincts were quickened by love of their kind, and its growth can be traced in the tendency of the ages. In America, it was the breath of life to the people. For the first time it found a region and a race where it could be professed with the earnestness of an indwelling conviction, and be defended with the enthusiasm that had marked no wars but those for religion. When all Europe slumbered over questions of liberty, a band of exiles, keeping watch by night, heard the glad tidings which promised the political regeneration of the world. A revolution, unexpected in the moment of its coming, but prepared by glorious forerunners, grew naturally and necessarily out of the series of past events by the formative principle of a living belief. And why should man organize resistance to the grand design of Providence?[4]

Mayhew was the boldest, most articulate, and most influential of those New England clergymen who helped to transform a set of political ideas into "an indwelling conviction" and "a living belief." This political faith he defended with "the enthusiasm that had marked no wars but those for religion." His untimely death a decade before the American Revolution reminds us that the second paragraph of the Declaration of Independence was a creedal statement of the religion of freedom propagated by Mayhew and others in the preceding generation. A conservative faith which taught that revolution against tyrants was a legitimate (almost constitutional) process as well as a religious obligation, it was true to the developing ethos of American civilization. As a result, it could transcend most sectarian differences. From 1765 to 1776, the majority of Americans awoke to the fact that they, catechized by their free institutions and rising economy, had long since become converts.

To nonbelievers, Jonathan Mayhew remained the first commander of the "black Regiment" of Congregational preachers who incessantly sounded "the Yell of Rebellion in the Ears of an ignorant & deluded People." [5]

A BIBLIOGRAPHICAL NOTE

BIBLIOGRAPHY OF JONATHAN MAYHEW

NOTES　•　INDEX

A BIBLIOGRAPHICAL NOTE

I HOPE that the notes in this volume will answer most of the questions scholars may have concerning the sources for a study of Jonathan Mayhew. A few additional comments may be helpful. Much of Mayhew's correspondence has been lost or destroyed. He either did not make or failed to preserve draft copies of most letters he wrote. He seems to have given little thought to the preservation of his personal papers; what remains is the result of chance. After carrying out the instructions of Thomas Hollis to destroy his letters to her husband, Mayhew's widow rescued a small file of manuscripts. These apparently remained in private hands until they were acquired in 1950 by Boston University. Regrettably, this collection of 139 items contains more letters to Mayhew than by him, but as a whole it constitutes the most important single collection for the study of his life.

These papers were available to Alden Bradford when he wrote his *Memoir of the Life and Writings of Rev. Jonathan Mayhew, D.D.* (Boston, 1838). In addition, the *Memoir* made use of Mayhew's printed sermons and the recollections of Mayhew's surviving friends. Bradford did not use his sources fully or critically. He sought to present Mayhew as an American patriot and a pioneer of the Unitarian movement. The *Memoir* consists largely of quoted materials connected by the author's personal observations. Its value as a source book is somewhat lessened by Bradford's insistence on rewriting the long extracts he quoted from Mayhew's manuscripts and printed sermons.

Fortunately, Thomas Hollis preserved the letters he received from Mayhew along with copies of his letters to Mayhew. This collection is now at the Massachusetts Historical Society and has been printed in the Society's *Proceedings*, LXIX (1956), 102–193. The manuscript diary of Thomas Hollis, 1759–1770, is an invaluable supplement to the Hollis Papers. Privately owned in England, the diary is available in this country through a microfilm copy in the possession of the Institute of Early American History and Culture.

The Henry E. Huntington Library has eight of Mayhew's manuscript sermons, preached from 1749 to 1764. These amplify the contents of his printed sermons and show that he preached much the same message in and out of print. Another small collection of manuscript sermons, formerly in the possession of the Wainwright family of Rye, New York, has apparently been lost in recent years. There are only a very few other known Mayhew manuscripts, and these are widely scattered in American and English institutions.

Anyone with more than a casual interest in Mayhew should go directly to the Boston newspapers published during his ministry at the West Church—the *Evening Post, Gazette, News-Letter,* and *Post-Boy*. The space he received in their pages is the best (and most neglected) evidence of the impact he made on his society. No published account of Mayhew made full use of the newspapers until the appearance of Clifford K. Shipton's sprightly sketch in volume XI of *Harvard Graduates*.

Harrison Gray wrote a short but interesting "Memoir" of Mayhew and presented it to the widow in November 1766. Mrs. Mayhew sent it to Hollis, who replied that it "should not be used I think, at this time; but it shall lie by me carefully preserved"—and so it was. The original, now in Dr. Williams's Library, London, has been published (Louis Leonard Tucker, ed., "Memoir of Dr. Jonathan Mayhew, by Harrison Gray," *Proceedings of the Bostonian Society*, Jan. 17, 1961, pp. 26–48). A manuscript copy is in MP, no. 137.

Readers interested in further study of Mayhew's world are fortunate in having available a number of significant works published in recent years. My interest in Mayhew was aroused by Max Savelle's thorough study of American thought from 1740 to 1760, *Seeds of Liberty: The Genesis of the American Mind* (New York, 1948). Clinton Rossiter, in *Seedtime of the Republic* (New York, 1953), traces the rise in the colonies of the political ideas of the American Revolution. *The Stamp Act Crisis* (Chapel Hill, N.C., 1953), by Edmund S. and Helen M. Morgan, demonstrated that Americans were far more united in principle in 1765 than appeared to be the case from the writings of earlier historians. No recent study in historical theology was so needed as Conrad Wright's *The Beginnings of Unitarianism in America* (Boston, 1955), which is the first adequate presentation of the theological position of eighteenth-century New England Arminians. Every student of the ideological background of the American Revolution is indebted to Caroline Robbins for the prodigious research summarized in *The Eighteenth-Century Commonwealthman* (Cambridge, Mass., 1959). The subtitle is self-explanatory: *Studies in the Transmission, Development and Circumstance of English*

Liberal Thought from the Restoration of Charles II until the War with the Thirteen Colonies. Gerald R. Cragg, *Reason and Authority in the Eighteenth Century* (Cambridge, 1964), is the best general introduction to the political and religious thought of the English Enlightenment that provided the climate of ideas in which Mayhew and other eighteenth-century colonial intellectuals worked.

Students of the episcopate question will want to read both Arthur Lyon Cross, *The Anglican Episcopate and the American Colonies* (New York, 1902) and Carl Bridenbaugh, *Mitre and Sceptre: Transatlantic Faiths, Ideas, Personalities, and Politics, 1689–1775* (New York, 1962). Bridenbaugh's book should make it impossible for future historians to neglect "the important historical truth that religion was a fundamental cause of the American Revolution." For an answer to his contention that the Church of England was partially responsible for the loss of the colonies, see Thomas P. Govan, "The Historian as Partisan, Prosecutor, and Judge," *Historical Magazine of the Protestant Episcopal Church,* XXXII (March 1963), 49–56. Alice M. Baldwin, *The New England Clergy and the American Revolution* (Durham, S.C., 1928; reprinted New York, 1958) is outdated in spots but still essential.

Two of Mayhew's important clerical friends have been the subjects of recent biographical studies. In *The Gentle Puritan, A Life of Ezra Stiles, 1727–1795* (New Haven, 1962), Edmund S. Morgan shows that Stiles was subjected in his youth to much the same intellectual currents as Mayhew, but after a period of skepticism found his way back to Puritan orthodoxy. Clifford K. Shipton's masterful sketch of Samuel Cooper in volume XI of *Harvard Graduates* (reprinted in Shipton's *New England Life in the 18th Century* [Cambridge, Mass., 1963]) suggests that Cooper's role in the Revolution was hardly less important than that of Samuel Adams. An interest in religion and the American Revolution must inevitably lead one to Perry Miller's important essay, "From the Covenant to the Revival," in *The Shaping of American Religion,* volume I of *Religion in American Life,* James Ward Smith and H. Leland Jamison, eds. (Princeton, 1961), pp. 322–368.

BIBLIOGRAPHY OF
JONATHAN MAYHEW

With Short Titles Used in the Notes

Christian Sobriety   *Christian Sobriety: Being Eight Sermons on Titus II.6. Preached with a Special View to the Benefit of the Young Men usually attending the public worship at the West Church in Boston. Published more particularly at their Desire, and dedicated to them.* Boston, 1763.
——— Dublin, 1767 and London, 1767 with title *Sermons to Young Men*, 2 vols.
Death of Frederick   *A Sermon Preached at Boston in New-England, May 26. 1751. Occasioned by The much-lamented Death of His Royal Highness Frederick, Prince of Wales.* Boston, 1751.
Death of George II   *A Discourse Occasioned by the Death of King George II. And the Happy Accession of His Majesty King George III. to the Imperial Throne of Great-Britain; Delivered Jan. 4th 1761. And Published at the Desire of the West Church and Congregation in Boston, New-England.* Boston, 1761.
Death of Stephen Sewall   *A Discourse Occasioned by the Death of The Honourable Stephen Sewall, Esq; Chief-Justice of the Superiour Court of Judicature, Court of Assize, and General-Goal-Delivery; as also A Member of His Majesty's Council for the Province of the Massachusetts-Bay in New England: Who departed this Life on Wednesday-Night, September 10. 1760. Aetatis 58. Delivered the Lord's-Day after his Decease.* Boston, 1760.
Defence   *A Defence of the Observations on the Charter and Conduct of the Society for the Propagation of the Gospel in Foreign Parts, against an anonymous Pamphlet falsly intitled, A Candid Examination of Dr. Mayhew's Observations, &c. and also against the Letter to a Friend annexed thereto, said to contain a short Vindication of said Society. By one of its Members.* Boston, 1763.
——— London, 1764.
Discourse Occasioned by the Earthquakes   *A Discourse on*

Rev. XV. 3ᵈ, 4ᵗʰ. Occasioned by the Earthquakes in November 1755. Delivered in the West-Meeting-House, Boston, Thursday December 18, following. In five Parts, with an Introduction. Part I. Of the Greatness of God's Works. Part II. Of their marvellous and unsearchable Nature. Part III. Of the moral Perfection and Government of God. Part IV. Of our Obligation to fear, glorify and worship Him. Part V. Practical Reflections upon the Subject, relative to the Occasion. Boston, 1755.

Divine Goodness   *Two Sermons on the Nature, Extent and Perfection of the Divine Goodness. Delivered December 9. 1762. Being the Annual Thanksgiving of the Province, &c. On Psalm 145. 9. Published with some Enlargements.* Boston, 1763.

Election Sermon   *A Sermon Preach'd in the Audience of His Excellency William Shirley, Esq; Captain General, Governour and Commander in Chief, The Honourable His Majesty's Council, and the Honourable House of Representatives, of the Province of the Massachusetts-Bay, in New-England. May 29th 1754. Being the Anniversary for the Election of His Majesty's Council for the Province. N.B. The Parts of some Paragraphs, passed over in the Preaching of this Discourse, are now inserted in the Publication.* Boston, 1754.

—————— London, 1755.

Expected Dissolution   *The Expected Dissolution of all Things, a motive to universal holiness. Two Sermons Preached in Boston, N.E. on the Lords-Day, Nov. 23, 1755; Occasioned by the Earthquakes Which happen'd on the Tuesday Morning, and Saturday Evening preceeding.* Boston, 1755.

God's Hand and Providence   *God's Hand and Providence to be religiously acknowledged in public Calamities. A Sermon Occasioned by The Great Fire in Boston, New-England, Thursday March 20. 1760. And preached on the Lord's-Day following.* Boston, 1760.

Letter of Reproof   *A Letter of Reproof to Mr. John Cleaveland of Ipswich, occasioned by A defamatory Libel Published under his Name, intitled, An Essay to defend some of the most important Principles of the reformed System of Christianity, &c.— against the injurious Aspersions cast on the same by Jonathan Mayhew, D.D. in his late Thanksgiving Sermons on Psalms CXLV, 9. In which, &c.* Boston, 1764.

Observations   *Observations on the Charter and Conduct of the Society For the Propagation of the Gospel in Foreign Parts; designed to shew Their Non-conformity to each other. With Remarks on the Mistakes of East Apthorp, M.A. Missionary at Cambridge, in Quoting, and Representing the Sense of said Charter, &c. As also Various incidental Reflections relative to the Church* of England, and the State of Religion in North-America, particularly in New-England. Boston, 1763.

———— London, 1764.

On hearing the Word Sermons Upon the following Subjects, Viz. On hearing the Word: On receiving it with Meekness: On renouncing gross Immoralities: On the necessity of obeying the Gospel: On being found in Christ: On Justification by Faith: On the nature, principles and extent of Evangelical Obedience. On the deceitfulness of the Heart, and God's knowledge thereof. On the shortness and vanity of Human Life: And On the true value, use and end of Life; together with the conduciveness of Religion to prolong, and make it happy. Boston, 1755.

———— London, 1756.

Popish Idolatry Popish Idolatry: A Discourse Delivered in the Chapel of Harvard-College in Cambridge, New-England, May 8. 1765. At the Lecture founded by the Honorable Paul Dudley, Esquire. Boston, 1765.

Practical Discourses Practical Discourses Delivered on Occasion of the Earthquakes in November, 1755. Wherein is particularly shown, by a Variety of Arguments, The great Importance of turning our Feet unto God's Testimonies, and of making Haste to keep his Commandments; Together with the Reasonableness, the Necessity, and great Advantage, of a serious Consideration of our Ways. Boston, 1760.

Remarks Remarks on an Anonymous Tract, Entitled An Answer to Dr. Mayhew's Observations on the Charter and Conduct of the Society for the Propagation of the Gospel in Foreign Parts. Being a Second Defence of the said Observations. Boston, 1764.

———— London, 1765.

Seven Sermons Seven Sermons upon the Following Subjects; viz. The Difference betwixt Truth and Falshood, Right and Wrong. The natural Abilities of Men for discerning these Differences. The Right and Duty of private Judgment. Objections considered. The Love of God. The Love of our Neighbour. The first and great Commandment, &c. Preached At a Lecture in the West Meeting-House in Boston, Begun the first Thursday in June, and ended the last Thursday in August, 1748. Boston, 1749.

———— London, 1750.

Snare Broken The Snare broken. A Thanksgiving-Discourse Preached at the Desire of the West Church in Boston, N.E. Friday May 23, 1766. Occasioned by the Repeal of the Stamp Act. Boston, 1766; second edition, Boston, 1766.

———— London, [1766].

Striving to enter Striving to enter in at the strait Gate

explain'd and inculcated; And the Connexion of Salvation therewith, Proved From The Holy Scriptures. In Two Sermons On Luke XIII. 24. Boston, 1761.

Two Discourses November 23d. 1758   Two Discourses Delivered November 23d. 1758. Being the Day appointed by Authority to be Observed as a Day of public Thanksgiving: Relating, more Especially, to the Success of His Majesty's Arms, And those of the King of Prussia, the last Year. Boston, [1758].

Two Discourses October 25th. 1759.   Two Discourses Delivered October 25th. 1759. Being the Day appointed by Authority to be observed as A Day of public Thanksgiving, for the Success of His Majesty's Arms, More particularly in the Reduction of Quebec, the Capital of Canada. With an Appendix, Containing a brief Account of two former Expeditions against that City and Country, which proved unsuccessful. Boston, 1759.

——— London, 1760.

Two Discourses October 9th, 1760   Two Discourses Delivered October 9th, 1760. Being the Day appointed to be observed As a Day of public Thanksgiving For the Success of His Majesty's Arms, more especially In the intire Reduction of Canada. Boston, 1760.

——— London, 1760.

Unlimited Submission   A Discourse Concerning Unlimited Submission and Non-Resistance to the Higher Powers: With some Reflections on the Resistance made to King Charles I. And on the Anniversary of his Death: In which the Mysterious Doctrine of that Prince's Saintship and Martyrdom is Unriddled: The Substance of which was delivered in a Sermon preached in the West Meeting-House in Boston the Lord's-Day after the 30th of January, 1749–50. Published at the Request of the Hearers. Boston, 1750; second edition, Boston, 1750.

——— Newry, 1775, with title *A Mysterious Doctrine Unriddled, or Unlimited Submission.* . . .

——— in Richard Baron, ed., *The Pillars of Priestcraft and Orthodoxy Shaken* (London, 1752 and 1767).

——— Boston, 1818.

——— in J. W. Thornton, ed., *The Pulpit of the American Revolution* (Boston, 1860).

——— Boston, 1867.

——— Boston, 1876.

ABBREVIATIONS

Acts and Resolves	*Acts and Resolves of the Province of the Massachusetts Bay* (21 vols., Boston, 1869–1922).
Adams Papers	L. H. Butterfield, ed., *Diary and Autobiography of John Adams* (4 vols., Cambridge, Mass., 1961).
Adams Works	Charles Francis Adams, ed., *The Works of John Adams* (10 vols., Boston, 1850–1856).
CSM Pubs.	*Publications of the Colonial Society of Massachusetts.*
EM	Experience Mayhew.
FP Transcripts	Fulham Palace Transcripts, Library of Congress.
Harvard Graduates	Clifford K. Shipton, *Sibley's Harvard Graduates* (12 vols., Boston, 1873–1962).
Hollis Diary	Diary of Thomas Hollis, 1759–1770, microfilm copy, The Institute of Early American History and Culture, Williamsburg, Virginia.
HP	Thomas Hollis Papers, 1759–1771, Massachusetts Historical Society.
Huntington Sermons	Manuscript sermons of Jonathan Mayhew, Henry E. Huntington Library and Art Gallery.
Hutchinson, *History*	Thomas Hutchinson, *The History of the Colony and Province of Massachusetts-Bay*, Lawrence Shaw Mayo, ed. (3 vols., Cambridge, Mass., 1936).
JM	Jonathan Mayhew.
LC	Library of Congress.
LC Transcripts	Library of Congress Transcripts.
Mass. House Journals	*Journals of the House of Representatives of Massachusetts* (31 vols., Boston, 1919–1956).
Mather Letters	Letters of Rev. Samuel Mather to his Son, 1759–1785, Massachusetts Historical Society.
MHS	Massachusetts Historical Society.
MHS Colls.	*Collections of the Massachusetts Historical Society.*
MHS Procs.	*Proceedings of the Massachusetts Historical Society.*
MP	Jonathan Mayhew Papers, Boston University.
NEHG Reg.	*The New England Historical and Genealogical Register.*
Overseers' Records	Harvard College Overseers' Records, Harvard University Archives.
Perry, *Papers*	William Stevens Perry, ed., *Papers Relating to the History of the Church in Massachusetts, AD 1676–1785* (n.p., 1873).
Stiles Papers	Ezra Stiles Papers, Yale University.
TH	Thomas Hollis.

NOTES

PROLOGUE

1. [Joseph Green] *An Eclogue Sacred to the Memory of the Rev. Dr. Jonathan Mayhew* (Boston, 1766), p. 8.

2. *MHS Colls.*, LXXIV (1918), xxiv. See the many references to JM in *Adams Papers* and *Adams Works*. For the comparison of JM with Webster, see the Channing Hall lecture by Andrew P. Peabody in *Unitarianism: Its Origin and History* (Boston, 1890), p. 162.

3. *Adams Works*, X, 287–288.

4. E.g., Charles Chauncy to Ezra Stiles, May 6, 1768, Stiles Papers.

CHAPTER I. MARTHA'S VINEYARD

1. *Practical Discourses*, p. 61.

2. See the letters of Thomas Mayhew in *MHS Colls.*, XXXVII (1865), 30–33. Nearly all the sources for the early history of Martha's Vineyard have been conveniently assembled at the MHS in Documents Relating to Marthas Vineyard, 1600–1899; 18 volumes with an Index; Transcripts made by Charles E. Banks. These transcripts were used by Banks in writing *The History of Martha's Vineyard* (vols. I, II, Boston, 1911; vol. III, Edgartown, Mass., 1925), one of the most complete and accurate local histories ever written. On details of Vineyard history, I generally follow Banks's Documents and *History*, with additional documentation as noted. A few documents have come to light since Banks did his work. These have been used in Warner F. Gookin, *Capawack alias Martha's Vineyard* (Edgartown, Mass., 1947).

3. Ida M. Wightman, *The Mayhew Manor of Tisbury* (Baltimore, 1921), is helpful in understanding feudal problems on the Vineyard.

4. *A History of the Expansion of Christianity*, III (New York, 1939), 218.

5. Thomas Mayhew, Jr., to John Winthrop, Aug. 15, 1648, MP. EM and Thomas Prince, *Indian Converts* (Boston, 1727), *passim*.

Henry Whitfield, *Strength out of Weakness* (London, 1652), p. 31. John Eliot and Thomas Mayhew, Jr., *Tears of Repentence* (London, 1653), *passim*. John Eliot and Thomas Mayhew, Jr., *The Glorious Progress of the Gospel Amongst the Indians in New England* (London, 1649), *passim*.

6. Henry Whitfield, *The Light Appearing* (London, 1651), p. 2. Thomas Mayhew to John Winthrop, Jr., *MHS Colls.*, XXXVII (1865), 34–35. *An Act For the promoting and propagating the Gospel of Jesus Christ in New England* (London, 1649), *passim*. See the following by George Parker Winship: "Samuel Sewall and the New England Company," *MHS Procs.*, LXVII (1945), 55–110; *The New England Company of 1649 and John Eliot* (Boston, 1920), *passim*. Frederick L. Weis, "The New England Company of 1649 and its Missionary Enterprises," *CSM Pubs.*, XXXVIII (1959), 134–218. William Kellaway, *The New England Company, 1649–1776* (Glasgow, 1961), *passim*.

7. *Indian Converts*, pp. 291, 298–300. Letters of Thomas Mayhew to John Winthrop, Jr., *MHS Colls.*, XXXVII (1865), 34–37. Thomas Balch, *A Sermon Preach'd . . . July 29th, 1747* (Boston, 1747), p. 3.

8. *Indian Converts*, pp. 293–295. MS Agreement between Thomas Mayhew and five Indians, March 15, 1669/70 (Huntington Library).

9. *Indian Converts*, pp. 301–306. "Diary of Rev. William Homes," *NEHG Reg.*, XLVIII (1894), 447.

10. EM to Paul Dudley, March 20, 1722, *NEHG Reg.*, XXXIX (1885), 13–14. Cotton Mather, *Magnalia Christi Americana* (London, 1702), bk. VII, p. 110. John Eliot, *A Biographical Dictionary* (Boston, 1809), p. 319.

11. *A Discourse Shewing that God Dealeth with Men as with Reasonable Creatures* (Boston, 1720).

12. "The Diary of Samuel Sewall," *MHS Colls.*, XLV (1878), 502; XLVI (1879), *passim*; XLVII (1882), 266. "Letter-Book of Samuel Sewall," *MHS Colls.*, LI (1886), 231–233. Cotton Mather to William Ashurst, Oct. 10, 1712 (Huntington Library). *Some Correspondence Between The Governors and Treasurers of the New England Company in London and the Commissioners of the United Colonies in America* (London, 1896), pp. 97–127. *Acts and Resolves*, IX, 494, 631. *Harvard Graduates*, VII, 635.

13. EM to Cotton Mather, Aug. 28, 1723, MHS Miscellaneous Papers, IX, 1721–1729. Thomas Mayhew, Jr., to John Winthrop, Aug. 15, 1648, MP.

14. See EM's account with the Society in *MHS Procs.*, LXVII (1945), 94–95. The trips can often be traced in Sewall's "Diary," *MHS Colls.*, XLV–XLVII. See also *Acts and Resolves*, X, 532;

EM to Thomas Foxcroft, May 18, 1742, Foxcroft MSS (Princeton University Library).

15. "Diary of Rev. William Homes," *NEHG Reg.*, L (1896), 156–157.

16. EM, *A Discourse Shewing that God Dealeth with Men as with Reasonable Creatures*, pp. 24–27, *passim.*

17. "The Diary of Samuel Sewall," *MHS Colls.*, XLVII (1882), 345. *Acts and Resolves*, X, 523.

18. Quenames is spelled variously as Quinames or Quanaimes. The deed is in Banks, *Documents, Deeds*, I, 396. See also EM to Paul Dudley, March 20, 1722, *NEHG Reg.*, XXXIX (1885), 16.

19. MS account of Mayhew family by Zachariah Mayhew in a copy of *Indian Converts* at Boston Public Library. Jonathan Marsh to Peter Wainwright, Aug. 9, 1845, MP. *Vital Records of Tisbury Massachusetts to the Year 1850* (Boston, 1910), p. 232.

20. *Vital Records of Chilmark Massachusetts to the Year 1850* (Boston, 1904), pp. 22, 24, 25. *New England Courant*, Jan. 22, 1722. "Diary of Rev. William Homes," *NEHG Reg.*, XXXIX (1885), 12; L (1896), 158. Frederick Freeman, *The History of Cape Cod* (Boston, 1869), I, 677–681.

21. *Indian Converts*, p. 307. EM to ——, July 20, 1741, MP. "Diary of Rev. William Homes," *NEHG Reg.*, L (1896), 158.

22. "Letter-Book of Samuel Sewall," *MHS Colls.*, LIII (1888), 208. "Harvard College Records," *CSM Pubs.*, XVI (1925), 547–548, 590–591. *Harvard Graduates*, VII, 635; IX, 70–71.

23. Harvard Faculty Records, I, 16. "Harvard College Records," *CSM Pubs.*, XV (1925), 98; XVI (1925), 599.

CHAPTER II. HARVARD COLLEGE

1. MP, no. 61, pp. 54–55.

2. *Boston News-Letter*, April 5, 1739. There is a suggestion of EM's interest in farming in a letter from Paul Dudley in *Transactions of the Royal Society*, no. 385 (Oct.–Dec. 1724).

3. "Diary of Rev. William Homes," *NEHG Reg.*, L (1896), 159–162.

4. Duke's County Papers, 1722–1800 (MSS, LC), *passim* for 1722–1740. *New England Courant*, April 1, June 3, 1723.

5. "Letter-Book of Samuel Sewall," *MHS Colls.*, LI (1886), 340; LII (1888), 163, 232. JM to EM, March 11, 1746, MP. EM to ——, July 20, 1741, MP. Experience Mayhew MSS (MHS), *passim.* Duke's County Probate Records, IV, 60. Nathan Mayhew's copy of *Lyra Prophetica David* is at MHS.

6. The inkstand is on display at MHS. For its identity see *MHS Procs.*, IV (1860), 107–108. See also MP, no. 137.

7. *Acts and Resolves,* XI, 530, 595; XII, 618; XIII, 56. *Mass. House Journals,* XVII, 169.

8. *Boston News-Letter,* June 26, 1740.

9. "Harvard College Records," *CSM Pubs.,* XV (1925), 134. Diary of Andrew Eliot (MS, MHS), Sept. 11, 1741. Daniel D. Addison, *The Life and Times of Edward Bass* (Boston, 1897), p. 7. *MHS Procs.,* XVIII (1881), 150.

10. Benjamin Peirce, *A History of Harvard University* (Cambridge, Mass., 1833), p. 238n. Samuel E. Morison, *Three Centuries of Harvard, 1636–1936* (Cambridge, Mass., 1946), p. 104. "Diary of Rev. William Homes," *NEHG Reg.,* L (1896), 165.

11. *Boston News-Letter,* July 31, 1740. Harvard Faculty Records, I, 149–150. "Harvard College Records," *CSM Pubs.,* XXXI (1935), 383–384.

12. *Harvard Graduates,* XI, *passim.*

13. "Harvard College Records," *CSM Pubs.,* XV (1925), cxli. Diary of Robert Treat Paine (MS, MHS), May 1, 1746. Harvard Faculty Records, I, 149–150. Morison, *Three Centuries,* p. 104.

14. "Harvard College Records," *CSM Pubs.,* XV (1925), 135. Diary of Jeremy Belknap (MS, MHS), March 15, 1760. Harvard Faculty Records, I, 157–158. Steward's Quarter-Bill Book, 1720–1756 (Harvard University Archives), *passim.*

15. Harvard Faculty Records, I, 186–187.

16. Harvard Faculty Records, I, 186–190, 198, 214. JM to EM, April 6, 1744, MP. Peirce, *History of Harvard,* p. 263.

17. Harvard Faculty Records, I, 156–158, 169, 186, 191. "Harvard College Records," *CSM Pubs.,* XV (1925), lxxxix, 140, 204; XVI (1925), 713, 721, 740. EM to ——, July 20, 1741, MP. Eliot Diary for 1740–1741.

18. JM's classmate, Jacob Green, kept a complete diary of his activities for one typical week during his third year at Harvard (*Christian Advocate,* IX [1831], 635–637). Harvard Faculty Records, I, 149. "Harvard College Records," *CSM Pubs.,* XV (1925), 138–139. *Harvard Graduates,* IX, 67–70. Peirce, *History of Harvard,* pp. 244–249. Morison, *Three Centuries,* p. 9.

19. JM's alphabetical list is in MP, no. 9; a commonplace book is in MP, no. 10. Harvard Faculty Records, I, 178. Arthur O. Norton, "Harvard Text-Books and Reference Books of the Seventeenth Century," *CSM Pubs.,* XXVIII (1935), 360–438. Perry Miller, *The New England Mind, The Seventeenth Century* (New York, 1939), pp. 196–206, 396–397. Samuel E. Morison, *Harvard College in the Seventeenth Century* (Cambridge, Mass., 1936), pp. 260–263.

20. *A Continuation of the Reverend Mr. Whitefield's Journal From Savannah June 25, 1740* (Boston, 1741), p. 55. *A Letter*

GREAT AWAKENING 247

to the *Reverend Mr. George Whitefield* (Boston, 1745), pp. 30–31.
Boston Gazette, April 20, 1741. Colman MSS (MHS), II.
21. *New England Courant,* June 8, July 20, Dec. 7, 1724.
Clifford K. Shipton, "Literary Leaven in Provincial New England,"
New England Quarterly, IX (1936), 203–217.
22. Winthrop's diary is in the Harvard College Library. *Harvard Graduates,* IX, 240–264. Winthrop wrote the obituary notice
of Mayhew that appeared in the *Boston Post-Boy,* July 14, 1766,
and other Boston newspapers for the same week.
23. *Seven Sermons,* p. 31.

CHAPTER III. GREAT AWAKENING

1. JM to Zachariah Mayhew, Dec. 26, 1741, MP.
2. Jonathan Edwards, *A Faithful Narrative of the Surprising
Work of God* (Boston, 1737). Thomas Prince, ed., *The Christian
History, Containing Accounts of the Revival* (Boston, 1743),
pp. 358–400. Benjamin Colman, *Souls flying to Jesus Christ* (Boston, 1740), p. 5. "Diary of Paul Dudley, 1740," *NEHG Reg.,*
XXXV (1881), pp. 29–30. Joseph Tracy, *The Great Awakening*
(Boston, 1842), pp. 87, 90. *A Continuation of the Reverend Mr.
Whitefield's Journal From Savannah June 25, 1740* (Boston,
1741), p. 56. Diary of Andrew Eliot (MS, MHS), *passim* for
1741–1742. John Moorhead to Willison, July 30, 1742, in *Glasgow-Weekly History* (Glasgow, 1743). Edwin S. Gaustad, *The Great
Awakening in New England* (New York, 1957), *passim.*
3. *Christian Advocate,* IX (1831), 523–524, 580. *Glasgow-Weekly History,* no. 1, p. 3. *Boston Gazette,* April 20, 1741. See
the letters concerning the Awakening in *MHS Procs.,* LIII (1920),
197–198, 203, 208–210, 214. Overseers' Records, I, 189–190.
4. Flynt Diary (MS, Harvard College Library), "Dec. & Jan.
1740."
5. JM to Zachariah Mayhew, Dec. 26, 1741, MP.
6. March 26, 1742, MP.
7. Oct. 1, 1747, MP.
8. EM to ——, July 20, 1741, MP. "A Letter to a Minister of the
Gospel," MP, no. 8. EM to Thomas Foxcroft, May 18, 1742, Foxcroft MSS (Princeton University Library). Thomas Balch, *A Sermon Preach'd . . . on July 29th. 1747* (Boston, 1747), pp. (6)–(7).
9. MP, no. 13.
10. Flynt Diary, Oct. 12, 1740. *The Testimony and Advice of
a Number of Laymen respecting Religion, and the Teachers of it*
(Boston, 1743), p. 3. Nathanael Appleton, *Faithful Ministers of
Christ* (Boston, 1743), *passim.* Chester Williams to Thomas Foxcroft, Dec. 18, 1744, Foxcroft MSS (Boston University). Benjamin
Colman, *The Great God has magnified his Word to the Children*

of Men (Boston, 1742). *The State of Religion in New England, Since the Reverend Mr. George Whitefield's Arrival there* (Glasgow, 1742), pp. 14, 42. Faculty Records, I, 210–212. *Harvard Graduates,* XI, 359–364.

11. Huntington Sermons, Jan. 1764, sermon 1, pp. 19, 26–27.

12. *Remarks,* p. 80.

13. Overseers' Records, II, 2, 6. Steward's Quarter-Bill Book, 1720–1756, *passim* for 1744–1747. Flynt Diary, Oct. 23, 1746. Sketches of Brandon, Cooper, Hitchcock, and Brown are in *Harvard Graduates,* XI. JM to Samuel Cooper, Dec. 5, 1743, MP.

14. *The Alienation of Affections from Ministers* (Boston, 1747), p. 26.

15. Diary of Joseph Andrews (MS, MHS), *passim. Harvard Graduates,* VI, 62. "Diaries of Rev. William Smith," *MHS Procs.,* XLII (1909), 465. Samuel A. Eliot, *Heralds of a Liberal Faith* (Boston, 1910), I, 1–19. Frederick Lewis Weis, "The Reverend Ebenezer Gay . . . ," *Unitarian Hist. Soc. Procs.,* IV (1936), part ii, p. 9.

16. March 11, 1746 and March 31, 1746, MP.

17. *Early Records of the Town of Worcester* (Worcester, 1880), II, 52, 74. Diary of David Hall (MS, MHS), *passim* for 1743–1746. C. E. Stevens, *Ecclesiastical History of the City of Worcester* (Philadelphia, 1889), pp. 3–4. E. Smalley, *The Worcester Pulpit* (Boston, 1851), pp. 52–54. *Adams Works,* II, 5–7.

18. In addition to sources cited in the preceding note, see the following: Ezra Stiles to Francis Alison, Aug. 16, 1761, Stiles Papers. *MHS Colls.,* XIII (1815), 211. Franklin B. Dexter, ed., *Extracts from the Itineraries . . . of Ezra Stiles* (New Haven, 1916), p. 205.

19. JM to EM, Oct. 1, 1747, MP. *Boston News-Letter,* Sept. 10, 1747. "History and Description of Cohasset . . .," *MHS Colls.,* XXII (1830), 94.

CHAPTER IV. WEST CHURCH

1. *Christian Sobriety,* p. iii.

2. On the growth of West Boston compare the 1722 and 1743 editions of John Bonner's map; and see the sketch facing the title page in Justin Winsor, ed., *The Memorial History of Boston* (Boston, 1881), III. See also *Boston News-Letter,* Feb. 13, 1746; Carl Bridenbaugh, *Cities in the Wilderness* (New York, 1938), pp. 146, 308; and Walter Muir Whitehill, *Boston, A Topographical History* (Cambridge, Mass., 1959), ch. 2.

3. Perry, *Papers,* pp. 398–402. *Trinity Church in the City of Boston, Massachusetts 1733–1933* (Boston, 1933), pp. 8–9, 34–35.

Carl Bridenbaugh, ed., *Gentleman's Progress, the Itinerarium of Dr. Alexander Hamilton* (Chapel Hill, 1948), p. 130.

4. Harrison Gray to Elizabeth Mayhew, May 2, 1783, Mayhew MSS (Harvard College Library). Diary of Benjamin Walker (MS, MHS), Sept. 1, 1936. "Diary of the Rev. Thomas Prince," *CSM Pubs.*, XIX (1918), 335–336. *Boston News-Letter*, Sept. 16, 1736; Jan. 6, 1737. *New England Weekly Journal*, May 17, 1737. Bowditch Title Books (MHS), XLI, 399.

5. Bridenbaugh, *Gentleman's Progress*, p. 109.

6. *Boston Gazette*, April 18, 1737. *Boston News-Letter*, May 19, 1737. "Diary of the Rev. Thomas Prince," p. 345. Richard D. Pierce, ed., "The Records of the First Church in Boston," *CSM Pubs.*, XXXIX (1961), 142, 173, 177. *An Historical Catalogue of the Old South Church* (Boston, 1883), p. 36. *Records of the Church in Brattle Square* (n.p., 1901), pp. 26–27. Charles Lowell, *A Discourse Delivered in the West Church in Boston, Dec. 31, 1820* (Boston, 1820), *passim*.

7. Hooper to Colman, Feb. 13, 1740, and Colman to Hooper, Feb. 19, 1740, Colman MSS (MHS). Perry, *Papers*, pp. 412–413. "Diary of the Rev. Thomas Prince," p. 364. William Buell Sprague, *Annals of the American Pulpit* (9 vols., New York, 1859–69), V, 122–126.

8. *Boston News-Letter*, Nov. 28, Dec. 4, 1746. FP Transcripts, box I, no. 173; box II, no. 186. Perry, *Papers*, pp. 398–402. *Trinity Church*, p. 35.

9. *Alienation of Affections*, p. 2.

10. MP, no. 133. *Boston Evening-Post*, March 9, 1747. Diary of Benjamin Walker, Jan. 25, 1747.

11. Oct. 5, 1747.

12. Detailed sources on the Boston clergy are too numerous to cite fully here. Sketches of those mentioned may be found in *Harvard Graduates*. There is an excellent discussion of the "old guard" in Perry Miller, *The New England Mind, From Colony to Province* (Cambridge, Mass., 1953), pp. 451f.

13. Colman to West Church, June, 1747, Colman MSS (MHS). MP, no. 137, pp. 3–6. Colman to Foxcroft, May 15, 1747, *CSM Pubs.*, VIII (1906), 352–353. "Records of the First Church in Boston," p. 248. Diary of Benjamin Walker, May 20, 1747.

14. *Records of the Church in Brattle Square*, p. 37. Chandler Robbins, *A History of the Second Church* (Boston, 1852), p. 298.

15. Diary of Benjamin Walker, May 20, 1747. Diary of Robert Treat Paine, May 20, 1747. MP, no. 137, pp. 6–7. Lowell, *Discourse*, pp. 25–26.

16. June 22, 1747.

17. Colman to West Church, June, 1747, Colman MSS (MHS).

18. The ordination sermon was printed as *The Alienation of Affections from Ministers consider'd and improv'd* (Boston, 1747).

19. *Boston Gazette*, June 23, 1747. *Boston Evening-Post*, June 22, 1747. *Harvard Graduates*, XI, 193.

20. The original West Church records have been lost. Copies of the membership and baptism records are in City Hall, Boston, and these were printed in *NEHG Reg.* Relevant sections are XCI (1937), 340–354; XCII (1938), 10–28; XCIII (1939), 250–263; XCIV (1940), 290–297.

21. Knox MSS (MHS), L, *passim. Historical Sketch and Matters Appertaining to the King's Chapel Burying Ground* (Boston, 1903), p. 46. JM to TH, June 24, 1764, HP. Samuel E. Morison, "The Property of Harrison Gray, Loyalist," *CSM Pubs.*, XIV (1913), 320–350.

22. *Boston News-Letter*, Jan. 17, 1760; Feb. 18, Nov. 11, 1762; Nov. 10, 1763; Jan. 17, March 30, 1769. *Boston Gazette*, Jan. 17, Jan. 24, March 14, 1763.

23. W. T. Baxter, *The House of Hancock* (Cambridge, Mass., 1945), pp. 67–69, 75–77. Bridenbaugh, *Gentleman's Progress*, pp. 109, 133–134, 136–137, 139, 143–144. *Boston Record Commissioners Report*, XXVIII, 267. A print of the portrait of Mrs. Henderson Inches may be seen in *Loan Exhibition of One Hundred Colonial Portraits* (Museum of Fine Arts, Boston, 1930), p. 52.

24. Particularly helpful here is Bernard Bailyn, "The Blount Papers: Notes on the Merchant 'Class' in the Revolutionary Period," *William and Mary Quarterly*, 3rd series, XI (1954), 98–104.

25. The evidence on pulpit exchanges is voluminous; good examples are the Diary of Andrew Eliot and the Foxcroft MSS (Boston University). For JM's problem in this regard see the following: JM to EM, Oct. 1, 1747, MP. Elizabeth Mayhew to TH, Jan. 13, 1767 and Harrison Gray to TH, Dec. 15, 1767, HP. JM to Samuel Williams, Sept. 17, 1764 (LC). "Diary of Rev. Samuel Cooper," *NEHG Reg.*, XLI (1887), 388–391; LV (1901), 145–148.

26. The best brief treatment of the role of the clergy is Clifford K. Shipton, "The New England Clergy of the 'Glacial Age,'" *CSM Pubs.*, XXX (1933), 24–25. The subject is treated in more detail in Miller, *The New England Mind, Colony to Province.*

27. Winsor, *Memorial History*, II, ch. iv. *Boston Evening-Post*, May 27, 1754. Ezra Stiles to Charles Chauncy, July 21, 1761, Stiles Papers.

28. *On hearing the Word*, pp. ii–iii.

29. *Jonathan Edwards* (New York, 1949), p. 48.

30. To TH, July 28, 1766, HP.

31. Douglas Adair and John Schutz, eds., *Peter Oliver's Origin*

& *Progress of the American Rebellion* (San Marino, Calif., 1961), p. 43.

32. Oct. 1, 1747, MP.

33. The size of the congregation can be estimated only roughly from the number of names appearing for any reason on the church records.

34. There is a description of JM's practice in admitting members in a letter by Richard Cranch, Aug. 8, 1749, Cranch MSS (MHS). Edmund S. Morgan has an excellent discussion of this entire question in *The Gentle Puritan, A Life of Ezra Stiles, 1727–1795* (New Haven, 1962), pp. 183–191. For general background, see Morgan's *Visible Saints* (New York, 1963).

35. *Boston News-Letter*, June 4, 1747. "Harvard College Records," *CSM Pubs.*, XV (1929), 147. *Quaestiones*, 1747 (Harvard University Archives). *Harvard Graduates*, XI, 498. *Proceedings of the American Antiquarian Society*, LXXIII, Part 1 (April 1963), 84.

36. July 1, 1747.

37. Oct. 1, 1747, MP.

CHAPTER V. OUT OF NAZARETH

1. *Seven Sermons*, p. 44.

2. In this discussion of New England theology I am chiefly indebted to Perry Miller's writings, the most important of which on this topic are the following: "The Marrow of Puritan Divinity," *CSM Pubs.*, XXXII (1937), 247–300; "Preparation for Salvation in Seventeenth-Century New England," *Journal of the History of Ideas*, IV (1943), pp. 253–286; and the two volumes of *The New England Mind*. Also helpful is Leonard J. Trinterud, "The Origins of Puritanism," *Church History*, XX (March 1951), 37–57.

3. For a summary of Arminianism in New England before the Great Awakening see Conrad Wright, *The Beginnings of Unitarianism in America,* (Boston, 1955), ch. i.

4. Colman to several London ministers, Oct. 2, 1740, Colman Papers (MHS), II. Jonathan Dickinson, *The True Scripture-Doctrine* (Boston, 1741), pp. vi–vii. *Christian Advocate*, X (1832), 147. *The State of Religion in New England, Since the Reverend Mr. George Whitefield's Arrival* (Glasgow, 1742), p. 7.

5. Miller, "Marrow," p. 300. Perry Miller, *Jonathan Edwards* (New York, 1949), pp. 101–126. Conrad Wright, in his *The Beginnings of Unitarianism in America*, was the first scholar to document fully the conclusion that the eighteenth-century Arminians were not nineteenth-century Unitarians but rather a movement with distinctive tenets of its own and out of which later Unitarianism would emerge. Past writers have missed this point

and have tended to read into the views of Mayhew, Chauncy, and others the mature concepts of the Unitarians, thus obscuring the actual beliefs of the Arminians in the eighteenth century.

6. EM, *Sermons to the Indians* (MS, MHS), *passim. Some Correspondence Between the Governors and Treasurers of the New England Company in London and the Commissioners of the United Colonies* (London, 1896), pp. 104–109. Ernst Benz, "The Pietist and Puritan Sources of Early Protestant Missions," *Church History*, XX (June 1951), 44–45.

7. *A Discourse Shewing that God Dealeth with Men as with Reasonable Creatures* (Boston, 1720).

8. EM, *Grace Defended* (Boston, 1744), p. iii. "A Discourse concerning Human Liberty, Or an Essay on the Proposition, that Man is a Free Agent," EM MSS (MHS), *passim*. Dickinson's book was *The True Scripture-Doctrine*. The Mayhew-Dickinson controversy can be traced in the correspondence of the participants in MP and the Thomas Foxcroft MSS (Princeton University Library). Cf. Conrad Wright, "Arminianism in Massachusetts, 1735–1780" (unpublished dissertation, Harvard University, 1943), pp. 21–28.

9. *Grace Defended,* pp. iii, 138.

10. *Ibid.,* pp. 140, 154f. See also EM, *A Letter to a Gentleman on . . . Saving Grace* (Boston, 1747), *passim*.

11. EM to JM, Nov. 1741, MP. JM to EM, Oct. 7, 1741, MP. JM to EM, n.d., MP, no. 13. There is a MS note in Wigglesworth's handwriting in a copy of *Grace Defended* at MHS. The ordination charge is in Ebenezer Gay, *The Alienation of Affections from Ministers* (Boston, 1747).

12. *Harvard Graduates,* VI, 456.

13. JM to EM, Oct. 1, 1747, MP.

14. Huntington Sermons, March 1750, sermon 1, p. 1; sermon 2, pp. 10–11, 16.

15. *Independent Advertiser,* May 30, Oct. 7, 1748. MP, no. 137, pp. 10–12. *Boston News-Letter,* May 18, 1749. For the Revere incident see E. H. Goss, *The Life of Colonel Paul Revere* (Boston, 1909–1912), I, 17–18, and Esther Forbes, *Paul Revere* (Boston, 1942), p. 33. *Amer. Unitarian Assoc. Tracts,* 2nd series, no. 5.

16. Wright, *Unitarianism,* p. 135.

17. *Seven Sermons,* pp. 7–8. Huntington Sermons, March 1750, p. 8.

18. *Seven Sermons,* pp. 60–61, 72–73.

19. Huntington Sermons, March 1750, pp. 5, 23. *Seven Sermons,* pp. 17–21, 56–57.

20. *Ibid.,* pp. 22–40.

21. *Ibid.,* pp. 42–43.

22. *Ibid.*, pp. 43–50.
23. *Ibid.*, pp. 50–63.
24. *Ibid.*, p. 74.
25. *Ibid.*, pp. 85–88.
26. Huntington Sermons, March 1749, p. 6. *Seven Sermons,* pp. 15, 39, 107. Wright, *Unitarianism,* ch. iii. H. Shelton Smith, *Changing Conceptions of Original Sin* (New York, 1955), pp. 10–26.
27. Huntington Sermons, March 1750, p. 27.
28. *Seven Sermons,* p. 152.
29. *Ibid.*, p. 153.
30. *Ibid.*, pp. 144–157. Huntington Sermons, March 1749, pp. 5–8.
31. *Seven Sermons,* p. 95. EM to JM, Nov. 1741, MP.
32. Huntington Sermons, March 1750, pp. 17–18.
33. *Boston Evening-Post,* April 17, 1749.
34. Benjamin Avery to JM, July 17, 1750, MP. George Benson to JM, July 17, 1750, MP. Edward Sandercock to JM, Oct. 2, 1750, MP. JM to Benjamin Avery, Oct. 23, 1750, MP.
35. The diploma is in MP. *Boston Evening-Post,* April 16, 1750. *Boston Post-Boy,* June 4, 1750. Benson, *et al.* to the University of Aberdeen, Dec. 11, 1749, MP. Joseph Chalmers to Shirley, Jan. 3, 1750, MP. JM to George Benson, Dec. 6, 1751 (Unitarian College, Manchester). Hollis Diary, April 26, May 2, May 4, Sept. 20, Dec. 3, 1765; Jan. 1, 1766.
36. Gideon Richardson to R. T. Paine, April 24, 1750, R. T. Paine MSS (MHS).
37. Briant's sermon was printed in Boston, 1749. See also: Diary of R. T. Paine (MS, MHS), Aug. 12, 1750. John Adams to Thomas Jefferson, July 18, 1818 in Lester J. Capon, ed., *The Adams-Jefferson Letters* (2 vols., Chapel Hill, N.C., 1959), p. 527. Samuel Niles, *A Vindication* (Boston, 1752), p. 11. Lemuel Briant, *Some more Friendly Remarks* (Boston, 1751), pp. 28–29. John Porter, *A Vindication* (Boston, 1751), p. 46. Thomas Foxcroft, *Humilis Confessio* (Boston, 1750), pp. 59–62.
38. JM to EM, Aug. 21, 1752, MP. *Boston Gazette,* May 14, 1751. Diary of Joseph Andrews (MS, MHS), May 24, 1752. Samuel Niles, *The result of a late ecclesiastical council* (Boston, 1753), pp. 2–3. *The Report of a Committee of the First Church in Braintree* (Boston, 1753), *passim.*
39. JM to EM, Aug. 21, 1751, MP. Richard Cranch to JM, June 10, 1752 (MHS).

CHAPTER VI. CATECHISM OF REVOLUTION

1. Huntington Sermons, March 1749, p. 3.

2. Oct. 17, 1750, MP.

3. H. B. Parkes, "New England in the Seventeen Thirties," *New Eng. Quart.*, III (1930), 414–415. "Francis Goelet's Journal," *NEHG Reg.*, XXIV (1870), 50–63. S. E. Dwight, ed., *The Works of President Edwards* (10 vols., New York, 1830), I, 413. The hostility of Anglicanism toward Calvinism had been well publicized in New England by John Checkley's controversial book, *Choice Dialogues Between a Godly Minister, and an Honest Country-Man, Concerning Election & Predestination* (Boston, 1719).

4. Pages 10–12.

5. Pages 12–13.

6. Pages 20–24.

7. Pages 29–30.

8. Pages 38–39n. Peter Laslett has pointed out that "trust" is used much more frequently by John Locke than "contract" or "compact." In fact, Laslett concludes that the concept of "trust" and its implications for dissolving governments is the main theme of the *Two Treatises* (Peter Laslett, *John Locke, Two Treatises of Government,* [Cambridge, 1960], pp. 111–120).

9. Pages 39–40.

10. JM to George Benson, Oct. 17, 1750, MP. See also MP no. 10.

11. Pages 42–43.

12. Pages 44–50.

13. Page 52.

14. Page 54.

15. Pages 21–22.

16. *Boston Evening-Post,* Feb. 19, Feb. 26, March 12, March 19, April 2, April 23, June 18, July 9, 1750. *Boston Gazette,* April 3, 1750; April 24, 1753. *Boston News-Letter,* March 1, 1750. See also the advertisement prefixed to the second Boston edition of *Unlimited Submission* (1750).

17. Brockwell to Bishop of London, April 13, 1750; Jan. 31, 1751, FP Transcripts, box II, nos. 192, 193.

18. MP, no. 13. *Boston News-Letter,* March 22, 1750. *Boston Gazette,* March 13, March 20, 1750; May 4, 1761. *Boston Evening-Post,* March 5, March 12, March 19, April 2, April 9, April 16, 1750.

19. E.g., compare p. 24 in *Unlimited Submission* (1st Boston ed., 1750) with p. 83 in Hoadley's *Sixteen Sermons* (London, 1754). The sermon in question, *The Measures of Submission to the Civil Magistrate considered,* was first published in London in 1705.

20. Hoadley's influence on American political thought needs a full study. A start has been made by Caroline Robbins in *The Eighteenth-Century Commonwealthman* (Cambridge, Mass.,

1959), p. 84, *passim*. See also the sketch of Hoadley by Norman Sykes in *The Social & Political Ideas of Some English Thinkers of the Augustan Age*, F. J. C. Hearnshaw, ed. (New York, 1950).

21. Oct. 1750, MP.

22. *Boston Gazette*, May 8, May 29, 1750. *Boston Evening-Post*, May 21, 1750.

23. May 6, 1751, MP.

24. London, 1752, pp. 259–335.

25. Dec. 1789, pp. 1093–94.

26. *Adams Works*, X, 301. Capon, ed., *The Adams-Jefferson Letters*, p. 527. See also *Niles' Weekly Register*, XV (Oct. 1818), 149–150.

27. *Death of Frederick*, pp. 12–13, 16, 25–26, 29. The other printed sermons were by Henry Caner, Thomas Prince, and Samuel Mather; all were published in Boston in 1751.

28. Lindsay Swift, "The Massachusetts Election Sermons," *CSM Pubs.*, I (1895), 388–451.

29. Useful here are Alice M. Baldwin, *The New England Clergy and the American Revolution* (Durham, N.C., 1928), and Martha Louise Counts, "The Political Views of the Eighteenth Century New England Clergy as Expressed in their Election Sermons" (unpublished dissertation, Columbia University, 1956).

30. Pages 6–22, 40–43.

31. See the comments on JM's Election Sermon in *Monthly Review*, XI (1754), 480.

32. MP, no. 61, pp. 54–55. Clinton Rossiter, "The Life and Mind of Jonathan Mayhew," *William and Mary Quarterly*, 3rd series, VIII (1950), 552–553. Baldwin, *The New England Clergy and the American Revolution*, p. 44.

33. *Unlimited Submission*, pp. 33, 38.

CHAPTER VII. PROFITS AND PIETY

1. Huntington Sermons, March 1759, sermon 2, pp. 30–31.

2. The evidence here is widespread. For a quick summary see Lawrence H. Gipson, *The British Empire before the American Revolution* (10 vols., New York, 1936–1961), X, 12–19.

3. *Boston Evening-Post*, Sept. 23, Oct. 21, Oct. 28, Nov. 4, 1754. *Boston News-Letter*, April 1, May 13, 1756; Feb. 3, 1757; March 30, Dec. 28, 1758. Bridenbaugh, *Gentleman's Progress*, pp. 145–146. "Francis Goelet's Journal," *NEHG Reg.*, XXIV (1870), 53.

4. *Christian Sobriety*, p. 134. To sample the Sabbath observance problem see the following: Diary of Benjamin Bangs (MS, MHS), June 22, 1760. *Boston News-Letter*, June 12, 1746. *Boston Evening Post*, Dec. 7, 1761. *Boston Gazette*, July 28, 1760.

Antinomians (Boston, 1747), p. 10. *Boston Post-Boy*, April 12, April 26, 1742. *Boston News-Letter*, April 15, 1742. *Boston Evening Post*, April 19, April 26, 1742. Thomas Emlyn, *An Humble Inquiry into the Scripture Account of Jesus Christ* (London, 1702; Boston, 1756).

6. There is an interesting discussion of the contemporary views of Arians, Socinians, and Athanasians in the *London Chronicle*, Dec. 6, 1757, pp. 541–542; July 11, 1758, p. 29; Aug. 1, 1758, p. 99; July 12, 1760, p. 43. See also July 29, 1766, p. 100.

7. The *Scripture Doctrine of the Trinity* was published in London, 1712, and is also available in Clarke's *Works* (4 vols., London, 1738), IV. See also J. Hay Colligan, *The Arian Movement in England* (London, 1913), *passim;* and Roland N. Stromberg, *Religious Liberalism in Eighteenth-Century England* (London, 1754), pp. 41–46.

8. *On hearing the Word*, pp. 268, 269n.

9. *Ibid.*, pp. 83, 267–268, 276–277.

10. *Christian Sobriety*, pp. 59, 61. *On hearing the Word*, pp. 267, 403–404, 417–418n.

11. Abraham Taylor, *The Insufficience of Natural Religion* (Boston, 1755). *Adams Papers*, I, 15. *Boston News-Letter*, May 17, 1756. Jared Eliot to Ezra Stiles, March 14, 1757, Stiles Papers.

12. S. E. Dwight, ed., *The Works of President Edwards* (10 vols., New York, 1830), I, 410, 421–427. E. Francis Brown, *Joseph Hawley, Colonial Radical* (New York, 1931), pp. 20–21, 30. Hawley's account of his conversion to Arminianism is contained in a MS fragment in the New York Public Library. EM to Thomas Foxcroft, Feb. 21, 1755, Foxcroft MSS (Princeton University Library) and a fragment (pp. 31–75) of a MS book by EM in the same collection.

13. Joseph S. Clark, *Historical Sketch of the Congregational Church in Massachusetts* (Boston, 1858), pp. 181–182. The originals of this correspondence, formerly in the Congregational Library, Boston, are now missing.

14. MP, no. 132. Joseph Quincy, *The History of Harvard University* (5 vols., Cambridge, Mass. 1840), II, 67. Diary of Ebenezer Parkman, May 2, 1756, MSS (Amer. Antiquarian Soc.).

15. Clark, *Historical Sketch*, pp. 181–182.

16. Wigglesworth's discourse was *Some Evidences of the Divine Inspiration of the Scriptures of the Old Testament* (Boston, 1755).

17. *All Power in Heaven, and in Earth given unto Jesus Christ* (Boston, 1756).

18. Clark, *Historical Sketch*, pp. 182–184.

19. Bellamy's sermons were *Sermons Upon the following Subjects, Viz. The Divinity of Jesus Christ* (Boston, 1758) and *True*

Religion delineated (Boston, 1750), pp. 263–265. See also *The Works of Joseph Bellamy, D.D.* (2 vols., Boston, 1850), I, 610.

20. *Boston Gazette*, March 14, April 11 (supplement), 1757.

21. MP, no. 124. *Christian Sobriety*, pp. 57–58. Wright, *Unitarianism*, pp. 200–209.

22. *Defence*, p. iii.

23. Taylor, *The Insufficience of Natural Religion*, preface. Bellamy's *Works*, I, 610.

24. *On hearing the Word*, 101, 171, 226, 282, 306. *Practical Discourses*, p. 333. *Expected Dissolution*, p. 69.

25. *Striving to enter*, pp. 6, 11–13, 18–20, 23, 49, 73.

26. Samuel Hopkins, *An Enquiry Concerning The Promises of the Gospel* (Boston, 1765), pp. 17, 46–49, 77, 108–110, 114. Stephen West, ed., *Sketches of the Life of the Late Rev. Samuel Hopkins, DD. . . . Written by Himself* (Hartford, 1805), pp. 93–94.

27. *Boston News-Letter*, Oct. 24, 1765. *Huntington Sermons*, Dec. 1762–Jan. 1764, pp. 11–12; Jan. 1763–Jan. 1764, pp. 4–5.

28. Huntington Sermons, Jan. 1763–Jan. 1764, pp. 6–20, 23–27. *Christian Sobriety*, pp. 100–104.

29. Huntington Sermons, Feb. 1764–April 1765, pp. 28–29.

30. *Christian Sobriety*, pp. 49, 68–70, 325–326. Edward Sandercock to JM, Oct. 2, 1750, MP. JM to TH, Jan. 7, 1766, HP.

31. Joseph Haroutunian, *Piety Versus Moralism* (New York, 1932), ch. iii.

32. Huntington Sermons, Jan. 1763–Jan. 1764, *passim*. *Striving to enter*, p. 6. *Christian Sobriety*, p. 93.

33. *Boston Gazette*, March 2, 1762. William Allen to JM, April 2, 1763, MP.

34. *Boston Gazette*, March 9, 1761.

35. *Boston News-Letter*, March 12, 1761. *Boston Gazette*, March 16, April 6, 1761.

36. *Ibid.*, April 13, 1761.

37. *Ibid.*, May 11, 1761.

38. *Ibid.*, May 4, 1761.

39. JM to George Benson, Jan. 7, 1754 (Unitarian College, Manchester). *Christian Sobriety*, p. 329.

40. *Seven Sermons*, p. 107. John Cleaveland, *An Essay to defend some of the most important Principles . . . of Christianity . . . against the injurious Aspersions cast . . . by Jonathan Mayhew* (Boston, 1763). Some contemporaries questioned Cleaveland's authorship of the *Essay*, but no definite evidence to support such doubts has come to light. See also the Boston newspapers published on May 30, 1763.

41. *Boston Gazette*, Jan. 9, 1764. *Boston Evening-Post*, Jan. 9,

1764. Wright, *Unitarianism*, pp. 185–187, 217–220. John Cleaveland, *A Reply to Dr. Mayhew's Letter of Reproof* (Boston, 1765), p. 62. *Divine Goodness*, pp. 86–87.

42. *Letter of Reproof*, pp. 3–5, 8–9, 29–31, 37, 47. Cleaveland, *Reply*, pp. 85–86, 92, 94–95.

43. Diary of David Hall (MS, MHS), March 9, 1766. *Defence*, p. 110n. *Observations*, p. 44.

CHAPTER IX. REAL WHIGGERY

1. *Christian Sobriety*, p. ix.

2. Election Sermon, pp. 35–37, 46–47.

3. Aug. 22, 1757.

4. *Two Discourses November 23d. 1758*, pp. 8–12, 22, 52. *Two Discourses October 9th, 1760*, p. 3.

5. *Two Discourses October 25th. 1759*, pp. 27–29.

6. *Christian Sobriety*, p. 159. *Death of George II*, p. 32. *Two Discourses October 9th, 1760*, pp. 42–43. W. T. Baxter, *The House of Hancock* (Cambridge, Mass., 1945), pp. 132, 141–142.

7. *Two Discourses October 25th. 1759*, pp. 39, 60–61.

8. Election Sermon, pp. 32–33, 37–39, 46–47. *Death of George II*, p. 40. JM to TH, Aug. 16, 1759, HP. John Reynolds to JM, Jan. 29, 1759, MP. Gipson, *The British Empire Before the American Revolution*, VI, 3–19.

9. *Death of George II*, passim.

10. *Two Discourses November 23d. 1758*, pp. 48–49. See also *Two Discourses October 25th. 1759*, poem at end of appendix.

11. *Two Discourses October 9th, 1760*, p. 45. Howard H. Peckham, "Speculations on the Colonial Wars," *William and Mary Quarterly*, 3rd series, XVII (Oct. 1960), p. 472.

12. *Unlimited Submission*, preface.

13. This concept of the plot against liberty was particularly rooted in the mind of Samuel Adams, as Carl Becker has pointed out in *Eve of Revolution* (New Haven, 1920), pp. 163–164.

14. Feb. 28, 1755, MP. See also George Benson to JM, Sept. 1, 1755, MP.

15. Jasper Mauduit to JM, Sept. 1, 1755; July 13, 1756; Nov. 8, 1757, MP. JM to TH, Aug. 16, 1759, HP.

16. [Francis Blackburne, ed.], *Memoirs of Thomas Hollis, Esq.* (London, 1780), I, 1, 4–6. For a modern account of Hollis see Caroline Robbins, "The Strenuous Whig, Thomas Hollis of Lincoln's Inn," *William and Mary Quarterly*, 3rd series, VII (June 1950), 406–453.

17. TH to JM, Aug. 27, 1760; Dec. 6, 1763, HP. Hollis Diary, Oct. 18, Nov. 5, 1759; Nov. 12, Dec. 5, Dec. 25, 1760. Hollis *Memoirs*, I, 6–60, 419.

18. MP, no. 118.

19. W. T. Franklin, ed., *Memoirs of the Life and Writings of Benjamin Franklin* (London, 1818), II, 44–45. Roger Ingpen, ed., *The Life of Samuel Johnson by James Boswell* (Boston, 1925), pp. 944–945. J. Nichols, *Illustrations of Literary History* (London, 1831), VI, 157. MP, no. 118.

20. Hollis Diary, April 10, 1765. Hollis *Memoirs*, I, 68–69. Caroline Robbins, *The Eighteenth-Century Commonwealthman* is the first full study of the Real Whigs of the eighteenth century. Pages 3–21, 221–270, 378–386 are most helpful in evaluating the Hollis-Mayhew relationship.

21. TH to Ed. Quincy, Oct. 1, 1766; TH to E. Holyoke, June 24, 1765, HP. Hollis *Memoirs*, I, 68–69, 85, 230–232, 492. Robbins, "The Strenuous Whig," pp. 425–426. Among other editorial achievements, TH republished in 1764 Locke's *Two Treatises* in an edition that remained the best available in English until 1960 (Laslett, *John Locke, Two Treatises of Government*, pp. 10–11).

22. TH to William Pitt, Nov. 23, 1760, Chatham Papers (Public Record Office, London). TH to JM, Aug. 27, 1760, HP.

23. TH to JM, Oct. 27, 1761, HP. Hollis Diary, April 27, 1759. Hollis *Memoirs*, I, 472. Charles Chauncy to Ezra Stiles, Nov. 7, 1768, Stiles Papers.

24. TH to JM, Aug. 27, 1760 & March 4, 1765; JM to TH, March 19, 1761, HP. Jasper Mauduit to JM, Nov. 8, 1757, MP.

25. Caroline Robbins, "Library of Liberty—Assembled for Harvard College by Thomas Hollis of Lincoln's Inn," *Harvard Library Bulletin*, V (1951), 5–23, 181–196. E. Holyoke to TH, Dec. 28, 1759; TH to JM, Aug. 27, 1760; JM to TH, March 9, 1761, HP.

26. See HP and Hollis Diary for 1764–1765, *passim*, and Overseers' Records, II, 196.

27. Based on the Hollis bibliography in Robbins, "Library of Liberty," pp. 188–196. See also Catalogues of Books Given by Thomas Hollis to Harvard College (photostats, MHS).

28. These letters, dated May 17, 1766 and May 8, 1766, are in HP.

29. TH to E. Holyoke, May 17, 1766; Holyoke to TH, July 9, 1766; JM to TH, Jan. 7 and April 8, 1766, HP. TH to Elizabeth Mayhew, July 12, 1769, MP. Robbins, "Library of Liberty," pp. 8–23. Robbins, "The Strenuous Whig," pp. 445–446. Catalogues of Books, *passim*.

30. TH to JM, July 28, 1762; Dec. 6, 1763, HP.

31. Hollis Diary, Aug. 3, Nov. 3, Nov. 10, Dec. 8, 1760; Jan. 1, Oct. 23, Oct. 27, 1761; April 20, 1766. HP, nos. 6, 9, 12, 13, 23, 69, 72, 75, 76, 81, 83.

32. TH to JM, Aug. 27, 1760; Oct. 27, 1761; July 28, 1762,

HP. JM to TH, May 21, Aug. 27, 1760; March 19, 1761; April 6, 1762, HP. Hollis *Memoirs*, I, 83–84, 501.

33. Samuel Mather to TH, Dec. 11, 1762; TH to Mather, May 14, 1763; TH to JM, May 17, 1763; JM to TH, Feb. 21, 1763, HP.

34. Hollis Diary, March 3, 1760.

35. Blackburne to Elizabeth Mayhew, Jan. 23, 1767; TH to Elizabeth Mayhew, July 12, 1769; Harris to TH, Sept. 7, 1764, MP. JM to TH, May 13, 1765; Oct. 17, 1764, HP. JM to TH, n.d., HP, no. 29. TH to JM, April 22, 1764, HP. Robbins, "The Strenuous Whig," p. 407n.

CHAPTER X. GOVERNOR BERNARD

1. "Circumstantial Narrative," MP, no. 61, p. 34.

2. *Boston News-Letter*, Oct. 2, 1760.

3. Hutchinson to Israel Williams, March 4, Aug. 24, 1760, Israel Williams MSS (MHS), II, 153–155. Samuel Mather to Samuel Mather, Jr., March 31, April 19, June 17, 1760, Mather Letters. On Bernard see Edmund S. and Helen M. Morgan, *The Stamp Act Crisis* (Chapel Hill, N.C., 1953), ch. ii.

4. On Pownall and Shirley see John A. Schutz, *Thomas Pownall* (Glendale, Calif., 1951) and *William Shirley* (Chapel Hill, N.C., 1961).

5. Hutchinson, *History*, III, 60–61.

6. *Boston Gazette*, Sept. 15, Sept. 22, 1760. *Boston News-Letter*, Sept. 11, Sept. 18, 1760. Hutchinson, *History*, III, 68. *Adams Works*, X, 183, 274. *Harvard Graduates*, VI, 565–566.

7. JM to EM, Aug. 21, 1752, MP. Douglass Adair and John A. Schutz, eds., *Peter Oliver's Origin & Progress of the American Rebellion*, p. 44. *Harvard Graduates*, VI, 565.

8. *Death of Stephen Sewall*, p. 7.

9. The literature on the writs case is too voluminous to cite fully here. Particularly important are the following: Horace Gray, "Writs of Assistance," in Josiah Quincy, *Reports of Cases . . . Between 1761 and 1772* (Boston, 1865). O. M. Dickerson, "Writs of Assistance as a Cause of the Revolution," in Richard B. Morris, ed., *The Era of the American Revolution* (New York, 1939). Gipson, *The British Empire Before the American Revolution*, X, 117–129. Clifford K. Shipton, "James Otis and the Writs of Assistance," *Proceedings of the Bostonian Society*, Jan. 17, 1961.

10. Hutchinson to Israel Williams, April 15, Nov. 17, 1763, Israel Williams MSS (MHS), II, 156–157. Hutchinson, *History*, III, 64. *Harvard Graduates*, XI, 254f.

11. This petition is not among the Indian papers in the Massachusetts Archives. There were at the time, however, Indian land

questions pending before the General Court (*Acts and Resolves*, IV, 634–635).

12. MP, no. 61. No reference to this affair has been located in Bernard's papers.

13. The "circumstantial Narrative" is divided into thirteen letters. Letter X was omitted, apparently through misnumbering. Unless other documentation is given, the following account of this incident is from the "Narrative."

14. JM's draft copy of this long letter to Bernard is with the "Narrative" in MP, no. 61.

15. Jan. 14, 1762, MP.

16. Overseers' Records, II, 91.

17. Minutes of a meeting to establish Hampshire County College (MS, LC). Oxenbridge Thacher to Benjamin Pratt, 1762, O. Thacher MSS (MHS). Israel Williams MSS (MHS), II, 176–181. Henry Lefavour, "The Proposed College in Hampshire County in 1762," *MHS Procs.*, LXVI (1942), 53–71. Franklin B. Dexter, *Miscellaneous Historical Papers* (New Haven, 1918), p. 220.

18. JM to TH, April 6, 1762, HP. Bernard to Lords of Trade, April 12, 1762, *MHS Colls.*, LXXIV (1918), 70. Memorial to English Dissenters, Miscellaneous Papers (MHS), XIII, 1761–1770. *Harvard Graduates*, XI, 256.

19. Overseers' Records, II, 92.

20. The Remonstrance is in the Overseers' Records, II, 94–117.

21. Overseers' Records, II, 120. TH to JM, July 28, 1762, HP. Israel Williams MSS (MHS), II, 108.

22. Charles Chauncy to Jasper Mauduit, Oct. 12, 1762, *MHS Colls.*, LXXIV (1918), 71–72.

23. *Boston Evening Post*, April 12, April 26, May 6, June 16, 1762; April 22, May 6, 1765. *Boston Gazette*, April 19, 1762.

24. Feb. 8, 1762.

25. JM to TH, April 6, 1762; Nov. 21, 1763; summer 1764, HP.

CHAPTER XI. DEEP IN THE PLOT

1. *Observations*, p. 45.

2. Rufus R. Wilson, ed., *Burnaby's Travels Through North America* (New York, 1904), pp. 100–102.

3. Cotton Mather, *Magnali Christi Americana* (London, 1702), bk. iii, p. 6.

4. *New England Courant*, July 10, 1727. The endless history of friction between Anglicans and Dissenters in America has been fully developed for the first time in Carl Bridenbaugh, *Mitre and Sceptre* (New York, 1962), which supplements but does not entirely replace Arthur Lyon Cross, *The Anglican Episcopate and the American Colonies* (New York, 1902).

5. The chief printed sources on the S.P.G. are the following: *Classified Digest of the Records of the Society for the Propagation of the Gospel in Foreign Parts, 1701–1892* (London, 1893). Ernest Hawkins, *Historical Notices of the Missions of the Church of England in the North American Colonies* (London, 1845). David Humphreys, *An Historical Account of the Incorporated Society for the Propagation of the Gospel in Foreign Parts* (London, 1730). A convenient summary of this and other material on the S.P.G. is Samuel Clyde McCulloch, "The Foundation and Early Work of the Society for the Propagation of the Gospel in Foreign Parts," *Huntington Library Quarterly*, VIII (1945), 241–258.

6. *Boston News-Letter*, Sept. 6, 1739. *Boston Gazette*, April 7, 1744; April 2, 1747. *Boston Evening Post*, Jan. 19, April 27, 1747; Jan. 14, 1760. *New England Courant*, Aug. 3, 1724. Hawkins, *Historical Notices*, pp. 180, 184, 203–204. Samuel Johnson, "An Impartial & Candid State of the Case between Dr. Mayhew and the SPG" (MS, N.Y. Hist. Soc.). Perry, *Papers*, pp. 398–404, 427–428.

7. H. B. Parkes, "New England in the Seventeen-Thirties," *New England Quarterly*, III (1930), 414–415. Clayton Hardin Chapman, "The Life and Influence of the Rev. Benjamin Colman" (unpublished dissertation, Boston University School of Theology, 1948), pp. 39–40, 88–89. *Burnaby's Travels*, p. 133. Perry, *Papers*, pp. 448–450. *Independent Advertiser*, Aug. 14, 1749. *Harvard Graduates*, VIII, 335. Diary of Robert Treat Paine, *passim*.

8. *Boston Evening Post*, March 6, 1741; Jan. 12, 1747. *Acts and Resolves*, II, 459–460, 783; III, 25. *Boston Gazette*, April 17, April 24, 1753; Sept. 17, Jan. 12, 1761; Sept. 24, 1764. Overseers' Records, II, 72–73. Perry, *Papers*, pp. 514–515.

9. *Classified Digest*, p. 11. John Duffy, "The Passage to the Colonies," *Miss. Valley Hist. Rev.*, XXVIII (1951), 35–37. A brief but excellent statement of the Anglican case for an American episcopate is *A Letter to the Right Honourable Horatio Walpole, Esq; Written Jan. 9, 1750–1, By the Right Reverend Thomas Secker, LL.D. Lord Bishop of Oxford: concerning Bishops in America* (London, 1769).

10. In addition to the relevant sections of Bridenbaugh, *Mitre and Sceptre* and Cross, *Anglican Episcopate*, see the following: *Boston Post-Boy*, June 24, Aug. 19, 1751. "Thoughts upon the present State of the Church of England in America, Sent to me by the Lord Arch Bishop of Canterbury, July 13: 1764" (MS, Clements Library). Matthew Hodgart, ed., *Horace Walpole, Memoirs and Portraits* (New York, 1963), pp. 5–6, 110. Sykes, *From Sheldon to Secker*, pp. 216–220.

11. Herbert and Carol Schneider, *Samuel Johnson* (4 vols., New

York, 1929), III, 259–260. To Bishop of London, Nov. 25, 1745, FP Transcripts, Mass., box I, no. 169.

12. JM to TH, April 6, 1762, HP. JM thought of Bernard as a tool of the Church's designs on America (MP, no. 61, p. 34). This was in marked contrast to the attitude of Governor Shirley, who, though an Anglican, opposed the episcopate (Schutz, *Shirley*, pp. 157–158).

13. Correspondence in *MHS Colls.*, LXXIV (1918), 37–38, 76–77. *Boston Gazette*, July 14, 1760. *Boston Post-Boy*, June 23, June 30, July 21, 1760. *Boston Evening Post*, July 7, July 14, 1760. Thomas Hutchinson to Israel Williams, Oct. 28, 1759, Israel Williams MSS (MHS).

14. *Acts and Resolves*, XVII, 194, 208. Correspondence in *MHS Colls.*, LXXIV (1918), 31–32, 37–38, 79–80. Hutchinson, *History*, III, 76n. TH to JM, July 28, 1762, HP. Jasper Mauduit to JM, July 31, 1762, MP.

15. Robert J. Taylor, "Israel Mauduit," *New England Quarterly*, XXIV (1951), 208–230. Correspondence in *MHS Colls.*, LXXIV (1918), 86–88, 179–180. Israel Mauduit to JM, April 8, 1763, MP. JM to TH, 1764 (no. 29); Dec. 18, 1764, HP. TH to JM, Dec. 6, 1763, HP. Thomas Hutchinson to Israel Williams, Nov. 17, 1763, Israel Williams MSS (MHS). *Boston Evening Post*, Jan. 24, 1763. *Boston Gazette*, Jan. 17, Jan. 24, Jan. 31, Feb. 21, Feb. 28, 1763; May 14, 1764. *Boston Post-Boy*, Jan. 24, 1763. *Boston News-Letter*, Jan. 31, 1765. *Acts and Resolves*, XVII, 587. Harrison Gray to Jasper Mauduit, Feb. 8, May 18, July 6, 1765, Miscellaneous MSS (Clements Library). *Adams Papers*, I, 234, 260–261. John Tomlinson, ed., *Additional Grenville Papers, 1763–65* (Manchester, 1962), pp. 258–259.

16. JM to EM, Aug. 21, 1752, MP. John E. Sexton, "Massachusetts Religious Policy with the Indians under Governor Bernard, 1760–1769," *Catholic Hist. Rev.*, XXIV (1938), 310–328. Schneider, *Samuel Johnson*, III, 281.

17. *Acts and Resolves*, IV, 520–523, 562. *Boston Gazette*, Feb. 21, May 2, 1763. JM to TH, April 6, 1762, HP. Charles Chauncy to Jasper Mauduit, May 4, 1763, *MHS Colls.*, LXXIV (1918), 117.

18. *Defence*, p. 142n. Perry, *Papers*, pp. 471–472. Schneider, *Samuel Johnson*, I, 328.

19. Perry, *Papers*, pp. 477–481.

20. Israel Mauduit to JM, April 8, 1763, MP. Lambeth MSS, 1123, III, no. 294, LC Transcripts. JM to TH, April 27, 1763, HP. Jasper Mauduit to James Bowdoin, April 7, 1763, *MHS Colls.*, LIX (1897), 14–16.

21. Lambeth MSS, 1123, III, nos. 276, 287, 308, LC Transcripts. Perry, *Papers*, p. 475. "Remarks on an Act lately passed in

the Massachusetts Government . . .," FP Transcripts, no. 179, Mass., box I. *Acts of the Privy Council of England, Colonial Series,* IV (London, 1911), 559–560.

22. JM to TH, April 6, 1762, HP. James Bowdoin to Jasper Mauduit, April 25, 1763, *MHS Colls.,* LIX (1897), 17. *Boston Gazette,* April 9, July 2, July 9, 1764. *London Chronicle,* Dec. 31, 1763; Jan. 17, Jan. 21, Feb. 11, Feb. 28, 1764. Perry, *Papers,* pp. 497–498.

23. *Remarks,* p. 80.

24. On Anglican plans to establish the Church of England in Canada, see vol. 59 of the Shelburne MSS (Clements Library) and Henry Caner to Thomas Secker, Oct. 6, 1760, Letterbook of Henry Caner (University of Bristol Library).

25. J. Richardson to Thos. Leverett, April 7, 1760, MP. See also the invoice in MP, no. 54. This portion of Galatians, ii, 4 was used on the title page of *Observations.*

CHAPTER XII. NO BISHOP, NO KING

1. *Observations,* p. 157.

2. *Boston Gazette,* Feb. 14, Feb. 21, March 7, March 14, March 21, March 28, 1763. *Boston Evening Post,* Feb. 28, March 7, March 14, 1763. *Boston News-Letter,* March 31, 1763. Wardens of Christ Church to S.P.G., March 7, 1763, S.P.G. MSS, series B, vol. I, no. 246, LC Transcripts. Perry, *Papers,* pp. 497–498. *Harvard Graduates,* VII, 93–100.

3. *Boston News-Letter,* Nov. 16, Nov. 24, 1758; Jan. 11, 1759. *Boston Post-Boy,* Jan. 8, 1759. Perry, *Papers,* pp. 452–453. Wendell D. Garrett, *Apthorp House, 1760–1960* (Cambridge, Mass., 1960), pp. 3–10.

4. *Considerations on the Institution and Conduct of the Society for the Propagation of the Gospel in Foreign Parts* (Boston, 1763), *passim.*

5. *Boston News-Letter,* March 24, 1763. *Boston Gazette,* April 4, 1763.

6. April 15, 1763, MP. Charles Chauncy to Ezra Stiles, July 21, 1761 and note by Stiles, July 1766, Stiles Papers. Stiles had been in touch with JM on the episcopate question in 1759; see Reynell to JM, Jan. 29, 1759, Stiles Papers. For a full account of Stiles's "Anglicophobia," see Morgan, *Gentle Puritan,* ch. 14. Carl Bridenbaugh devotes the opening chapter of *Mitre and Sceptre* to the *Christian Union.*

7. Pages 53–54.

8. Pages 107–131.

9. Pages 45, 86–96, 137.

10. Pages 6–7, 156.

11. *MHS Colls.*, LXXIV (1918), 103.

12. To N. Lardner, June 20, 1764, Stiles Papers.

13. Perry, *Papers*, pp. 497–498. Johnson to S.P.G., May 10, 1763, S.P.G. MSS, series B, vol. XXII, no. 170, LC Transcripts. Schneider, *Samuel Johnson*, III, 267–268; IV, 336.

14. Providence, 1763. See also *Boston Gazette*, June 20, 1763.

15. Portsmouth, 1763, p. 24.

16. This broadside is in MHS.

17. *Boston Gazette*, May 2, Aug. 1, Sept. 5, 1763. *Boston News-Letter*, June 30, Aug. 25, Sept. 15, 1763. *London Chronicle*, March 1, 1763, p. 208. Schneider, *Samuel Johnson*, III, 269, 276–278. Perry, *Papers*, pp. 494–496, 510–511. Lardner to JM, July 18, 1763, MP.

18. Boston, 1763, pp. 1–3, 57–58, 77–80. See also *Boston Gazette*, Oct. 10, 1763; *Boston News-Letter*, Oct. 6, 1763.

19. *Boston Gazette*, Oct. 17, 1763. Samuel Hopkins, *An Enquiry Concerning the Promises of the Gospel.* (Boston, 1765), p. 11. *Defence*, p. 112.

20. Pages 27–39, 49–58. See also *Boston Gazette*, Nov. 14, Nov. 21, 1763.

21. For authorship see Schneider, *Samuel Johnson*, I, 43–44.

22. Pages 4, 23–25, 40–41.

23. Pages 67–90, 107–109, 121–124.

24. Schneider, *Samuel Johnson*, III, 280. *London Chronicle*, Jan. 28, 1766, p. 95.

25. To sample the English phase of the controversy, see the following London newspapers: *Lloyd's Evening Post*, April 29, 1763, p. 408. *London Chronicle*, May 17, 1763, p. 471; Jan. 17, 1764, pp. 51–52; Jan. 21, 1764, p. 70; Feb. 11, 1764, pp. 138–139; March 30, 1765, p. 308; Jan. 7, 1766, p. 21; Jan. 11, 1766. *Public Advertiser*, April 23, July 10, July 17, 1766. See also Schneider, *Samuel Johnson*, III, 258.

26. Hollis Diary, *passim* for 1759–1764. TH to JM, Dec. 6, 1763; April 4, 1764, HP.

27. *An Answer to Dr. Mayhew's Observations* (London, 1764), pp. 57–66. For its authorship see: Schneider, *Samuel Johnson*, I, 345. Israel Mauduit to JM, Feb. 14, 1764, MP. TH to JM, April 4, 1764, HP.

28. Israel Mauduit to JM, Aug. 8, 1764, MP. Perry, *Papers*, pp. 508–509. S.P.G. Journals, XVI, 116–122, LC Transcripts. Samuel Dean to JM, Nov. 5, 1764, MP. Schneider, *Samuel Johnson*, III, 277.

29. *Remarks*, pp. 3, 12–13, 57–61. *Boston News-Letter*, April 13, May 24, June 21, 1764.

30. *Remarks*, p. 62. "Thoughts upon the present State of the

Church of England in America, Sent to me by the Lord Arch Bishop of Canterbury July 13:1764" (MS Clements Library).

31. Secker, *Answer,* p. 55. *Remarks,* p. 82–83.

32. Hollis Diary, Aug. 28, Aug. 30, Sept. 3, Sept. 7, Sept. 11, Oct. 5, Oct. 9, Oct. 11, Nov. 7, 1764. TH to JM, Dec. 6, 1763; Aug. 28, 1764, HP. Michael Towgood to JM, March 25, 1764, MP. See also MP, nos. 65, 71, 76, 80, 81.

33. JM to TH, June 24, Oct. 17, 1764, HP. *Boston Gazette,* Jan. 23, April 2, April 9, June 25, July 9, July 23, Oct. 15, 1764. *Boston News-Letter,* Oct. 20, 1763; June 21, Dec. 6, Dec. 20, 1764; April 11, 1765. MP, nos. 71, 77, 78, 82, 84.

34. *Boston News-Letter,* Sept. 13, 1764. TH to JM, April 4, 1764, HP. JM to TH, Oct. 17, 1764, HP. Apthorp to S.P.G., Jan. 9, 1764, S.P.G. MSS, series B, vol. XXII, no. 8, LC Transcripts. Caner to Bishop of London, Sept. 6, 1764, FP Transcripts, Mass., box II, no. 211.

35. London, 1765, pp. 48–56.

36. TH to JM, March 4, 1765, HP. Hollis Diary, May 20, 1766. *Boston News-Letter,* Nov. 8, 1764.

37. *Popish Idolatry,* pp. 48–49.

38. Hollis Diary, May 20, 1765. TH to JM, June 24, 1765, HP. *Halifax Gazette,* Dec. 20, 1764. *Public Advertiser* (London), April 17, 1765; April 26, May 19, May 23, 1766. *London Chronicle, passim* for 1765–1766.

39. See Franklin's *Cool Thoughts on the Present Situation of Our Public Affairs* (Philadelphia 1764), pp. 17–18. Carl Bridenbaugh has pointed out that Franklin underestimated the intensity of anti-episcopal opinion in the colonies (*Mitre and Sceptre,* p. 252n). A clear expression of Anglican bewilderment at the motives for Congregational hostility toward their Church is Samuel Johnson, "An Impartial & Candid State of the Case between Dr. Mayhew and the S.P.G." (MS, New York Hist. Soc.).

40. Schneider, *Samuel Johnson,* III, 280–288. "Thoughts upon the present State of the Church of England in America." Caner to Bishop of London, FP Transcripts, Massachusetts, box 1, no. 152.

41. Secker to Caner, Sept. 15, 1763, Lambeth MSS, 1123, III, no. 319, LC Transcripts. *Horace Walpole, Memoirs and Portraits,* p. 199. Bernhard Knollenberg, *Origin of the American Revolution: 1759–1766* (New York, 1960), ch. v.

42. William Allen to JM, Oct. 15, 1764, MP. Ezra Stiles to Samuel Langdon, May 24, 1766; Ezra Stiles to Charles Chauncy, Oct. 24, 1766; Stiles Papers. Bridenbaugh, *Mitre and Sceptre,* ch. ix.

CHAPTER XIII. SLAVERY

1. MP, no. 91.

2. *Boston Post-Boy,* July 1, 1765.

3. Samuel Mather to Samuel Mather, Jr., Sept. 15, 1764, Mather Letters. For recent studies of the revenue acts of 1764 and 1765 see: Morgan, *The Stamp Act Crisis;* Knollenberg, *Origin of the American Revolution,* chs. xi–xxi; Gipson, *The British Empire Before the American Revolution,* vol. X. Older but still important are Arthur M. Schlesinger, *The Colonial Merchants and the American Revolution, 1763–1776* (New York, 1939) and Charles M. Andrews, "Boston Merchants and the Non-Importation Movement," *CSM Pubs.,* XIX (1918), 159–259.

4. JM to TH, Aug. 8, 1765, HP.

5. JM to TH, Aug. 19, 1765, HP. Hutchinson to Israel Williams, April 26, 1765, Israel Williams MSS (MHS). Wm. Allen to JM, Oct. 15, 1764, MP.

6. JM to TH, Aug. 19, 1765, HP.

7. JM to TH, Aug. 19, 1765, HP. See also Diary of Benjamin Bangs (MS, MHS), Aug. 22, 1765; Andrew Eliot to TH, Aug. 27, 1765, HP; Samuel Mather to Samuel Mather, Jr., Aug. 17, 1765, Mather Letters.

8. Apparently JM delivered this sermon without notes, for afterwards he attempted to put in writing the substance of what he had said ("Memorandum," MP, no. 91). Important additions to the sermon are found in a letter to Hutchinson (Aug. 27, 1765, MP, hereafter cited as Hutchinson Letter) and in a letter to Richard Clarke (Sept. 3, 1765, *NEHG Reg.,* XLVI [1892], 16–20, hereafter cited as Clarke Letter).

9. Memorandum.

10. *Ibid.*

11. *Ibid.*

12. Hutchinson Letter.

13. Clarke Letter.

14. *Boston Gazette,* Sept. 2, 1765. Andrew Eliot to TH, Aug. 27, 1765, HP.

15. Bernard to Lords Commissioners for Trade and Plantations, Aug. 22, 1765, House of Lords MSS, 209 (LC Photostats). *The Conduct of the Late Administration Examined* (London and Boston, 1767), p. 102.

16. Hutchinson, *History,* III, 88–89. Adair and Schutz, *Peter Oliver's Origin & Progress of the American Rebellion,* p. 44. Andrew Eliot to TH, Aug. 27, 1767, HP. John Avery, Jr., and Benjamin Edes of the Loyal Nine attended West Church (*Adams Papers,* I, 294). Caner to Secker, Sept. 5, 1765, Caner Letterbook.

17. Andrew Eliot to TH, Aug. 27, 1767, HP. Hutchinson Letter.

Alden Bradford, *Memoir of the Life and Writings of Rev. Jonathan Mayhew, D.D.* (Boston, 1838), p. 422. Hutchinson to——, Mass. Archives, XXVI, 158. Hutchinson, *History*, III, 89.

18. Clarke Letter. Andrew Eliot to TH, Aug. 27, 1767, HP. Richard Clarke, father-in-law of John Singleton Copley, later became notorious as a consignee of the shipment of tea that precipitated the Boston Tea Party of 1773.

19. JM to TH, Dec. 18, 1764; Sept. 26, 1765, HP. TH to JM, June 24, 1765, HP.

20. *Boston News-Letter*, Nov. 7, 1765. *Boston Gazette*, Dec. 23, 1765. Diary of Robert Treat Paine, Nov. 1, 1765.

21. Hollis Diary, Oct. 18, Oct. 21, 1765. HP, no. 65.

22. Hollis Diary, Oct. 22, Oct. 24, Oct. 25, Oct. 31, Nov. 1, Nov. 6, Nov. 14, Nov. 15, Nov. 16, Nov. 18, Dec. 13, 1765; Jan. 10, Jan. 17, Jan. 20, Jan. 24, Jan. 25, Feb. 6, 1766. TH to JM, Nov. 18, 1765, HP.

23. TH to JM, Nov. 18, 1765; May 8, 1766, HP. TH to Wm. Pitt, Jan. 20, 1766 and *passim* for 1761–1765 in Hollis-Pitt correspondence, Chatham MSS (Public Record Office). Hollis Diary, May 7, Sept. 28, Nov. 23, Dec. 28, 1762; April 17, 1763; Jan. 28, 1766.

24. Hollis Diary, Feb. 10, March 18, April 14, April 15, 1766. Hollis to Wm. Pitt, April 16, 1766, Chatham MSS. TH to JM, May 8, June 19, 1766, HP.

25. TH to JM, May 8, 1766, HP. TH to Edmund Quincy, Oct. 1, 1766, HP. L. H. Gipson, "The Great Debate in the Committee of the Whole House of Commons on the Stamp Act, 1766, as Reported by Nathaniel Ryder," *Pa. Mag. Hist. and Biog.*, LXXXVI (1962), 23–24.

26. JM to TH, Jan. 7, April 8, 1766, HP. *Boston News-Letter*, May 22, 1766. Diary of Robert Treat Paine, May 19, 1766. Anne R. Cunningham, ed., *Letters and Diary of John Rowe* (Boston, 1903), pp. 95–96.

27. *Boston News-Letter*, May 22, May 29, 1766. *Boston Gazette*, Aug. 21, 1766. *Rind's Virginia Gazette*, Aug. 15, 1766. *Snare Broken*, p. iv. Hollis Diary, June 30, 1766. TH to Elizabeth Mayhew, Oct. 4, 1766, MP.

28. *Snare Broken*, pp. 2–6.

29. *Ibid.*, pp. 2–23, 27, 39, 42.

30. *Ibid.*, pp. 9–10, 32–33.

31. *Ibid.*, pp. 25–26.

32. *Ibid.*, pp. 30–40.

33. *Ibid.*, pp. 35–37.

CHAPTER XIV. EVEN UNTO THE DEATH

1. JM to James Otis, June 8, 1766 (Amer. Antiquarian Soc.).
2. JM to TH, June 24, 1764, HP. Samuel Checkly to JM, April 25, 1766, MP. Elizabeth Mayhew to TH, Jan. 13, 1767, HP.
3. Elijah Mason to JM, Aug. 25, 1764, MP. Samuel Dean to JM, Nov. 5, Dec. 4, 1764, MP.
4. JM to James Otis, June 8, 1766 (Amer. Antiquarian Soc.).
5. Cf. William V. Wells, *The Life and Public Services of Samuel Adams* (3 vols., Boston, 1865), II, 62n.
6. "Copy of proceedings of an ecclesiastical council held in the Rutland District, June 18, 1766," MP.
7. *Boston News-Letter*, July 3, 1766. Samuel Mather to TH, July 8, 1766, HP. Samuel Mather to Samuel Mather, Jr., July 9, 1766, Mather Letters. Andrew Eliot to TH, Nov. 14, 1766, HP. Huntington Sermons, March 1764, no. 2, p. 26.
8. MP, no. 137, p. 25. *Christian Sobriety*, p. 337. Samuel Mather to TH, July 8, 1766, HP. *Boston Evening Post*, July 7, 1766. *Boston News-Letter*, supplement, July 10, 1766. *Adams Papers*, I, 15. Alden Bradford first recorded the story of Cooper's deathbed interview with JM (*Memoir*, p. 431). The story seems to have come from some of Mayhew's acquaintances from whom, in their old age, Bradford drew information.
9. *Boston Gazette*, July 14, 1766.
10. *A Discourse Occasioned by the Death of the Reverend Jonathan Mayhew, D.D.*, pp. 27–28. See also Chauncy to Ezra Stiles, May 6, 1768, Stiles Papers.
11. *Boston Post-Boy*, July 14, 1766, and other Boston newspapers for the same week. The obituary was reprinted in pamphlet form as *From the Public News-Papers* [Boston, 1766].
12. *Providence Gazette*, Aug. 30, 1766. *Boston Gazette*, Sept. 8, Sept. 15, 1766. *Boston News-Letter*, Sept. 11, Sept. 25, 1766. *Pennsylvania Gazette*, Oct. 13, Oct. 20, Oct. 27, 1768. Isaac Backus, *A Fish Caught* (Boston, 1768), p. 66n.
13. Hollis Diary, Aug. 21, Sept. 3, 1766. TH to Elizabeth Mayhew, Oct. 4, 1766, MP. Andrew Eliot replaced JM as TH's New England correspondent, thanks to JM's having sent TH a copy of Eliot's election sermon (JM to Andrew Eliot, Feb. 20, 1766, Waterston Autographs, MHS, III). When TH died in 1774, his will contained a bequest of £100 for Mrs. Mayhew (Thomas Brand Hollis to Elizabeth Mayhew, May 28, 1774, MP).
14. *Dict. Amer. Biog.*
15. *MHS Colls.*, III (1794), 263. TH to Elizabeth Mayhew, Oct. 4, 1766, MP.

16. *Adams Works*, X, 193. Harrison Gray to TH, Oct. 6, 1766; Dec. 15, 1767, HP. "Remariage of Elizabeth Mayhew," MP.

17. S. E. Morison, "The Property of Harrison Gray, Loyalist," *CSM Pubs.*, XIV (1913), 320–350. Gray to Elizabeth Mayhew, May 2, 1783; June 1, 1790, MP.

18. Simeon Howard, *A Sermon Preached before the Honorable Council, and the Honorable House of Representatives of the State of Massachusetts-Bay, . . . May 31, 1780* (Boston, 1780). The original wooden building of the West Church was replaced in 1806 with the present brick structure, a familiar landmark on Cambridge Street. Simeon Howard died in 1804 and was succeeded by Charles Lowell (father of James Russell Lowell). After Lowell's death in 1861, Cyrus Augustus Bartol served until the church was closed in 1889 because most of the members had moved away. In 1894 the City of Boston acquired the property, and from 1896 to 1960 it housed the West End Branch of the Boston Public Library. In 1962 the property was sold to the First Methodist Church of Boston, which renovated the building and opened it in 1964 for Sunday services and a variety of weekday social and cultural activities. (C. A. Bartol, *The West Church and Its Ministers* [Boston, 1856]. *Boston Globe*, April 13, 1964, p. 11. Boston Public Library archives. Fannie Goldstein, former librarian of the West End Branch, has prepared a history of the church and branch library, a typescript of which is available at the Boston Public Library.)

19. *Adams Papers*, III, 198. Hollis *Memoirs*, I, 465, 481.

EPILOGUE

1. Schneider, *Samuel Johnson*, I, 346, 354–355.

2. This phrase is from the tribute paid to JM at the 1792 Harvard Commencement by Robert Treat Paine, Jr. (*The Works, . . . of . . . Robert Treat Paine, Jun.* [Boston, 1812], pp. 70–77).

3. Wright, *Unitarianism*, p. 8.

4. (New York, 1884), IV, 3–4.

5. Adair and Schutz, *Peter Oliver's Origin & Progress of the American Rebellion*, p. 29.

INDEX

Aberdeen, University of, 77
Absurdity and Blasphemy of depretiating Moral Value, The, 78, 123
Adams, John, 118, 139; JM's influence on, 2, 93–94; and JM's character, 2–3; "A Dissertation on the Canon and Feudal Law," 209; religion of, 228
Adams, Samuel, 112, 139, 207
Age of Reason, 60, 115
Aix-la-Chapelle, peace of, 98, 133
Allen, Jonathan, 17
Allen, William, 197, 200
American Revolution, 2, 93; future leaders of, 23; Hollis blamed for, 141; ends episcopate controversy, 196; and JM's friends, 223; completes Puritan and Glorious revolutions, 229; and Great War for Empire, 229; and JM, 231
American Society, 175–178, 180
American Unitarian Association, 68
Amherst, Jeffrey, 144
Ancient and Honorable Artillery Company, 164
Anglicans. *See* Church of England
Anne, Queen of England, 170
Appleton, Nathaniel, 32, 49, 51, 169
Apthorp, East, 181–184, 186, 190, 194–195
Archbishop of Canterbury, and the SPG, 167
Arianism, 115–116, 118, 119, 222
Arminianism, 121, 178; in England, 61, 76, 130; in New England, 61–63, 78–79; and E. Mayhew, 64–65; and political philosophy, 82; and Congregational clergy, 115; and definition of sin, 125; and Deism, 126; importance of, in Massachusetts, 227
Athanasian Creed, 116; and JM, 117, 118, 122, 130
Atonement, doctrine of, 130–131, 132

Bancroft, George, 230–231
Banks, Charles E., 243n2
Baptist Church (Boston), 56
Baron, Richard, 93, 143
Barton's Point (Boston), 44
Bayle, Pierre, 146
Beacon Hill (Boston), 44, 47
Belcher, Jonathan, 108
Bellamy, Joseph, 121, 122, 131, 132
Benson, George, 139, 143; recommends JM for degree, 77; reaction to *Unlimited Submission,* 92–93; quoted, 113
Bernard, Francis, 219; receives books from Hollis, 144; arrives in Mass., 150–153; accused of taking bribe, 153–161, 229; and Hampshire Co. college, 161–164; and episcopate, 172, 265n12; and selection of agent, 173–174; and American Society, 174, 175; and Stamp Act, 201, 205, 206, 208

DATE DUE

MAR 1 '65			
AP 16 '65			